Venezuela

LATIN AMERICAN PERSPECTIVES
IN THE CLASSROOM

Series Editor: Ronald H. Chilcote

Venezuela

Hugo Chávez and the Decline of an "Exceptional Democracy"

Edited by
Steve Ellner and Miguel Tinker Salas

ROWMAN & LITTLEFIELD PUBLISHERS, INC.
Lanham • Boulder • New York • Toronto • Plymouth, UK

ROWMAN & LITTLEFIELD PUBLISHERS, INC.

Published in the United States of America
by Rowman & Littlefield Publishers, Inc.
A wholly owned subsidary of The Rowman & Littlefield Publishing Group, Inc.
4501 Forbes Boulevard, Suite 200, Lanham, Maryland 20706
www.rowmanlittlefield.com

Estover Road, Plymouth PL6 7PY, United Kingdom

Copyright © 2007 by Rowman & Littlefield Publishers, Inc.

British Library Cataloguing in Publication Information Available

Library of Congress Cataloging-in-Publication Data

Venezuela : Hugo Chávez and the decline of an "exceptional democracy" / edited by
Steve Ellner and Miguel Tinker Salas.
    p. cm. — (Latin American perspectives in the classroom)
    Includes bibliographical references and index.
    ISBN-13: 978-0-7425-5455-9 (cloth : alk. paper)
    ISBN-10: 0-7425-5455-4 (cloth : alk. paper)
    ISBN-13: 978-0-7425-5456-6 (pbk. : alk. paper)
    ISBN-10: 0-7425-5456-2 (pbk. : alk. paper)
    1. Venezuela—Politics and government—1974–1999. 2. Venezuela—Politics and
government—1999– 3. Chávez Frías, Hugo—Influence. 4. Democracy—Venezuela.
I. Ellner, Steve. II. Tinker Salas, Miguel.
    F2328.V43 2007
    987.06'42—dc22

                                                                          2006031590

Printed in the United States of America

⊗™ The paper used in this publication meets the minimum requirements of American
National Standard for Information Sciences—Permanence of Paper for Printed Library
Materials, ANSI/NISO Z39.48-1992.

Contents

v

Acknowledgments

We would like to thank *Latin American Perspectives* editor Ronald Chilcote for having encouraged us to work on a diversity of topics related to the impact of the phenomenon of President Hugo Chávez. In addition, we are grateful to Barbara Metzger of Sage Publications and Susan McEachern, vice president of Rowman & Littlefield, both of whom worked closely with us at different stages of this project. Finally, we acknowledge the support and encouragement we have received from our respective institutions, the Consejo de Investigación of the Universidad de Oriente and the Pomona College Research Committee.

Acronyms

ACILS	American Center for International Labor Solidarity
AD	Acción Democrática (Democratic Action)
BDM	Banco de Desarrollo de la Mujer (Women's Development Bank)
CD	Coordinadora Democrática (Democratic Coordinating Committee)
CIPE	Center for International Private Enterprise
CNE	Consejo Nacional Electoral (National Electoral Council)
CONIVE	Consejo Nacional Indio de Venezuela (National Indian Council of Venezuela)
COPEI	Comité de Organización Política Electoral Independiente (Committee of Independent Political Electoral Organization)
CREOLE	Creole Petroleum Corporation, a subsidiary of Standard Oil Company of New Jersey
CTV	Confederación de Trabajadores de Venezuela (Venezuelan Workers' Confederation)
FBT	Fuerza Bolivariana de Trabajadores (Bolivarian Workers' Force)
FEDECAMARAS	Federación Venezolana de Cámaras y Asociaciones de Comercio y Producción (Venezuelan Federation of Chambers and Associations of Commerce and Production)
FEDEPETROL	Federación de Trabajadores Petroleros (Federation of Petroleum Workers)

FTAA	Free Trade Area of the Americas
FUT	Frente Unitario de Trabajadores (Unitary Workers' Front)
IAD	Inter-American Dialogue
ILO	International Labor Organization
IRI	International Republican Institute
IVIC	Instituto Venezolano de Investigaciones Cientificas (Venezuelan Institute of Scientific Investigations)
MBR–200	Movimiento Bolivariano Revolucionario–200 (Revolutionary Bolivarian Movement–200)
MERCOSUR	Mercado Común del Sur (Common Market of the South)
MVR	Movimiento Quinta República (Fifth Republic Movement)
NDI	National Democratic Institute
NED	National Endowment for Democracy
OAS	Organization of American States
OPEC	Organization of Petroleum Exporting Countries
PDVSA	Petróleos de Venezuela, Sociedad Anónima (Petroleum of Venezuela, Joint Stock Company)
PPT	Patria para Todos (Nation for All)
PROVEA	Programa Venezolano de Educación y Acción en Derechos Humanos (Venezuelan Program for Education and Action on Human Rights)
SINUTRAPETROL	Sindicato Único Nacional de Trabajadores Petroleros (Sole National Union of Petroleum Workers)
SUTISS	Sindicato Único de Trabajadores de la Industria Siderúrgica (Sole Union of Steel Industry Workers)
UNT	Unión Nacional de Trabajadores (National Workers' Union)
URD	Unión Republicana Democrática (Republican Democratic Union)

Series Introduction

This series evolves from themes emanating from the bimonthly journal, *Latin American Perspectives*, which since its inception has desired to make its material available for classroom use. The goal of this series has been to introduce curious readers and students to some of the important themes and issues about Latin America that have appeared in the journal and to integrate them with new material into coherent anthologies for classroom use. Pedagogically, we try to trim articles to their essential content, reorganize them into teachable clusters, work in contextualized commentary, and prepare introductory essays. With this coherence and organization, we intend that our series be different from the often-abortive efforts of other publishers to develop textbook anthologies. We also want these volumes to be relevant to a broad range of interests in the social sciences and humanities, with particular attention to Latin America.

The chapters in this volume on Venezuela have been drawn from two recent popular journal issues that focus on and analyze the dynamic changes in that country under its progressive president, Hugo Chávez. Not only has Chávez resisted reactionary efforts to overthrow his legitimately elected government, but he has successfully implemented deep reforms that have increasingly gained him majority support, especially from the country's disadvantaged and poor peoples. The editors of this volume, Miguel Tinker Salas and Steve Ellner, provide a stimulating context around the half-truths, misconceptions, and fallacies of a prevailing thesis of exceptionalism that appears in the traditional literature on Venezuela and affirms that, unlike its neighbors, the country has emerged as a stable democracy. Their critique facilitates a critical appraisal of the exceptionalism thesis as a means of leading the reader into the exciting events and issues around the contemporary

Venezuelan experience. Several of the journal editors have reviewed the essays, including the volume editors and myself. The result of all this effort is a highly readable volume of timely information, analysis, and debate.

Ronald H. Chilcote
Series Editor

Introduction:
New Perspectives and the
Chávez Phenomenon

Steve Ellner and Miguel Tinker Salas

Prior to the election of Hugo Chávez in December 1998, when people in the United States reflected on Venezuela, positive images generally came to mind: an abundant supply of oil, a trusted political ally of the United States, a reservoir of highly skilled baseball infielders (such as Chico Carrasquell, Luis Aparicio, David Concepción, and Omar Vizquel) and a rich vein of beautiful women (during the 1980s and 1990s the country had an uncanny ability to win international beauty pageants). For better or for worse, oil, baseball, and the dubious Miss Venezuela phenomenon framed most Americans' limited knowledge of the country. With the election of Chávez this popular portrayal changed literally overnight. From trusted U.S. ally, Venezuela became in the mind of Washington policymakers a dangerous nation that needed to be cut off from its neighbors.

So what happened in Venezuela to set off such as dramatic shift? How did a trusted ally become a pariah? The transition did not occur overnight and it was not a sudden lurch to the left, but rather a gradual process of disillusionment with Venezuelan political institutions especially during the course of the 1980s and the 1990s.

Venezuela had long been promoted as a model democracy for Latin America, but it soon became obvious that below the surface Venezuelan society exhibited deep social fissures and the political system had become unresponsive to the needs of the general populace. This disparity was only made worse by the popular perception that, as a leading supplier of oil, the country had ample resources with which to redress poverty. Recurrent national scandals involving government corruption and the collapse of banking institutions, and the complete impunity surrounding these cases, further incensed most Venezuelans. As Venezuela experienced an intensification of class polarization, the continued growth of the informal sector, popular disillusionment with traditional politics, and a wave of social protest, the nation increasingly resembled others throughout Latin America. Mass disturbances in opposition to government-imposed austerity measures beginning on February 27, 1989 (the *Caracazo*), and the democratic government's ensuing brutal repression placed in sharp relief the social tensions that undermined the Venezuelan political system. Subsequently, two unsuccessful military coups in February and November 1992 (the former led by Chávez) also put in evidence widespread discontent.

Throughout the 1990s the traditional political class scurried to repair the system without fundamentally addressing the causes of the problem. Yet even under these circumstances, many political leaders at all levels assumed that no significant changes had occurred in Venezuelan politics. This complacency explains why Venezuela's largest party, Acción Democrática (Democratic Action—AD), nominated a lackluster, old-time politician, Luis Alfaro Lucero, and the Christian Democratic Comité de Organización Política Electoral Independiente (Independent Electoral Political Organizing Committee—COPEI) supported former beauty queen and former mayor of Chacao, Irene Saenz, as their presidential candidates in 1998 in spite of the formidable challenge posed by the candidacy of Hugo Chávez.

The presidential election of octogenarian Rafael Caldera in 1993, former leader of COPEI, at the head of a diverse coalition of traditional political figures and erstwhile leftists, had initially increased the expectation of meaningful change. Throughout this period, however, parties ranging from the social democratic AD to the left-leaning Movimiento al Socialismo (MAS) abandoned their support for state interventionist policies in the economy and embraced neoliberal reform, thus leaving an important space on the political spectrum virtually unoccupied. Indeed, Venezuela became the only country in Latin America in which two presidents in the 1990s (Caldera and his predecessor Carlos Andrés Pérez) won elections on antineoliberal platforms only to end up embracing neoliberal strategies. In the end, Caldera's presidency served to further expose the rigidity of the political system and the calcified nature of the traditional parties that held power since 1958.

The escalating political crisis and the election of Hugo Chávez Frías as president in 1998, with his policy of favoring the poor, forced scholars to reexamine many of the widely held assumptions concerning the country and its once heralded democratic institutions. Chávez's opponents resorted to social stereotypes including racially tinged propaganda aimed at the president and the lower classes, which constituted the core of his supporters. Reliance on the race card shattered the widely held belief that Venezuela was and had long been a racial democracy. The belief (known as the Venezuelan exceptionalism thesis) that Venezuela after 1958 represented an exception to the backward political culture that predominated elsewhere in Latin America eventually proved untenable for scholars and policy officials. For his part, the new president seldom missed an opportunity to highlight the opportunistic nature of the traditional political class and the failures of the once powerful parties.

Although the election of Hugo Chávez has gone a long way in dispelling misconceptions regarding Venezuela's long-standing status as a model democracy, other equally problematic assumptions are now being used to analyze events in the post-1998 period. Reporting in the private media, as well as statements by the Venezuelan opposition and the U.S. State Department, reflect the notion that democracy is not well served when elections favor candidates who galvanize social tensions and privilege the poor strata of the population. Venezuelans who have voted for Chávez on multiple occasions or attended mass rallies are often categorized as lower class, ill informed, or worse, simply an ignorant mass that willfully succumbs to the whims of an all-powerful charismatic leader. These same accounts tend to racialize Chávez's supporters and depict them in stereotypical fashion. This perspective is reminiscent of approaches used in the scholarly literature to discount the followers of populist leaders from Lázaro Cárdenas in Mexico to Juan Domingo Perón in Argentina. In both cases, race and lower-class status were also conflated to stereotype the adherents of these populist leaders. At the root of this approach continues to be the failure to recognize the country's pressing social ills.

The simplifications and Manichean depictions put forward by the opposition during the Chávez presidency and reflected in much political writing recall the nineteenth-century positivist duality of barbarism versus civilization that influenced the thesis of Venezuelan exceptionalism. Just as the exceptionalism writers who lauded Venezuelan democratic governments (the embodiment of "civilization") contrasted them with the nation's dictatorial past ("barbarism"), anti-Chavistas compare the same democratic experience of previous decades with the alleged praetorianism of Chávez's rule. In another comparison with the past, Chávez's adversaries view the president as a throwback to nineteenth-century caudillo rule. Thus, the anti-Chavistas, who have portrayed Chávez's sympathizers as an unruly mass susceptible to demagogic appeals, conjure up images of the peons who fought in the armies of caudillos in the civil wars of the nineteenth century. Such a view passes over the democratic features of the Chavista experience, namely the high degree of popular mobilization, the frequency of the elections that have been held, and the system of recall elections and other aspects of "participatory democracy" incorporated in the Constitution of 1999.

The chapters in this volume examine how the experiences of the recent past and specifically those of the presidency of Hugo Chávez beginning in 1999 have encouraged a reexamination of long-held assumptions regarding

Venezuelan politics and society. Collectively, the chapters refute the "Venezuelan exceptionalism" thesis, which shaped political analysis following the founding of the nation's democracy in 1958. Some exceptionalism writers went so far as to assert that the Venezuelan political system and culture were conducive to stable democracy that was in some ways comparable to the political environment of Western Europe. The instability and violence that have marked Venezuela over the last two decades have undermined the credibility of exceptionalism thinking.

The chapters grapple with other notions that distort objective political analysis, including the troublesome tendency on the part of policy and opinion makers to claim that elections, when they do not produce the desired results, do not represent the real democratic will of the people. This line of thinking has dictated Washington's repudiation of the democracy that is taking shape in Venezuela under Chávez. The U.S. imposition of a particular model of democracy must be seen in the context of the face-off between liberal democracy, which has always been embraced by Washington, and Rousseau-style democracy, which finds greater acceptance in Latin America. Under the U.S.-endorsed model, not only is the margin of votes that results in the triumph of a given president unimportant, but a president's efforts to lessen inequality and promote the direct participation of popular sectors become irrelevant in the classification of the government as democratic or undemocratic. The debate over democratic models has a direct bearing on the portrayal of the Chávez government.

This book brings together ten chapters with the aim of covering key themes, specifically the global context, history, economic policy, organized labor, race, social movements, electoral politics, and foreign relations. The chapters question the validity of simplistic concepts that have long been used to extol the nation's post-1958 democratic governments and minimize their deficiencies, and that are now contributing to misleading descriptions and analyses of the Chávez phenomenon. The contributors to this volume underline the complexity of the subject matter of their respective chapters and the need to emphasize social and racial sources of conflict, which were largely downplayed by political analysts in the past.

By demonizing Chávez, the Bush administration and much of the media, as well as some scholars in Venezuela and elsewhere, have reached easy answers that belie the complexity of his presidency. Indeed, the Chávez movement since its founding in the early 1980s has had unique features and since reaching power in 1998 has carried out novel policies. The very complexity of the Chávez phenomenon opens great possibilities for researchers in diverse fields, providing them with the opportunity to go beyond simplified notions and contribute to a much needed clarification of issues.

Part I

THEORETICAL, HISTORICAL, AND INTERNATIONAL BACKGROUND

The deterioration of political conditions and growing social inequality in the 1980s and 1990s debunked the myth of Venezuela's "exceptional" democracy and set the stage for Chávez's rise to power. Chapter 1 questions the notion of Venezuelan exceptionalism that contrasted the alleged backwardness of the nineteenth century and the first decades of the twentieth with the "model" democracy after 1958. Chapter 2 shows that the aggravation of social tensions in the 1980s and 1990s in Venezuela was due not only to declining oil prices but also to a global process characterized by the erosion of living standards for the popular classes.

CHAPTERS 1 AND 2:
THEORETICAL, HISTORICAL, AND INTERNATIONAL
DIMENSIONS OF VENEZUELAN EXCEPTIONALISM

The chapter by Steve Ellner and Miguel Tinker Salas provides a critical appraisal of the salient features of the thesis of Venezuelan exceptionalism. Those who defended the notion of exceptionalism exalted a set of favorable natural circumstances including geographic position, rich oil and mineral deposits, and a set of historical experiences that included Venezuela's social composition, patterns of miscegenation, foreign presence, and the absence of extreme nationalism to construct an image of a country distinct from others in the region. After 1958, the image included a political process, born out of a pacted democracy and sustained by petroleum revenues, that appeared to conserve social peace, ensure the peaceful transfer of power, and mollify class and racial differences, while maintaining close ties to the United States.

1

Contrasts with other countries of the region, in the throes of military dictatorships or violent uprising, only served to confirm the exceptionalism view-
point. Yet as the authors point out, the thesis consisted of "half-truths, misconceptions, and fallacies from the beginning and proved incapable of
providing an adequate interpretation of the complexities of Venezuelan history." This became painfully evident in February of 1989 (the *Caracazo*)
when the government used military troops to suppress Venezuelans who
protested the imposition of neoliberal measures. Ellner and Tinker Salas trace
the rise of exceptionalism, how it influenced the political discourse and was
used to reinterpret Venezuelan history, and how in the end it impeded the nation's assertion of its Latin American identity.

Edgardo Lander's chapter assesses the Venezuelan experience from the
perspective of the broader developments in Latin America since the mid-
1970s. While the nations of South America languished under dictatorships,
Venezuela avoided military rule, as well as the repression and popular demobilization that accompanied these regimes. The mid-1980s witnessed the rise
of a divided society, in which greater income disparity, enclosed communities, high levels of violence, and an expanding lower class became common
features of a nation in crisis. Race and class took on new meanings in a society that refused to recognize the existence of these contradictions. Oil revenues initially permitted Venezuela to elude the full force of orthodox neoliberal structural adjustments, measures imposed on other countries. Tracing
the strategies pursued to maintain stability, Lander argues that the application
of neoliberalism during the governments of Carlos Andrés Pérez (1989–1993)
and Rafael Caldera (1994–1999) set the stage for the election of Hugo
Chávez to the presidency in 1998.

Chapter One

The Venezuelan Exceptionalism Thesis: Separating Myth from Reality

Steve Ellner and Miguel Tinker Salas

The notion of Venezuela as a privileged Third-World nation is rooted in concrete historical, social, economic, political, and geographical circumstances. Venezuela's status as a major oil producer far removed from the political turbulence of the Middle East, where most of the Third World's petroleum reserves are located, places it practically in a category unto itself. As an export commodity, oil stands out as superior to, and qualitatively different from, all other Third-World products. Specifically, the historical stability of the international oil market, and the strategic importance of petroleum that has impacted world politics over the last half century, has no equivalent among the raw material and agricultural products exported by other Third-World nations.[1] Venezuela has other advantages, including its strategic geographical location, its regional diversity, and a host of raw materials other than oil, such as natural gas, iron, gold, diamonds, and bauxite.

Historically, Venezuela is distinguished by having greater social mobility than its more socially stratified neighbors. This characteristic has its roots in the colonial period, when Venezuela existed largely on the periphery, and the nineteenth century, when the independence war and subsequent civil wars devastated the established aristocracy. With independence, the Venezuelan army ceased to be the exclusive domain of the upper classes; its relatively popular social makeup was reflected in the leftist-inspired military revolts in the early 1960s and the one led by Hugo Chávez in 1992. Venezuela's protracted democratic stability after 1958 also set it off from the military dictatorships that dominated Latin America from the 1960s to the 1980s. Furthermore, though racism continued to frame social relations, Venezuela experienced a high degree of miscegenation and, on the surface, seemed to avoid the racial tensions evident elsewhere in Latin America.

Another salient characteristic exalted by some observers is the absence of extreme nationalism, which contributed to extended periods of armed conflict and economic disruptions in Mexico and elsewhere (Alexander, 1964: 315). Interaction with foreigners, whether from Spain, Portugal, Italy, or the United States, dramatically stamped Venezuelan culture and lifestyles. In particular, the presence of U.S. residential enclaves (or "oil camps") left an indelible mark on Venezuelan society, making baseball the nation's number one sport and whisky the number one alcoholic beverage among the middle class.

These diverse factors have molded the way many Venezuelans view their nation, its past and future, and its relations with the United States and the rest of Latin America. Favorable conditions have generated high expectations among Venezuelans and, in certain sectors, faith in the steady improvement in their standard of living. During an extended period of relatively stable oil prices, the optimism was translated into support for the capitalist system and rejection of antisystem movements such as Communism (Bergquist, 1986: 206–214). The self-image of being privileged shaped attitudes toward the rest of Latin America and was reflected in policies adopted by various presidents. Thus Venezuelans applauded the "generosity" displayed by the first administration of Carlos Andrés Pérez (1974–1979), who provided aid to poorer Latin American nations at a time when Venezuela experienced a relative boom in the aftermath of the Arab oil embargo. Under the presidency of Jaime Lusinchi (1984–1989), however, the government rejected the proposal (originally formulated by Fidel Castro) of collective negotiation of new terms for the foreign debt on the ground that association with the poorer nations of the continent would increase the perception of risk, to Venezuela's disadvantage.

The notion of being privileged was a double-edged sword: while it contributed to political stability during periods of stable oil prices, it also generated discontent when prices began to fluctuate sharply and economic conditions deteriorated beginning in the mid-1980s. Venezuelans who considered material improvement a birthright blamed politicians for the nation's failure to live up to expectations.

A brief overview of Venezuela's modern democratic period serves to place the optimistic, exceptionalism view in perspective. For several decades after the overthrow in 1958 of the nine-year-old military dictatorship led by General Marcos Pérez Jiménez, the nation's two dominant parties, the social democratic Acción Democrática (AD) and the social Christian Comité de Organización Política Electoral Independiente (COPEI), alternated in power several times. Both parties supported the model of import substitution and government intervention in the economy, which enhanced regime legitimacy and the popularity of pro-establishment political leaders. However, the second administrations of President Carlos Andrés Pérez (1989–1993), who belonged to AD, and the former COPEI leader Rafael Caldera (1994–1999) unexpectedly implemented neoliberal formulas that aggravated social inequality. These turnarounds created political and social tensions that led to the electoral triumph of the leftist, former coup leader Hugo Chávez in 1998. Venezuela's reputation as a privileged Third-World country with "responsible" political leadership appeared in question.

EXCEPTIONALISM IN SCHOLARLY AND NONSCHOLARLY ANALYSES

Notions of Venezuelan exceptionalism influenced the work of political scientists and other scholars. Three basic formulations underpinned exceptionalism writing: that Venezuela was privileged with respect to the rest of Latin America, that it remained free of acute class and racial conflict and cleavages that threatened political stability elsewhere, and that its democratic system and political culture were healthy and solid. These writers not only lauded Venezuelan democracy, but compared the nation's democratic prospects favorably with those of the rest of Latin America, even drawing comparisons in a number of areas with Western Europe (Levine, 1977: 10). Two Venezuelan scholars, for instance, claimed that the majority of those Venezuelans not involved in the guerrilla warfare of the 1960s "supported a social and political peace that was worthy of the envy of any non-industrialized nation" (Naím and Piñango, 1984: 553). A U.S. political scientist asserted that no other country in the continent could match the levels of popular participation achieved in Venezuela (Martz, 1984: 392). He also argued that Venezuela's "mobile, active, participatory, and optimistic" population demonstrated a "public vigor and political vibrancy unparalleled in Latin America" (Martz, 1980: 1–2).

Exceptionalism writers contrasted Venezuela's situation with the ungovernability that led to military coups in other Latin American nations. They argued that Venezuela had created institutional mechanisms and practices, principally in the form of political parties and electoral politics, that contained conflict. Political parties exhibited "autonomy" from powerful interest groups and, more than elsewhere in the continent, developed organic ties to organized sectors of the population (Abente, 1988: 149; Levine, 1978: 102; 1989: 284; Salgado, 1987). According to the "institutional" argument, Venezuela owed its success to the sequence of democratic development: first the incorporation of centrist parties into the political system in 1958; then the exclusion, isolation, and defeat of the right (in the military) and the left (the guerrillas) during the 1960s; and, after the consolidation of democratic rule, the government's receptivity to the popular demands embraced by the leftists. With the elite firmly in control, the general populace's behavior changed "in

response to new leadership perspectives." Venezuela was thus spared the re-
lentless radical demands that spurred unruly politics throughout the rest of the
continent (Levine, 1973: 257–259; 1978: 85, 105–107).

Political scientists offered two distinct explanations for the apparent stability of Venezuelan democracy. One thesis attributed Venezuela's success to the
democratic commitment and skills of those who had learned from the sectar-
ian errors committed during the democratic period of 1945–1948, when AD
came to power through a coup. These writers extolled the political behavior
of AD's polemical Rómulo Betancourt and other leaders whom the left
sharply criticized in the 1960s for violating human rights and adopting pro-
U.S. policies. According to this line of thinking, these politicians exhibited
outstanding leadership qualities by establishing a "pacted democracy" consisting of a coalition of pro-establishment parties and institutions that guaranteed political stability. Many other countries in Latin America adopted the
same approach more than two decades later.[2]

A second optimistic thesis regarding democracy in Venezuela centered on
its oil-producing status. According to this argument, Venezuela's transformation from an agricultural to oil-based economy lessened the possibilities for
class-based politics in that it weakened the oligarchy and produced a productive but numerically small working class. This development lent itself to the
formation of multiclass parties with leadership exercised by an "unusually
large middle class fostered by petrodollars," a makeup that contained class
tensions and proved conducive to stability (Karl, 1987: 87).

The notion of exceptionalism also reflected the way Venezuelans constructed their past, exalting the modernity of Venezuelan society and the politics allegedly modeled after the developed countries, and disparaging everything that came before the outset of the modern period in 1936. For decades,
historians and political actors discounted the significance of all political developments in the years between the death of Simón Bolívar in 1830 and the
end of the Juan Vicente Gómez dictatorship in 1935. The Gómez regime was
considered the last in a series of repressive and retrograde governments that
spanned the nineteenth century. By pointing to the perniciousness of this cen-
tury-long rule, AD and Communist leaders who wrote influential books on
Venezuelan political history accentuated the importance of the anti-Gómez
movements, since their parties emerged out of these protests.

AD, in particular, profited from such a depiction since it highlighted the
party's rise to power in 1945 as a veritable "revolution," a break with one
hundred years of backwardness (Betancourt, 2001: 864–867). Similarly,
Communist theoretician Salvador de la Plaza denied that structural changes
of any type, specifically with regard to the semifeudal system of land tenancy,
had occurred since colonial rule—not even under the land-grabbing governments of Conservatives (after 1830), Liberals (after 1863), or Gómez's clique

(after 1899) (de la Plaza, 1973: 102–111). Historians also stressed continuity during the same extended period. Guillermo Morón, for instance, reduced Venezuela's two principal regime changes in 1863 and 1899 to "personalism in the form of ambition to gain power" (referred to as *caudillismo*), "which was made possible by the state of backwardness of the population," specifically "intellectual backwardness" (Morón, 1961: 371, 402, 441).

The end result of these analyses was a monotonous account that minimized the social content and political ideals of a host of struggles that erupted during what might be termed Venezuela's "lost century." The tendency to play down resistance to political oppression and an oppressive world order during the century following 1830 was manifested in a speech by Carlos Andrés Pérez during his first presidency (1974–1979): "Our history was characterized by perpetual personalism . . . the same authoritarianism, oppression and reduction of the people to insignificance. . . . The people were apathetic spectators and failed to control their destiny, as if their lives and futures were the booty of the caudillo" (Pérez, 1988: 162).

This historical interpretation lent itself to exceptionalism thinking, which viewed modern Venezuela as following in the footsteps of developed nations, having left behind virtually all vestiges of its past. In this respect, exceptionalism was firmly rooted in concepts borrowed from nineteenth-century positivism. Latin American positivists extolled U.S. and European-style progress while disparaging and repudiating Latin America's cultural and political heritage, which they often equated with barbarism.

Any thorough examination of the scholarly literature on Venezuela has to place exceptionalism in the context of the Cold War. In the first place, the Cold War's Manichean prism of good versus evil was compatible with the notion that Venezuelan politics after 1830 represented the embodiment of evil. More important, the showcase reputation of Venezuelan democracy obeyed Cold War imperatives. In the 1960s, Rómulo Betancourt, more than any other Latin American leader, succeeded in achieving the type of democracy and implementing the type of policies that the United States favored for Latin America (Alexander, 1964: 319). The glorification of Venezuela for having emulated the U.S. model and avoiding extreme nationalism began at a time when the rest of the continent seemed to be on the verge of choosing between military dictatorship and Cuban-style Communism. Robert Jackson Alexander, one of Betancourt's staunchest academic supporters and a longtime anti-Communist, wrote at the time: "The rivalry between the Cuban Totalitarian Revolution and the Venezuelan Democratic Revolution [sic] will go far to determine the future of the whole of Latin America" (Alexander: 1964: 4). Indeed, the Kennedy administration very much appreciated the role played by Betancourt in backing U.S. efforts to isolate Cuba, at a time when the other principal Latin

American democracies were reluctant to take a position on the issue (Schlesinger, 1965: 177–178, 225).

REEXAMINATION OF THE EXCEPTIONALISM THESIS

The surprise that many academics shared when confronted by the events of February 1989 was expressed in the headline "South America's Most Stable Democracy Explodes" (*Newsweek*, 1989). The mass disturbances in opposition to neoliberal austerity measures known as the *Caracazo* led Venezuelans and especially scholars to question the premises of the exceptionalism paradigm. Events during the 1990s, including two military coup attempts in 1992 and a wave of street protests, obliterated Venezuela's image as a model democracy while they confirmed its status as a Third-World nation. The thesis that institutional mechanisms legitimately channeled conflict and guaranteed democratic stability on a par with developed nations had become untenable, and some scholars questioned whether the proposition had ever been fully applicable (Ellner, 1993: 224–231). The institutional argument assumed widespread participation in impartially managed elections, but events in the 1990s invalidated this presumption. In 1993 popular pressure forced new gubernatorial elections in various states, and the outcome reversed the officially announced results, buttressing allegations of widespread fraud.[3] During the same period, electoral abstention more than doubled from that of the 1988 presidential race, itself high with respect to previous years.

Exalting the quality of political leaders and the interparty pacts they fashioned in the 1960s and 1970s proved less convincing in the political context of the 1990s. Political scientists came to see "pacted democracy" as elitist and exclusionary (Crisp, Levine, and Rey, 1995: 148–158), while public opinion polls placed parties at the bottom of the list of Venezuelan institutions in credibility (Buxton, 2001: 59–104). The political class's loss of prestige was related to the fact that Venezuela was the only nation in Latin America in which presidents on two separate occasions campaigned on antineoliberal platforms only to embrace neoliberalism once in office (Pérez in 1989 and Caldera in 1994). Finally, the argument that Venezuela was exempt from the levels of violence that shook nations elsewhere in the continent was shattered by the *Caracazo* and the two subsequent abortive military coups.

Although some scholars writing in the 1990s argued that exceptionalism was no longer applicable to Venezuela (Levine, 1994), they nonetheless failed to expose its fundamental flaws. Those who had previously defended exceptionalism generally came to recognize that the system of "pacted democracy" was fashioned by political elites and was therefore inherently exclusionary. They failed, however, to draw the connection between political exclusion and the related phenomenon of clientelism, on the one hand, and undemocratic practices, such as the violation of human rights, electoral manipulation, and corruption, on the other. Indeed, they took the legitimacy of the institutional mechanisms that guaranteed stability for granted. Nevertheless, the same defects of electoral fraud, corruption, and repression (as occurred during the disturbances of February 1989) that scholars pointed to as contributing to the crisis of the 1990s had been apparent in previous decades. Thus, for instance, the popular belief that party representatives at the polls determined the outcomes of elections underscored that electoral abuse was not a recent phenomenon. In short, the exceptionalism assertion that Venezuelan democracy had created efficacious mechanisms to channel conflict failed to take into account the dubious legitimacy of certain procedures.

Several examples of the link between political exclusion and undemocratic behavior will suffice. The political pact that ushered in the democratic period in 1958 shunted aside the Communist Party in spite of its leadership role in the struggle against the previous military dictatorship. Some scholars and politicians (like Rómulo Betancourt at the time) argued that the exclusion of leftists from the decision-making process facilitated democratic consolidation in the 1960s (Levine, 1978: 106–107; 1989: 259–260, 283). The nonparticipation of the leftists throughout the decade was partly due to their own decision to take up arms, but that action was taken only in the context of flagrant violation of human rights during the AD governments of Betancourt (1959–1964) and Raúl Leoni (1964–1969).

In another example of the combination of exclusion, self-exclusion, and undemocratic measures, the Matanceros (a worker contingent of the "Causa R" Party) emerged in the industrial Guayana region as the nation's most important insurgent workers' movement in the 1970s and 1980s. In spite of the spectacular inroads made by the Matanceros, the AD leadership in organized labor declined to incorporate them into national and regional structures, thus increasing their intransigence. This isolation was due in part to the Matanceros' declared policy of spurning "unrepresentative" bodies but also to the undemocratic and even repressive measures taken against them. In 1981 the AD-controlled national labor federation took over the all-important Matanceros-controlled union representing workers in the state-run steel company SIDOR. The intervention and resultant reprisals against Matanceros militants backfired, as they returned to the union's leadership when elections were held again in 1987 and retained control of the organization throughout the following decade.

Clientelism and undemocratic practices also ensured that the conservative Betancourt-led faction of AD, favored by exceptionalism writers, maintained control of the party for decades in the face of a series of left-leaning factional challenges in the 1960s and 1970s.[4] The most important schism occurred in

1967, when Betancourt insisted on overturning the results of internal elections that favored a pro-leftist as the party's presidential candidate. The resultant split-off of the left-leaning Movimiento Electoral del Pueblo (People's Electoral Movement—MEP) and its subsequent electoral decline represented a triumph for the AD party machine over the will of the rank and file.

Elected president in December 1998, Hugo Chávez did much to puncture the myths surrounding Venezuelan exceptionalism. Most important, his fiery nationalism reaffirmed Venezuela's status as a Latin American nation and rejected the importation of values, culture, and models from the United States. Chávez embraced the concept of a "multipolar" world in which Latin American nations formed a bloc to defend their interests. On this basis, he vigorously opposed the U.S.-promoted Free Trade Area of the Americas (FTAA), which favored foreign investments and tariff reduction on a hemispheric scale. At the same time, he successfully petitioned for Venezuelan entrance in MERCOSUR (consisting of southern South American nations) and advocated Latin American unification modeled after the European Union. On the cultural front, Chávez and his movement reaffirmed Venezuela's indigenous, African, and Latin American identities. Thus the 1999 Constitution granted Indian groups territorial autonomy and officially recognized their languages. The Constitution also stipulated that "popular culture embodying the essence of Venezuela would enjoy special attention" (Article 100) and that the communications media would be responsible for "transmitting the values of popular tradition" as well as the works of Venezuelan artists (Article 101).

REINTERPRETING THE PAST

President Chávez questioned the tendency of traditional historiography (which reflects exceptionalism thinking) to denigrate the nation's past, specifically its exaggeration of the passivity of the Venezuelan people during the years between 1830 and 1936. Chávez proclaimed the nineteenth-century general Ezequiel Zamora, who raised the cry "Horror to the Oligarchy!" and promoted land redistribution, as one of the main inspirations of his movement. Chávez also lauded Cipriano Castro, who headed Venezuela from 1899 to 1908 and had long been considered capricious, lustful, and corrupt. Chávez celebrated Castro's resolve in confronting foreign investors and his efforts to rally national sentiment against European creditor nations that blockaded Venezuelan ports in 1902. In addition, Chávez rejected the notion that the 1830–1936 years represented nothing more than uninterrupted strong-man (or "caudillo") rule. In doing so, he singled out the case of his own great-grandfather, Pedro Pérez Delgado ("Maisanta," whose father had served in Zamora's army). For three decades, Maisanta participated in uprisings (including one that opposed Gómez's overthrow of Castro) and died in prison in 1924. Chávez claimed that far from being a bloodthirsty caudillo, as he was sometimes described, Maisanta was a "revolutionary" fighter for democracy. "To call someone '*caudillo*,'" Chávez stated, "is to throw him into the garbage heap of history as a stigma. . . . I believe we have imported a bourgeois democratic model that consists of the elimination of [our historical] leaders" (Blanco Muñoz, 1998: 103).

A critical analysis of the exceptionalism thesis points in the direction of a balanced approach to postindependence Venezuelan history that avoids two antithetical positions. On the one hand, scholars cannot ignore the corrupt dealings and authoritarianism of historical figures such as Cipriano Castro, whom Chávez views as a national hero due to his nationalistic stands. On the other hand, monochromatic historiography, with its backward versus modern dichotomy, reduces nineteenth-century politics to personal ambition and resistance to progress and pays insufficient attention to the ideals that inspired the period's principal political and social movements. Thus, for instance, the Liberals before and after reaching power in 1863 constituted an antioligarchic movement committed to achieving national unification, identity, and development (Carrera Damas, 1983). It is hard to exaggerate the self-serving qualities of the main Liberal leader, Antonio Guzmán Blanco, who discarded the party's democratic ideals during his rule from 1870 to 1888. Nevertheless, Guzmán Blanco dealt a heavy, long-lasting blow to the Church, a bulwark of the aristocracy, reined in the power of regional caudillos for the first time in the nation's history, promoted public education, and, according to one Venezuelan revisionist account, favored the "advanced," enterprising sectors of the elite over the traditional oligarchy (Carrera Damas, 1983: 113–117).

The classical populism represented by AD in the 1940s shared the tendency to belittle the importance of all struggles after 1830. The party thus lost the opportunity to strengthen its nationalist appeal by glorifying post-1830 Venezuelan leaders and struggles as the *Peronista* populists had Juan Manuel de Rosas and other nineteenth-century Argentine caudillos (Ellner, 1999: 130–131). Part of the reason for the difference between Venezuelan and Argentine populism was that AD (unlike *Peronismo*) emerged as a civilian reaction to military rule, and therefore denigrated military figures of the past even when they were identified with national and popular causes. Along these lines, AD writers praised the nineteenth-century civilian leader José María Vargas (president on two occasions in the 1830s), even though he was of an aristocratic background and confronted military officers of popular extraction (Betancourt, 1979: 150). In addition, later AD leaders who fought against dictator Juan Vicente Gómez in the early 1930s clashed with the dictator's military enemies in exile, whom they denounced as "caudillos" (Sosa and Lengrand, 1981: 140–143). The antimilitarism and the liberal democratic model embraced by AD coincided with exceptionalism's idealization of Western-style democracy. A reexamination of antimilitarism (including that on the Venezuelan left) is of special relevance given the military origin of the Chavista movement.

Chávez's discourse signals a new tendency to extol nineteenth-century leaders (such as Cipriano Castro), rebels (such as Maisanta), and political movements. The glorification of these historical actors obviously simplifies complex historical reality and indeed may be an overreaction to exceptionalism thinking. On the positive side, Chávez's interpretation of Venezuelan history contributes to the eradication of the "black legend" of Cipriano Castro, among others (Pino Iturrieta, 1991: 10).[5] The end result may be a more balanced popular view of post-1830 Venezuela and an appreciation of its complexity. This revisionist historiography also underlines the importance of heroes such as Ezequiel Zamora, demonstrating that their struggles were not isolated incidents but rather formed part of a larger, ongoing movement with national goals and ideals.

The critical problems that Venezuelan democracy faced in the 1990s and the issues raised by the Chávez movement also encourage a reevaluation of the entire post-1958 democratic period and cast doubt on the validity of many of the postulates associated with Venezuelan exceptionalism. As president, Hugo Chávez has not missed an opportunity to denounce Venezuela's forty-year democratic regime as corrupt, repressive, and subservient to vested interests. Venezuelan democratic leaders as he depicts them recall the Cuban political class in the 1940s and 1950s, whose opportunism, lack of nationalistic sentiment, and moral depravity led to Fidel Castro's rise to power. We do not share, however, Chávez's complete dismissal of Venezuela's extended democratic experience. One major reason for our difference with Chávez is that the model of state intervention in the economy after 1958 (referred to in Venezuela as "*sembrar el petróleo,*" or "sow the oil") promoted development and contained a dosage of economic nationalism that contrasted favorably with the neoliberal formulas implemented after 1989 (Collier and Collier, 1991: 572). A balanced picture of the period of democratic rule that avoids the exaggerated praise of the exceptionalism writers and the satanization encouraged by Chávez is needed to place the democratic experience in proper perspective. Such an analysis would rescue the interventionist model from the dogmatic assertions of neoliberals. At the same time, it would demonstrate that the failures of state interventionism in the economy were due as much to the aberrations of the political system, such as the cleintelistic practices of the dominant political parties, as to the shortcomings of the economic policies of the period. Most important, the political leaders who directed the interventionist model during those years lacked a well-developed long-term strategy for overcoming dependence. The proposed analytical approach would point to the correctives necessary to make state interventionism successful in the future.

NOTES

1. Many writers on the left have recognized the uniqueness of oil's role in sharp contrast with other Third-World export commodities, whose cheap prices—as Lenin pointed out—buttressed the capitalist economies of developed nations (Bergquist, 1986: 273; Klare, 2004).

2. Venezuela and Colombia both pioneered in designing interparty pacts, but political scientists recognize that the agreements of the former were more viable and long-lasting than those of the latter (Herman, 1988: 5–12).

3. As a corrective to electoral fraud, the Constitution of 1999 recognized the electoral authorities as a separate branch of the state (known as the Poder Electoral) on a par with the executive, legislative, and judicial powers.

4. The four left-leaning factions that emerged during the period accused the party machine dominated by the "Betancouristas" (Rómulo Betancourt's followers) of employing undemocratic methods against them. The first three of these internal currents broke off from the party to form the Movimiento de Izquierda Revolucionaria (MIR) in 1960, the "Grupo ARS" in 1962, and the MEP in 1967. A fourth internal current, located on the party's left, consisted of the followers of Carlos Andrés Pérez prior to his embracement of neoliberal policies in 1989.

5. Historian Elías Pino Iturrieta points out that the "literature adverse to Cipriano Castro is overwhelming and has weighed on the sentiment of Venezuelans to the extent that few recognize any merit in the Restoration [Castro's arrival to power in 1899]. Nevertheless one should be skeptical of the books" on Castro since they generally "fail to consider the nuances of both his personality and the era" (Pino Iturrieta, 1991: 10).

REFERENCES

Abente, Diego
    1988 "Politics and Policies: The Limits of the Venezuelan Consociational Regime," pp. 133–154 in Donald L. Herman (ed.), *Democracy in Latin America: Colombia and Venezuela*. New York: Praeger.
Alexander, Robert Jackson
    1964 *The Venezuelan Democratic Revolution: A Profile of the Regime of Rómulo Betancourt*. New Brunswick, NJ: Rutgers University Press.
Bergquist, Charles
    1986 *Labor in Latin America: Comparative Essays on Chile, Argentina, Venezuela, and Colombia*. Stanford, CA: Stanford University Press.
Betancourt, Rómulo
    1979 *El 18 de octubre de 1945: génesis y realizaciones de una revolución democrática*. Barcelona: Editorial Seix Barral.
    2001 [1956] *Venezuela: política y petróleo*. Caracas: Monte Avila.
Blanco Muñoz, Agustín [interviewee]
    1998 *Habla el comandante*. Caracas: Universidad Central de Venezuela.
Buxton, Julia
    2001 *The Failure of Political Reform in Venezuela*. Aldershot, England: Ashgate.

Carrera Damas, Germán
    1983 *Una nación llamada Venezuela*. Caracas: Monte Avila.
Collier, Ruth Berins and David Collier
    1991 *Shaping the Political Arena: Critical Junctures, the Labor Movement, and Regime Dy-namics in Latin America*. Princeton, NJ: Princeton University Press.
Crisp, Brian F. and Daniel H. Levine and Juan Carlos Rey
    1995 "The Legitimacy Problem," pp. 139–170 in Jennifer McCoy, Andrés Serbin, William C. Smith, and Andrés Stambouli (eds.), *Venezuelan Democracy under Stress*. New Brunswick, NY: Transaction.
de la Plaza, Salvador
    1973 *Venezuela: país privilegiado*. Caracas: UCV.
Ellner, Steve
    1993 *Organized Labor in Venezuela, 1958–1991: Behavior and Concerns in a Democratic Setting*. Wilmington, DE: Scholarly Resources.
    1999 "The Heyday of Radical Populism in Venezuela and Its Aftermath," pp. 117–137 in Michael Conniff (ed.), *Populism in Latin America*. Tuscaloosa: University of Alabama Press.
Herman, Donald L.
    1988 "Democratic and Authoritarian Traditions," pp. 1–15 in Herman (ed.), *Democracy in Latin America: Colombia and Venezuela*. New York: Praeger.
Karl, Terry Lynn
    1987 "Petroleum and Political Pacts: The Transition to Democracy in Venezuela." *Latin American Research Review* 22 (1): 35–62.
Klare, Michael
    2004 *Blood and Oil: The Dangers and Consequences of America's Growing Dependency on Imported Oil*. New York: Metropolitan Books.
Levine, Daniel H.
    1973 *Conflict and Political Change in Venezuela*. Princeton, NJ: Princeton University Press.
    1977 "Venezuelan Politics: Past and Future," pp. 7–44 in Robert D. Bond (ed.), *Contemporary Venezuela and Its Role in International Affairs*. New York: New York University Press.
    1978 "Venezuela since 1958: The Consolidation of Democratic Politics," pp. 82–109 in Juan J. Linz and Alfred Stepan (eds.), *The Breakdown of Democratic Regimes: Latin America*. Baltimore, MD: Johns Hopkins University Press.
    1989 "Venezuela: The Nature, Sources, and Future Prospects of Democracy," pp. 247–289 in Larry Diamond, Juan J. Linz, and Seymour Martin Lipset (eds.), *Democracy in Developing Countries: Latin America*. Boulder, CO: Lynne Rienner.
    1994 "Goodbye to Venezuelan Exceptionalism." *Journal of Inter-American Studies and World Affairs* 36 (4): 145–182.
Martz, John D.
    1980 "The Evolution of Democratic Politics in Venezuela," pp. 1–29 in Howard R. Penniman (ed.), *Venezuela at the Polls: The National Elections of 1978*. Washington, DC: American Enterprise Institute for Public Policy Research.
    1984 "Venezuela, Colombia, and Ecuador," pp. 381–401 in Jan Knippers Black (ed.), *Latin America: Its Problems and Its Promises*. Boulder, CO: Westview.
Morón, Guillermo
    1961 *Historia de Venezuela*. 3rd edition. Caracas: n.p.
Naím, Moisés and Ramon Piñango
    1984 "El caso Venezuela: una illusión de armonía," pp. 539–579 in Naím and Piñango (eds.), *El caso Venezuela: una illusion de armonía*. Caracas: Ediciones IESA.
Newsweek
    1989 "South America's Most Stable Democracy Explodes." March 13, 35.

Pérez, Carlos Andres
    1988 *El quehacer y la historia*. Caracas: Alfadil.
Pino Iturrieta, Elías
    1991 "Rasgos y limites de la restauración liberal," pp. 9–25 in *Cipriano Castro y su época*.
    Caracas: Monte Avila.
Salgado, René
    1987 "Economic Pressure Groups and Policy-Making in Venezuela: The Case of FEDECA-
    MARAS Reconsidered." *Latin American Research Review* 22 (3): 91–105.
Schlesinger, Arthur M., Jr.
    1965 *A Thousand Days: John F. Kennedy in the White House*. Boston: Houghton Mifflin.
Sosa A., Arturo and Eloi Lengrand
    1981 *Del garibaldismo estudiantil a la izquierda criolla: los orígenes marxistas del
    proyecto de A.D. (1928–1935)*. Caracas: Ediciones Centauro.

Chapter Two

Venezuelan Social Conflict in a Global Context

Edgardo Lander

Having escaped the harsh experience of military rule during the 1970s and 1980s, Venezuela did not undergo the political demobilization and abandonment of social democratic policies that occurred in most of Latin America over the same period. As a consequence, it appears to have been unprepared for the neoliberal programs promoted by the United States as part of the "Washington Consensus." Authoritarian regimes throughout the continent sought to restructure the principal dimensions of social life to adapt to the new exigencies of the global economy. Policies of deregulation, liberalization, privatization, reduction of the state's activity, and the limitation of social rights, which could only be partially implemented in the United States and Europe, were imposed with few constraints in Latin America, in some cases after all resistance had been crushed through repression. Chile represents the most extensive and painfully "successful" experiment of this type. The Popular Unity government was overthrown, the multifarious popular movement was routed, power relations among diverse social groups were radically altered, and a fundamental change occurred in the political culture. As the fourth post-Pinochet president (and second Socialist Party member) Michelle Bachelet was sworn into office at the beginning of 2006, the main directions of the neoliberal economic policies established by the military dictatorship remained firmly on course.

The democratic transitions and processes of state reform and decentralization carried out in most Latin American countries were implemented only after military regimes had modified the economic model of state intervention that had existed previously. The new civilian governments did not alter basic policies that had excluded vast sectors of the population and promoted concentration of power and wealth. It is therefore hardly surprising that to this day democracy generates little enthusiasm throughout most of the continent, that political parties are in crisis, and that the population in general expects little from elections. Throughout Latin America, more vitality can be found in movements such as the *Zapatistas* in Mexico, and the "Sin Tierra" movement in Brazil and novel forms of struggle such as the blocking of traffic in Argentina and the indigenous/popular mobilizations that paralyzed Ecuador in 2000 and Bolivia in 2000 and 2002 (CLACSO, 2000). Before the 2002 elections in Brazil, Bolivia, and Ecuador, only in Venezuela, under the government of Hugo Chávez that came to power in 1998, had electoral politics played an important role in resisting neoliberalism.

After the transitions to democracy throughout Latin America in the 1980s, it was only the longevity of Venezuela's political institutions that seemed unusual. Nevertheless, the Venezuelan political process appeared to be out of sync with the rest of the continent. The Venezuelan armed forces became restive just as the military was returning to the barracks elsewhere in the continent. Already in 1982 (when Hugo Chávez began organizing within the armed forces) the military unrest that would shake the Punto Fijo democracy was taking form. The election of Chávez in December 1998 brought to power a leader determined to oppose neoliberalism at home and global concentration of power abroad. In contrast to the case of the Southern Cone and most other parts of Latin America, Venezuelan electoral politics had not been tamed by terror and transition. Even though two attempted coups d'etats, popular explosions, and declarations of radical populist content initiated Chavismo, from 1998 onward the movement remained within democratic institutional limits, with seven national elections carried out over the course of two years (Parker, 2001). Chávez aroused suspicion among most of the other leaders of the hemisphere, but he also produced hope among its popular movements. With Cuba excluded from participation in hemispheric and multilateral meetings, and given the fact that he came to power through competitive elections, Chávez has arguably been the most effective national leader espousing resistance to the Washington Consensus.

This chapter explores three main issues. In the first place, it presents several general hypotheses on the global geopolitical and economic context within which the Venezuelan political system has operated over the last decades. Second, it discusses some of the particular conditions that help explain the relative stability and success of the first decades of Venezuelan democracy after 1958 and that gave rise to notions of "Venezuelan exceptionalism." Finally, it describes the conditions leading to the breakdown of this experiment and the extraordinary popular resistance that confronted attempts to impose neoliberal adjustment policies in the country in the 1990s, leading to the election of Hugo Chávez as president in 1998.

THE GLOBAL CONTEXT

During the postwar period, especially in the 1960s, significant changes in the global arena fostered a relative redistribution of power in favor of the underprivileged sectors. The bipolar nature of the Cold War permitted a degree of freedom favorable to national liberation movements, which triumphed in many parts of the world. With regard to the distribution of power, the world became somewhat more democratic. In Western Europe, the social welfare state became firmly established and was accompanied by democratization throughout the continent. In Latin America, the "oligarchic" regimes entered into crisis, and popular struggles—frequently through some form of populism—achieved levels of participation and social incorporation greater than previously known except during the Mexican Revolution.

Reduction in the enormous gaps in the distribution of wealth and income accompanied this political change (Cornia, 1999). In Western Europe, inequality declined during the 1950s, 1960s, and throughout most of the 1970s. Low levels of unemployment and the accelerated expansion of social security helped reduce inequality. In the United States, the concentration of wealth, measured in terms of the proportion of wealth in the hands of the richest 1 percent of the population, reached its postwar peak of 37 percent in 1965, but after that began to decline, with the wealthiest 1 percent accounting for 22 percent of assets in 1976 (Wolff, 1995). In Latin America income distribution improved in the 1960s until the 1982 foreign debt crisis. Between 1970 and 1982, the ratio of the average income of the wealthiest 20 percent to that of the poorest 20 percent of the population decreased from 23:1 in 1970, to 18:1 in 1982 (UNDP, 1999: 39). Although no major change in income distribution occurred in Venezuela during this period, the material conditions of the majority of the population steadily improved, largely as a consequence of oil rent. Increased oil revenue reflected the increased power of Third-World oil-exporting nations vis-à-vis the companies and consuming countries after the founding of the Organization of Petroleum Exporting Countries (OPEC) in 1960.

At the beginning of the 1970s the rate of profit for large corporations fell, much as Marx would have predicted, as a consequence of their more limited access to resources, workers, and markets in many parts of the world. The nationalist policies of the Third World, in the context of a bipolar world, the strengthening of organized labor, and increased taxes and state regulation put the brakes on the private sector's capacity for expansion. Global corporate executives felt threatened not only by Communism and reduced profits, but by democracy itself, which seemed to pose risks to liberal, industrialized societies. The Trilateral Commission diagnosed this crisis as one of "governability"—that is, an excess of democracy that needed to be contained (Crozier, Huntington, and Watanuki, 1975). Conservatives advocated an extraordinary offensive at all levels: military, political, technological, and economic. The governments of Ronald Reagan and Margaret Thatcher spearheaded this global counterrevolution (Quijano, 1996), initiating aggressive military policies against "rebel" governments and popular movements throughout the world.

The foreign debt, as manipulated by Washington, was a central political weapon in this global strategy. The Bretton Woods multilateral financial institutions broadened their functions and at the same time they imposed severe controls on countries that proved incapable of paying their debt and appeared to be in serious financial straits. The concentration of power and decision-making capacity by transnational corporations and their governments negatively affected the majority of the world population. This consolidation was reflected in further steps in the establishment of a global liberal legal order and in new, extremely powerful supranational institutions such as the World Trade Organization (Wallach and Sforza, 1999). Of particular consequence for Venezuela has been the International Energy Association (IEA), founded in response to OPEC's success in raising oil prices. The IEA eulogized the oil policies designed by Margaret Thatcher for the North Sea, which eliminated oil royalties and established a sliding scale for taxes, two key elements later embodied in Venezuela's "oil opening" (Mommer, 2003).

Multinational companies sought to restore the rate of profit through corporate mergers and through technological and organizational transformations designed to diminish labor costs and strengthen management's capacity to impose its will on workers. To meet these objectives corporations accelerated automation, introduced new communication technologies, implemented labor "flexibility," fractionalized and relocated different phases of the productive process, and increased capital mobility—all aspects of globalization. Both the processes of state deregulation and changes in labor legislation throughout the world increased the power of the owners of capital and limited that of the workers (MacEwan, 1999: 59). This successful corporate strategy for the recuperation of earnings rates required the establishment of firm barriers to protect capitalist enterprises from the alleged "excesses" of democratic politics—regulation, taxes, and other public policies that would restrict the economic liberty defended by neoliberal ideology.

All the available statistics indicate that a notable decrease in equality, both among and within most countries, has accompanied this concentration of power and capital over the past two or three decades (Cornia, 1999; 2000). The relationship between the average income of the fifth of the world population living in the wealthiest countries and that of the fifth of the population living in the poorest countries went from 30:1 in 1960 to 74:1 in 1997 (UNDP, 1999). According to a study of 124 countries representing 94 percent of the world's population, the income share of the wealthiest 20 percent of countries increased from 69 percent in 1965 to 83 percent in 1990 (UNCTAD, 1997). In Venezuela these patterns became evident after the collapse of oil prices and the devaluation of the currency in 1983. The ratio of the income from salary of the top tenth to that of the lowest tenth went from 12.5:1 in 1984 to 23.9:1 in 1991 (Lander, 1996b: 65).

In keeping with world trends, the rate of impoverishment in Venezuela persisted throughout the 1990s, along with the outbreak of popular protests. Since 1990, fifty-five countries, the majority of them in sub-Saharan Africa, Eastern Europe, and the Community of Independent States (CIS), have experienced declining per capita incomes (UNDP, 1999). The increase in inequality of the "transitional" countries of Eastern Europe and the CIS has been the greatest ever known historically (UNDP, 1999). Inequality has increased significantly in China, Indonesia, Thailand, and other countries of Southeast Asia that in past decades had achieved rapid growth and at the same time improved income distribution and reduced poverty (UNDP, 1999). Average family consumption in Africa at the end of the 1990s was 20 percent less than 25 years earlier (UNDP, 1999). In addition, in most Organization of Economic Cooperation and Development countries income inequality increased after 1980, most notoriously in the United Kingdom, the United States, and Sweden (UNDP, 1999).

Throughout Latin America, structural adjustment policies implemented by authoritarian and nonauthoritarian regimes alike exacerbated inequalities (Berry, 1997). The foreign debt gave creditors and multilateral financial organizations immense power over the governments of debtor countries. Democratic political processes became progressively emptier; the "recommendations" of the multilateral organizations came to be more important than the will of the voters, public opinion, or parliamentary decisions. Under these conditions, the states of the periphery and semiperiphery came to operate more like "a kind of subcontractor or franchise holder" (Sousa Santos, 1998: 33) than like democratic representatives of sovereign nations.

According to neoliberal discourse, the restoration of democracy combined with economic growth will improve the living conditions of the millions of excluded people of the continent. Given the unchanged relations of power in the continent, this is not a realistic expectation. Even where there has been sustained growth and where poverty-reducing policies have had some success, as in the case of Chile, the distribution of income has not been altered. Economic growth is now less progressively distributed in the region than it was in the past (Morley, 2000; Janvry and Sadoulet, 1995: 15). At the end of the 1990s, only Uruguay showed an improvement since the beginning of the 1980s in poverty levels and equity. In democratic Argentina, the income difference between the wealthiest 10 percent and the poorest 10 percent of the population increased from a factor of 15 to 24 between the years 1991 and

1997 (Gambina, 1999). In all Latin America, unemployment at the end of the 1990s was higher than during the crisis of the 1980s (Weller, 2000: 48), and there was a general tendency toward more precarious and heterogeneous jobs. Labor law "reforms" diminished job protection and workers' negotiating power. The International Labor Organization (ILO) has calculated that of every ten new jobs created in the 1990s, eight were low quality positions in the informal sector (Ocampo, 1998). Job security has been reduced, and there has been an increase in temporary jobs not protected by collective bargaining agreements (CEPAL, 2000, 98–99). At the same time, fewer workers are covered by some system of social security or employment insurance (CEPAL, 2000: 101). Venezuela has not escaped these tendencies, particularly the loss of traditional legal benefits (Ellner, 2003: 164–165). Faced with these results, it is hardly surprising that electoral democracy has until recently inspired little interest in most of the region. Electoral promises have rarely coincided with public policy; resistance has largely taken extraparliamentary form.

THE DECOMPOSITION OF THE
PUNTO FIJO REGIME IN VENEZUELA

Despite significant inequality, during the first years of the democratic regime installed in 1958 and especially during the period of greatest expansion of petroleum rent (1973–1978), the standard of living in Venezuela improved. Social indicators reflecting education levels, health standards, life expectancy, access to housing and public services, infant mortality, and employment (including levels of formal employment) all registered significant improvement. Public-sector employment and an important expansion of access to education at all levels, particularly university education, led to substantial social mobility. During part of this period, there was some improvement in income distribution (Rodríguez, n.d.). After the defeat of the armed insurgency in the 1960s, Venezuela assumed the role of a showcase democracy, an experience widely considered successful, institutionalized, stable, and legitimate. Historical patterns of growth and increase in oil prices were projected into the distant future. The upper and middle classes did not see their ever-increasing levels of consumption and cosmopolitan cultural orientations as threatened by popular demands, since state income continued to rise. Expanded education, health, and public works expenditure did not depend on taxing private wealth. Popular sectors of Venezuelan society, especially the new urban majority of the population, expected continued upward social mobility. A "modern" integrated society appeared possible in a not-too-distant future. A political culture of "national harmony" and its corresponding multiclass political party organizations achieved hegemony. A self-image of an inclusive, equalitarian, and racially democratic society became dominant. Optimism prevailed. The thesis of "Venezuelan exceptionalism" took firm hold.

Toward the end of the 1970s, these tendencies began to reverse themselves. A significant decline in per capita oil income and per capita income (Rodríguez, n.d.) anticipated the foreign debt crisis and devaluation in 1983. The financial crisis occurred later than those in most Latin American countries, but the political impact proved more profound because expectations of sustained growth and improved living conditions had sunk deep roots in the Venezuelan mode of thinking. In addition, the economic crisis became more prolonged, with deterioration in the living conditions of a majority of the population lasting more than two decades. Per capita income in 1997 was 8 percent less than in 1970; workers' income during this period was reduced by approximately half. Furthermore, there was a marked deterioration of income distribution. Capital's share of income derived from production increased by approximately 15 percentage points, implying a substantial increase in its power relative to labor (Rodríguez, n.d.). According to one estimate, total poverty in the country nearly doubled between 1984 and 1991, from 36 percent of the population to 68 percent (Martel, 1993). The impact of these changing conditions on Venezuelan political culture was profound.

A DIVIDED SOCIETY

An increasingly divided society took shape in Venezuela. Historical and more recent forms of social divisions and exclusions that had been forgotten in the dominant political discourse and political culture became increasingly difficult to ignore. As elsewhere in Latin America, social segregation was most visible in urban areas. A sensation of insecurity became generalized throughout the population, constituting "an emerging culture of violence . . . very distinct from the culture of tolerance and peace that dominated Venezuelan society in the past" (Briceño León et al., 1997: 213). Along with unemployment, personal safety topped the problems perceived as most serious by the population. Between 1986 and 1996 the number of homicides per 10,000 inhabitants jumped from 13.4 to 56, an increase of 418 percent, with most of the victims being young males (San Juan, 1997: 232–233). Countless streets in the middle- and upper-class neighborhoods were closed and privatized; increasingly, bars and electric fences surrounded houses and buildings in these areas. The threat represented by the "dangerous class" came to occupy a central place in the media—frequently with racist overtones—along with demands that drastic measures be taken, including the death penalty or direct execution by the police.

These processes of exclusion, segregation, and fragmentation led to socioeconomic decay—especially in the cities—and to the decomposition of the traditional mechanisms and forms of socialization and social integration, particularly the family, school, and work. At the same time new models of alternative socialization emerged to address the challenge of surviving extremely adverse conditions (Pedrazzini and Sánchez, 1992). The benefits of economic growth in the country, health, education, housing, well-compensated employment, and social mobility, once assumed by the popular sectors to be a real possibility for a better future, now appeared inaccessible. Poverty and exclusion ceased to be seen as temporary phenomena in a "developing" or "modernizing" society or as conditions that might be overcome through individual effort. These crises-like conditions increasingly became permanent features of society. We are dealing here not with the exclusion of a minority categorized as "marginal" in relation to society as a whole but with the living conditions and cultural reproduction of the great majority of the population. The result was the development of what Ivez Pedrazzini and Magaly Sánchez (1992) have called the "culture of urgency." They describe a practical culture of action in which the informal economy, illegality, illegitimacy, violence, and mistrust of official society are common. Alejandro Moreno (1995) characterizes this other cultural universe as the popular-life world that is *other*, different from Western modernity—organized in terms of a matriarchal family structure, with different conceptions of time, work, and community, and a *relational* (community-oriented) rationality distinct from the abstract rationality of the dominant society. This cultural context is scarcely compatible with the model of citizenship associated with liberal democracies of the West.

The declining legitimacy of the political system, evident since the early 1980s, prompted the elite to reform a presidential and centralized state that was increasingly ineffective, corrupt, and incapable of responding to the demands of a more diverse and complex society. Politicians from across the political spectrum embraced the goals of modernization and democratization, with the latter understood principally as decentralization. The Presidential Commission for the Reform of the State, founded in 1984, made this goal a priority. Thus, while society became increasingly fragmented, the idea of carrying out institutional changes to make the Venezuelan political system more decentralized, more democratic, and more participatory dominated political debate.

In a society increasingly characterized by social apartheid in the form of severe economic exclusion, cultural gaps, and differentiated individual and collective identities, institutional political reforms could only make a partial and limited contribution to the achievement of a nationally integrated political system. From a juridical and institutional point of view, new mechanisms of incorporation and participation were necessary. These reforms included steps to decentralize the state as well as the direct election of mayors and governors, and they promoted the emergence of diverse regional and local leaderships, bringing fresh air to the political system (López Maya and Lander, 1996: 174). However, the economic and cultural processes of exclusion proved much more potent than the democratizing impact of these political reforms.

Thus we encounter the apparent paradox of an increasingly divided society with an elite political debate centered on institutional democratization. However, since this elite debate did not deal with the structural and cultural determinants of exclusion and political illegitimacy, what had seemed as deeply rooted ideas about democracy and society had to be questioned. Social-democratic and Christian-democratic ideals, which for decades were located at different points on the political spectrum, by the 1990s had become infused with new meanings derived from neoliberal and neoconservative ideological frameworks. An antipolitical and antiparty discourse was reflected in the media, establishing a Manichean opposition between the state (characterized as corrupt, inefficient, and clientelist) and a mythical civil society (which included the media), understood as a synthesis of all virtue: creativity, initiative, efficacy, honesty, and participation.

The paradigmatic new subject of this "democracy of citizens" that would replace the "democracy of parties" was the neighbor-citizen, conceived on the basis of the experience of middle- and upper-class urban neighborhood organizations (Lander, 1996a: 55–56). The central concern of these organizations has been defense of property and protection from threats by the excluded sectors of the population. The normative horizon for this conservative idea of democracy is an apolitical society, free of ideological debates, in which the principal concerns of government have to do with the effectiveness and honesty of the administration, one in which participation and democratic decision-making about the collective good are tightly restricted to local arenas. The economy must be vigorously protected from "demagogic and irresponsible" demands formulated in the name of democracy. All social and redistributive policies by the state fall under suspicion as populist.

The social and political organizations (parties and unions) that in previous decades served as the principal channels of expression for popular demands not only were in crisis but tended to be treated in the new political discourse as illegitimate. For this model of citizenship the paradigmatic image is the middle- and upper-middle-class neighborhood, with its professional expertise, access to the media, personal political relations, and use of the Internet as an organizational instrument. With the increasing delegitimization of all redistributive public policies and most social policy, the country's underprivileged sectors had little opportunity for the articulation and expression of their interests. This political model could be called, paraphrasing Bonfil Batalla (1990), a *"Venezuela imaginaria"* that was disconnected from *"Venezuela profounda"* —the everyday life of the majority of the population.

This deep fissure in Venezuelan society was most sharply expressed in the social explosion of February 1989 known as the *Caracazo*. In the principal cities of the country, looting occurred on a scale previously unknown in Venezuelan history. Large-scale military repression produced hundreds if not thousands of deaths. The rioting constituted a symbolic breaking point in the legitimacy of the democratic regime associated with the Pact of Punto Fijo initiated in 1958 (López Maya and Gómez Calcaño, 1989). The absence of popular opposition to the coup attempts of February 1992 and November 1992 confirmed the decomposition and growing illegitimacy of a political system long considered a showcase for Latin America.

The *Caracazo* coincided with the imposition of strict conditions by the multilateral lending organizations, similar to those forced on most other countries of the continent. Faced with a severe crisis of international reserves, fiscal as well as trade and balance-of-payment deficits, and an external debt that under these conditions could not be paid, the government of Carlos Andrés Pérez (1989–1993) signed a letter of intention with the International Monetary Fund. Pérez made a commitment to carry out an orthodox policy of structural adjustment, despite having appealed for votes in his campaign by presenting images of the abundance of his first government. These agreements were not submitted to parliamentary consultation and were made public only after being signed (Lander 1996b: 52–53). The significance of these structural adjustment policies cannot be understood apart from global trends in capitalism. Concurrent with a massive transfer of resources toward financial capital, and measures involving a commercial opening, privatization, and deregulation, the range of national decisions that could be taken through democratic procedures was severely limited (Lander, 1996b: 66–68). During the three years of the implementation of the structural adjustment policies, regressive distribution of wealth and income and the levels of poverty took a qualitative leap (Lander, 1996b: 63–66; Valecillos, 1992: 205).

Without a doubt, the transformations in the petroleum arena were the most significant. As a result of the nation's growing crisis after 1983, the state gradually lost control over the petroleum sector (Mommer, 2003). The state company, Petróleos de Venezuela (PDVSA) began to impose its own agenda departing from its role as a public enterprise and increasingly becoming a transnational corporation adhering to the liberalizing agenda of multilateral economic institutions including the World Bank and the International Monetary Fund. PDVSA succeeded in reorienting public policies with respect to this activity in the following ways: (a) opening the petroleum sector to direct foreign investment and limiting possibilities for the participation of national private capital; (b) substituting the policy of defending OPEC prices for one oriented toward capturing markets by offering increasing quantities of crude oil at lower prices; (c) disregarding Venezuela's OPEC commitment on production quotas and making a sustained effort to have the country withdraw from this organization or make it irrelevant; (d) introducing, despite their evident unconstitutionality, provisions for international arbitration over contracts signed with foreign investors; and (e) replacing the system of special compensations required from private enterprises for the exploitation of nonrenewable resources with a liberal regime with tax rates similar to those of any other economic activity (Mommer 1999: 70–98). All this translated into a significant reduction in the state's capacity to regulate petroleum activity and in its share of petroleum earnings.

These polices of structural adjustment demonstrate that Venezuela's political system, along with its counterparts elsewhere in the continent, found the range of possible autonomous decisions limited by international economic and political forces. This predicament endowed Chávez's slogans of popular and national autonomy with special significance, positions that explain in large part his immense popular support as well as the strong resistance to his government from elite sectors.

VENEZUELAN OPPOSITION TO THE FTAA

Among the multiple issues that have created tensions between the Venezuelan and the U.S. governments (Plan Colombia, OPEC, diplomatic and economic relations with "axis of evil" countries, Washington's role in the April 2001 coup, etc.) the Free Trade Area of the Americas (FTAA) turned out to be one of the main issues leading to acute confrontations. As negotiations advanced and popular opposition throughout the continent increased, the Venezuelan position became more and more critical of the treaty. In the Third Summit of the Americas held in Quebec in April 2001, for the first time the final statement was not approved unanimously among the heads of state of the thirty-four countries represented. Venezuela reserved its position on both the FTAA negotiating schedule and the definition of democracy as exclusively "representative democracy." Further criticisms of the FTAA negotiating process were formulated in the Quito Ministerial Meeting of November 2002, which demanded transparency in the negotiations and pointed out that the Venezuelan Constitution (Article 73) required the holding of a national referendum before such an important policy decision could be made (Rosales Linares, 2002). A global critique of the FTAA was presented at its Trade Negotiations Committee meeting held in Puebla in April 2003.

By 2003 opposition to the main aspects of the FTAA had extended beyond social movements to many governments in the region. In a response to this growing resistance, FTAA defenders put forward a proposal of a two-tier treaty in the November ministerial meeting in Miami. The first level would be a watered down version of the treaty with all countries participating. Only nations willing to assume the full obligations of the FTAA would form part of the second level. Negotiations in early 2004 in Puebla, Mexico, broke down without producing a final declaration. The U.S. government's unwillingness to accept negotiations over the issue of its massive subsidies to its agricultural producers even though it insisted on open markets from other nations in the hemisphere represented the main obstacle to an agreement. Informal meetings in Buenos Aires in early 2005 failed to make any headway.

In one final attempt to save the FTAA plan, President George Bush tried to reach an agreement at the Summit of the Americas in Mar del Plata, Argentina, in November 2005. Bush's efforts were thwarted by popular resistance in the form of massive mobilizations that included representatives from social movements throughout the Americas, as well as the firm opposition from the presidents of Venezuela and the other nations of MERCOSUR (Brazil, Uruguay, Paraguay, and Argentina) who attended the summit. This appeared to be the final nail in the coffin of the FTAA negotiations.

CONCLUSION

The political phenomenon represented by Chávez cannot be understood apart from the basic split—both material and cultural—between elites and popular sectors within Venezuelan society, a distance that increased during recent governments. The neoliberal policies of the 1990s accentuated exclusion and inequality in the nation. The expectations generated during the first years of the democratic regime initiated in 1958 were increasingly frustrated, and initial advances toward a more democratic society suffered severe reverses.

The key word in Chávez's speeches, to which he returns again and again in the most diverse contexts, is *pueblo* (people), which is a synthesizing term taking in the popular and the national. He often uses the concept "el soberano" (sovereign) synonymously with "el pueblo." This reiterated appeal to the popular and the national (in which he defends sovereignty by invoking the founding myths of the nation) generates contrasting interpretations and reactions among different sectors of Venezuelan society. For the upper-middle and upper classes and a large proportion of the country's intellectuals, the recurrent appeal to sovereignty is a source of division and animosity, instigating a separation between rich and poor that threatens democratic stability as well as their own personal security and property. Their consumption patterns, value orientations, and enjoyment of the "modern" global good life resemble more closely those prevailing in the core countries. Not surprisingly, they agree with Washington's characterization of Chávez's nationalism as an anachronism in a globalizing world and a return to unfeasible and historically obsolete Third-World postures.

The popular sectors to a large degree interpret this discourse in opposite terms. In this second, popular reading, the divisions within Venezuelan society and the exclusion of the majority are not simply a product of Chavista discourse. On the contrary, Chavismo's recognition of the wide gap between rich and poor and its appeals to the majority (*el pueblo, el soberano*) have a powerful integrating effect. Even though the material conditions of the majority of the population did not improve during the first years of the Chávez government, the president continued to be popular among nonprivileged sectors because his symbolically integrative discourse cultivates an extraordinary sense of belonging. The appeal to the *national* (and to the founding leaders of the nation), far from being perceived as anachronistic, contributes to a powerful sense of identity. There has been, however, much more than what has been disqualified as a "merely" symbolic integrating effect. For a large number of the underprivileged, new historical levels of participation and organization have been achieved and, perhaps more significant, the diffuse process of cultural decolonization appears to be taking place among them. The extensive mobilizing and organizing experiences, as well as the significant cultural and political transformations involving the excluded majority of the population, are by far the most significant changes in Venezuelan society.

It is beyond the goals of this chapter to analyze the degree of consistency of Chávez's discourse, the relationship between his discourse and the principal forces favoring political change and government policy, or the viability of his proposals given the global geopolitical context within which Venezuela finds itself. However, some ideas can be advanced. For many reasons, most of the popular material expectations in relation to Chávez's government have not been fulfilled. Only since mid-2003, with the massive social programs know as the *misiones* (literacy, expanded educational access at all levels, land reform, substantial social and community health programs, employment, and the promotion of cooperatives), made possible by ever-rising oil prices, did this begin to change. On the government's side, its major failures can be attributed to the lack of an organized political party and a coherent, practical, and viable political and economic project for the country. Equally lacking has been a sustained political effort at coalition-building directed at expanding the government's base of support toward the middle class and some sectors of the business community. This has gone hand in hand with inexperienced —and sometimes corrupt—handling of a weak and severely inefficient state apparatus. In many areas of government, improvisation has prevailed. The downturn in the world economy during the early years of the government made matters worse.

Chávez's radical, confrontational discourse, while effective in terms of rallying popular support, has contributed to a profound distrust in the business community and the upper and middle classes. Since the end of 2001, this rhetoric has been systematically characterized by the Venezuelan media and wide sectors of the opposition as an authoritarian Castro-Communist threat to both liberty and property. Even though the new constitution defined an ample role for private enterprise and guarantees private property, and the word "socialism" was initially absent from Chávez's discourse, significant proportions of these sectors have taken the threats seriously. As a consequence, there has also been an extraordinary level of organization and mass mobilization in the upper and middle classes. A very intensive media and Internet crusade has contributed to the creation of high levels of anxiety and even paranoia about the imminent threats posed by Chavista mobs (*turbas, hordas*) that are allegedly poised to assault their neighborhoods and ransack their houses.

The long-held dream of a society in which the upper and middle classes could continue their journey toward global citizenship and First-World abundance, while preserving the allegiance of the excluded as a guarantee of the legitimacy and stability of their rule, has come to an end. The myth of true social integration and genuine citizenship without significant alterations in the societal distribution of power has become untenable, and thus the bases of so-called Venezuelan exceptionalism have been eroded. The country's celebrated racial and social democracy, as expressed in the informal and familiar social intercourse in various sectors of society, has turned out to be a superficial veneer. Social exclusion and derogatory expressions based on class and race, once rare except in private conversations and jokes, have now achieved the status of a legitimate public political discourse as the excluded sectors mobilize and refuse to assume their place in the social hierarchy. Another myth, that of a country with a left-of-center and center political culture without significant conservative or right-wing political tendencies, is also rapidly vanishing.

It is in the context of this extreme political polarization and mutual distrust that broad sectors of the opposition have attempted to overthrow the government by any means at their disposal. Thus, many of the so-called democratic sectors of the opposition have repeatedly demanded that the armed forces step in to oust Chávez. They have not been successful in overthrowing the government, but violence, political polarization, and instability have increased.

To conclude, two points are worth emphasizing about the current Venezuelan political process. One is that Chávez and his government have given renewed urgency to certain essential matters that cannot be avoided in any strategy for change or in debates over the challenges of constructing more democratic societies in the continent. Issues such as national sovereignty, autonomous development, equality, social integration, and the need for participatory democracy to transcend the limitations of representative democracy have been highlighted. In the process, Chávez has earned the mistrust of influential groups throughout the continent. Perhaps what most concerns the

U.S. government is that he has awakened interest among popular sectors in Latin America and shown that elections can, under the right circumstances, be used to challenge the Washington Consensus, as occurred in the case of the election of Evo Morales in Bolivia. The second point is that the present global geopolitical context, characterized by the U.S. government's new national security strategy and the concept of "preemptive attacks" on potential enemies, places severe limitations on national-popular options throughout the world. This casts a profound uncertainty on the future of the country. Will Washington decide that Venezuela is a rogue state, belonging to the "axis of evil," and act accordingly? This possibility seems to be the hope of major sectors of the Venezuelan opposition.

REFERENCES

Berry, Albert
   1997 "The Income Distribution Threat in Latin America." *Latin American Research Review* 32 (3): 3–40.
Bonfil Batalla, Guillermo
   1990 *México profundo: una civilización negada*. México: Grijalbo.
Briceño León, Roberto et al.
   1997 "La cultura emergente de la violencia en Caracas." *Revista Venezolana de Economía y Ciencias Sociales* 3, nos. 2–3.
Comisión Económica para América Latina (CEPAL)
   2000 *Panorama social de América Latina 1999–2000*. Santiago de Chile.
Consejo Latinoamericano de Ciencias Sociales (CLACSO)
   2000 *Observatorio social de América Latina*. Buenos Aires.
Cornia, Giovanni Andrea
   1999 "Liberalization, Globalization and Income Distribution." Helsinki: UNU/WIDER (March) (mimeo).
   2000 "Inequality and Poverty in the Era of Liberalisation and Globalisation." Meeting of G-24 held in Lima, Peru, February 29 to March 2.
Crozier, Michel J. and Samuel Huntington and Joji Watanuki
   1975 *The Crisis of Democracy: Report on the Governability of Democracies to the Trilateral Commission*. New York: New York University Press.
Ellner, Steve
   2003 "Organized Labor and the Challenge of *Chavismo*," in Steve Ellner and Daniel Hellinger (eds.), *Venezuelan Politics in the Chávez Era: Class, Polarization, and Conflict*. Boulder, CO: Lynne Rienner.
Gambina, Julio C.
   1999 "La crisis y su impacto en el empleo," in Atilio Borón, Julio Gambina, and Naun Minsburg (eds.), *Tiempos violentos: neoliberalismo, globalización y desigualdad en América Latina*. Buenos Aires: CLACSO-EDUDEBA.
Janvry, Alain de and Elizabeth Sadoulet
   1995 "Poverty, Equity and Social Welfare in Latin America: Determinants of Change over Growth Spells." *Issues in Development*. Geneva: Development and Technical Cooperation Department, International Labor Office.

Lander, Edgardo
1996a "Urban Social Movements, Civil Society and New Forms of Citizenship in Venezuela." *International Review of Sociology* 6 (1): 51–65.
1996b "The Impact of Neoliberal Adjustment in Venezuela 1989–1993." *Latin American Perspectives* 23, no. 3 (Summer): 50–73.

López Maya, Margarita and Luis Gómez Calcaño
1989 *De punto fijo al pacto social: desarrollo y hegemonía en Venezuela (1958–1985).* Caracas: Fondo Editorial Acta Científica de Venezuela.

López Maya, Margarita and Edgardo Lander
1996 "La transformación de una sociedad 'petrolera-rentista': desarrollo económico y viabilidad democrática en Venezuela," pp. 159–188 in Pilar Gaitán, Ricardo Pearanda, and Eduardo Pizarro (eds.), *Democracia y reestructuración económica en América Latina*. Bogotá: Universidad Nacional.

MacEwan, Arthur
1999 *Neo-liberalism or Democracy? Economic Strategy, Markets, and Alternatives for the 21st Century*. London: Zed Books.

Martel, Armando
1993 "Metodologías de estimación de la pobreza en Venezuela." Paper presented to the *COPRE-ILDIS Workshop on Methodologies on Poverty in Venezuela*. Caracas, February.

Mommer, Bernard
1999 "Venezuela, política y petróleos." *Cuadernos del CENDES* 16, no. 42 (September–December): 63–107.
2003 "Subversive Oil," in Steve Ellner and Daniel Hellinger (eds.), *Venezuelan Politics in the Chávez Era: Class, Polarization, and Conflict*. Boulder, CO: Lynne Rienner.

Moreno, Alejandro
1995 *El aro y la trama: episteme, modernidad y pueblo*. Caracas: Centro de Investigaciones Populares.
1999 "Resistencia cultural del pueblo venezolano a la modernidad." *Revista Venezolana de Economía y Ciencias Sociales* 5, nos. 2–3 (April–September).

Morley, Samuel A.
2000 "Efectos del crecimiento y las reformas económicas sobre la distribución del ingreso en América Latina." *Revista de la CEPAL* 71 (August).

Ocampo, José Antonio
1998 "Income Distribution, Poverty and Social Expenditure in Latin America." Paper prepared for the First Conference of the Americas convened by the Organization of American States. Washington, March 6.

Parker, Dick
2001 "El chavismo: populismo radical y potencial revolucionario." *Revista Venezolana de Economía y Ciencias Sociales* 1 (January–April).

Pedrazzini, Ives and Magaly Sánchez
1992 *Malandros, bandas y ni os de la calle: cultura de urgencia en la metrópolis latinoamericana*. Valencia: Hermanos Vadell.

Quijano, Aníbal
1996 "El fin de cuál historia?" *La República*. Lima, December 8.

Rodríguez, C. Francisco
n.d. "Factor Shares and Resource Booms: Accounting for the Evaluation of Venezuelan Inequality." Department of Economics, University of Maryland (mimeo).

Rosales Linares, Ramón
2002 "Carta a Heinz Moeller Frelle," Presidente de la Séptima Reunión Ministerial del Area de Libre Comercio de las Américas, Caracas, October 30, 2002.

San Juan, Ana María

1997 "La criminalidad en Caracas: percepciones y realidades." *Revista Venezolana de Economía y Ciencias Sociales* 3, nos. 2–3 (April–September).

Sousa Santos, Boaventura de

1998 *La globalización del derecho: los nuevos caminos de la regulación y la emancipación.* Bogotá: Universidad Nacional de Colombia e Instituto Latinoamericano de Servicios Legales Alternativos.

UNCTAD

1997 *Trade and Development Report 1997.* New York: United Nations Conference on Trade and Development.

UNDP

1999 *Human Development Report 1999.* New York: United Nations Development Program.

Valecillos, Héctor

1992 *El reajuste neoliberal en Venezuela.* Caracas: Monte Avila.

Wallach, Lori and Michelle Sforza

1999 *Whose Trade Organization? Corporate Globalization and the Erosion of Democracy.* Washington, DC: Public Citizen.

Weller, Jürgen

2000 "Tendencias del empleo en los a os noventa en América Latina y el Caribe." *Revista de la CEPAL* 72 (December).

Wolff, Edward N.

1995 "How the Pie Is Sliced: America's Growing Concentration of Wealth." *The American Prospect* 22 (Summer): 58–64.

Part II

OIL AND ECONOMIC POLICY

Oil is central to any understanding of Venezuelan politics and economic policy. The strategy that parties and political leaders pursued, first with the private foreign oil companies and later with the state-owned enterprise, reveal much about their political vision for the country. An analysis of the government's investment of oil profits to address social inequality also contributes to an understanding of political developments in the country. Chapter 3 provides a critical overview of how oil policy developed in the last half of the twentieth century, and chapter 4 demonstrates how it has been radically transformed since the election of Hugo Chávez.

CHAPTERS 3 AND 4: OIL AND ECONOMIC POLICY

Miguel Tinker Salas's chapter demonstrates how the oil companies, with millions invested in the country, adapted to governments controlled by military dictatorships or middle-class reformers. He questions the validity of the exceptionalism argument that established AD's advent to power in 1945 and 1958 as "significant breaks in the construction of Venezuelan politics and the implementation of oil policy." As nationalism became a force in Latin America, oil companies quickly recognized the rise of new social and political actors in the region. Companies such as Creole Petroleum Corporation (Standard Oil) took an active role and sought to influence the course of reforms before they threatened the company's fundamental economic interests. Promoters of exceptionalism failed to recognize the convergence of interests between the foreign oil companies, Venezuelan middle-class reformers, and U.S. policymakers opposed to the left in Latin America. In the process,

Venezuela became a model for the U.S. government and the oil industry worldwide. While some writers have questioned the notion that AD promoted a veritable "revolution," no one until now has closely looked at the flexible role of the oil companies in accepting certain concessions to national interests while influencing the government in a way that ensured superprofits for their operations.

Dick Parker's chapter assesses the neoliberal framework that characterizes the writings of Chávez's academic critics. Indeed, many of them failed to recognize that an alternative to neoliberalism was possible, or that antineoliberalism would resonate among the populace and produce the election of Hugo Chávez. Even after his election in 1998, many refused to acknowledge the thrust of antineoliberal policies of the Chávez government and instead sought to compare him to past populist leaders. Parker draws a connection between their refusal to recognize the antineoliberal thrust of the Chávez government's policies and the tendency associated with neoliberalism to "pass over social differences and conflict." He indicates that the latter shortcoming is also at the heart of the exceptionalism thesis. Parker analyzes efforts on the part of the Chávez government to develop economic models as an alternative to neoliberalism that include broad levels of participation. He subsequently turns to the all-important oil policy and government efforts to stabilize world oil prices. He breaks with the assumption that, since the industry was nationalized, it operated in the interest of the nation. He goes on to trace the government's struggle to regain control over the company apparatus, which operated as a "state within a state."

Chapter Three

U.S. Oil Companies in Venezuela: The Forging of an Enduring Alliance

Miguel Tinker Salas

The history of the oil industry is critical to an understanding of contemporary Venezuelan society and politics. The rise of the oil industry influenced the formation of social classes, the petroleum workers movement, relations with the United States, and alliances that developed between various classes. Since the 1940s, the government's petroleum policy became linked to the success of the nation and, by extension, the social standing of oil workers and the upper and middle classes. Thus, oil not only sustained the Venezuelan economy, but it also shaped the political attitudes and the social values that held sway over important sectors of the population. Throughout the twentieth, and into the twenty-first century, oil remained inseparable from the evolution of Venezuelan state building and was linked to the rise of nationalism. Without a critical assessment of the historical context of oil policy it is difficult to grasp the political divide in present-day Venezuela.

Traditional studies of oil have focused on the struggle of Venezuelans to gain control over the industry, the struggles of oil workers, and the role of Acción Democrática (AD) (the country's leading party after 1958) in this process. These earlier assessments tended to promote the notion of AD as the leading nationalist force in the country that championed Venezuelan interests and resisted pressures from the foreign petroleum companies. The works, however, failed to recognize the convergence between foreign economic concerns, the U.S. policymakers, and the interests of emerging middle and upper classes and their political parties. A critical reappraisal of the history of oil policy in the post–World War II period provides an important point of comparison from which to understand the development of oil policy under the government of Hugo Chávez.

Proponents of "Venezuelan exceptionalism" viewed the so-called October Revolution of 1945 led by Rómulo Betancourt and the AD party, and the ouster of General Marcos Pérez Jiménez in 1958 as important watersheds, producing changes that U.S. oil interests opposed (Alexander, 1964: 22). According to Edwin Lieuwen, the events of October 1945 were "the most fundamental in Venezuelan history" (1963: 64). Robert Alexander likewise argued that 1945 had produced "a profound revolutionary change in the country" (1982: 195). For his part, John Martz contended that the 1945 Trienio "marked a structural transformation that . . . provided the basis for future national development" (1966: 62). A handful of Venezuelan leftist critics, including Salvador de la Plaza, Juan Bautista Fuenmayor, and the members of the group Ruptura disagreed with these assessments, asserting that AD policy amounted to a capitulation to U.S. interests. They argued that middle-class nationalist rhetoric served to obscure the fact that AD did not fundamentally challenge the power relations that existed between the state and the foreign corporations. Within the mainstream academy, these critical voices were largely dismissed as partisan polemics and silenced by the prevailing triumphalism that greeted the return of AD and the Betancourt presidency (de la Plaza, 1999; Bautista Fuenmayor, 1981; Marquez and Bravo, 1977).

While the earlier critics focused on AD and its leadership, this work draws special attention to the adaptive role of the oil companies during this period. It underscores how the three big oil companies that operated in Venezuela, Creole (Standard Oil of New Jersey), Shell, and Mene Grande (Gulf), compelled political leaders to moderate their views in order to consolidate political power and achieve U.S. recognition. In particular it demonstrates how Creole adapted to political changes in Venezuela and sought to directly influence the course of these reforms before they threatened the company's fundamental economic interests. This experience also explains why in some cases Creole opted for negotiation rather than confrontation with the Venezuelan government, political parties, and labor unions. It also shows that the oil companies constituted important allies of U.S. government policy in the region. In 1953 the U.S. National Security Council asserted, "Oil operations, are for all practical purposes, instruments of our foreign policy toward these countries."[1] Analyzing the oil companies' internal documents and industry publications, this work offers an alternative interpretation and provides a more nuanced view of how the oil companies developed policy in Venezuela. In doing so it reinforces the argument of AD critics that the party in spite of its nationalist rhetoric failed to develop a truly independent oil policy.

Efforts to analyze the events of the early and middle twentieth century join a growing body of work that questions some of the assumptions that have traditionally framed our understanding of Venezuelan history (Valero, 2001; López Maya, 1996; Vivas Gallardo, 1993). Since 1980, as Steve Ellner (1995) points out, Venezuelan scholars have been critically reexamining historical events and the individuals involved in them. Rather than a legacy marked by profound ruptures with an immediate past, a new perspective is emerging that stresses a greater degree of continuity in the country's history. The other critical factor propelling this reexamination has been the demise of the traditional political parties that dominated Venezuela since 1958 and the election of Hugo Chávez Frías, whose rise to power breaks with the notion of Venezuelan exceptionalism and compels a new reading of the past.

Despite efforts to provide a more complex view of contemporary Venezuelan history, the role of U.S. oil firms has not been the object of critical reassessment, in part because of the difficulty in gaining access to corporate archives. According to the traditional interpretation, foreign corporations benefited from the policies of Venezuelan dictators such as Juan Vicente Gómez (1907–1935), opposed the reforms initiated by Acción Democrática during the Trienio (1945–1948), and resumed their cozy relationship with Marcos Pérez Jiménez (1948–1958). Not only is this interpretation simplistic, but it fails to consider the central role of Venezuela in the formulation of U.S. foreign policy. Venezuela assumed new importance for the United States after the nationalization of Mexican oil in 1938, during the course of World War II, and again as a result of the Cold War. According to the probusiness National Planning Association, companies like Creole, "operated successfully under the governments ranging from the personal and non-ideological dictatorship of Gómez to the professedly leftist regime of A.D." (Taylor and Lindeman, 1955: 23). Foreign oil companies, with millions invested in the country, adapted and proved capable of operating under different political arrangements. Confronting a wave of nationalization in the continent and fearful of emerging Arab nationalism, the U.S. government and the oil industry made Venezuela central to their concerns. By the late 1940s, according to *Fortune*, "if there had been no perfect illustration of what U.S. technical and capital resources could do for the world's underdeveloped areas, it would have been necessary to invent the Republic of Venezuela" (*Fortune*, 1949b: 101).

FOREIGN OIL AND THE TRIENIO, 1945–1948

Juan Vicente Gómez, Venezuela's long-time dictator, died peacefully in his sleep in December 1935. His successor, General Eleázar López Contreras (1936–1941), initiated a limited political liberalization: restricting the presidential term to five years and permitting labor unions and political parties to function openly (Burggraaff, 1972: 41). Under López Contreras Venezuela's transformation from an agricultural exporter to a monoexporter of oil, initiated under Gómez, accelerated, and the nation became a net importer of food. In matters of oil policy, however, López did little to break with the past. In fact, he committed some of the same missteps that had characterized previous administrations. In November 1937 Manuel Egaña, dispatched to Washington to confer with the U.S. companies, wrote Minister of Hacienda Cristóbal Mendoza to express his outrage at learning that President López Contreras, through indirect channels, had already assured Shell and Standard that "he had no problem with them and would pursue no policy that might endanger their position in the country."[2] Egaña insisted that the president's actions undermined his efforts to extract concessions from the companies, gave the appearance of a divided government, and strengthened the position of hard-liners in the U.S. firms.

In 1941, López Contreras designated General Isaías Medina Angarita as his successor. Medina Angarita freed political prisoners, legalized the Communist Party, instituted an important petroleum reform law (in 1943), and gained popular support. However, his attempt to impose a successor on the nation incited protests. A group of young military officers known as the Union Patriótica Militar (Patriotic Military Union) formed an alliance with AD and staged a coup in October 1945 (*New York Times,* October 20, 1945).[3] Within a week Creole, Shell, and Mene Grande held a private meeting with Rómulo Betancourt who, according to the U.S. embassy, was "in the driver's seat." A company official summarized the results of the meeting as follows: "Received [the] impression junta will be realistic and that no change is contemplated in the oil law and concessions contracts. . . . They feel, therefore, be wiser concede everything reasonable at once instead of have measures forced on them later, including collective contracts they would have opposed had nothing changed" (*FRUS,* 1969–1987: 1945, vol. 9, pp. 1405–1406). Hoping to avert any fundamental changes to their operations, the companies agreed to mild labor reforms and tax increases (Philip, 1982: 3). In fact, shortly after the coup the oil companies, the Ministry of Labor, and representatives of the labor unions entered into an interim agreement. Standard acknowledged that, "in view of the general labor attitude prevailing, it was absolutely necessary for the Junta to take certain steps in favor of labor," and considered the agreement of December 8, 1945, a "conservative step under these circumstances."[4] To prevent strikes, in January 1946 the junta issued a decree prohibiting work stoppages and requiring compulsory arbitration for work-related disputes.[5]

Throughout the late 1930s and 1940s, Standard prepared for a change in the political climate. As early as 1937, the directors recognized that "a growing feeling of nationalism and its inevitable reaction of antagonism to foreigners [had] made it an imperative for any foreign company operating in Latin America to give more attention to industrial and public relations."[6] By 1940 they had concluded that "by cooperation, and not unyielding opposition, private industry [would] do more to mold the trend of modern legislation in foreign countries, especially Latin America."[7] This, however, is not a matter of a benevolent transnational corporation's altering its business practices and deliberately undercutting the profits it derived from oil production. Rather, its strategy represented business acumen, given that new social actors had arisen in the region and their social agendas could often be co-opted to avoid fundamental change. At a February 1946 meeting, one consultant described the situation as follows:

> The political reality throughout Latin America today is the emergence of new political elements representing the people who, under semifeudalistic society, had no chance for expression. . . . It is necessary to base policy judgment on this political reality whether you like it or not, and forget "wishing for the good old days" when those days are gone forever. . . . I would recommend that all the Company's affiliates do their utmost to cultivate acquaintance and friendship with the growing middle class and the labor movement.

To this end, Standard proposed building a close relationship with its employees, "developing as many channels of contact with them as possible for better mutual understanding and to improve free exchanges of information on company-worker problems."[8] This policy, it concluded, would "reduce the need for outside assistance of either the labor authorities or the syndicates." It also opted to increase relations with other oil companies such as Shell and Mene Grande in order to "establish uniform practices on basic policy matters." Despite having signed a new labor contract with the Oil Workers Federation that improved the economic conditions of workers, in the end Creole officials felt that "all attempted encroachments on management's prerogatives were denied."[9] Several factors appear to have driven the U.S. oil companies' policy in Venezuela, among them the desire to limit the rise of a militant independent labor movement, eliminate Communist influences, and avoid the nationalization of oil that had occurred in Mexico (Singh, 1989: 100). A new, higher price for doing business was considered acceptable in order to avoid another Mexico and discontinuation of a policy that allowed them access to Venezuelan oil.

Interviewed by the industry's *Oil and Gas Journal* shortly after the coup, the minister of development, Juan Pablo Pérez Alfonzo, reassured foreign investors:

> The defense of our national economy and the necessity of using foreign capital for the development of our national resources can be harmonized without trouble. . . . It is in [the country's] best interest to permit development of its oil petroleum resources under the present arrangement of foreign capital and technicians. There is no intention to nationalize the industry or to expropriate properties. (*Oil and Gas Journal*, 1945: 63)

This official government view contrasted sharply with Creole's own internal polling data of the Venezuelan population, which in 1947–1948 indicated that "82% of the [university] students as a group were for nationalization of the industry, while the national average was only 72%."[10] It should therefore come as no surprise that Standard's president asked the U.S. ambassador to thank Betancourt for these assurances. The ambassador refused, indicating that the U.S. government should stay "out of the forefront of the oil picture" in order not to fuel anti-Americanism (*FRUS*, 1969–1987: 1945, vol. 9, p. 1417).

AD's policy was "no more concessions." (It did not apply to the transfer of existing "exploration concessions" that the company could place under production.[11]) This policy, according to Pérez Alfonzo, was neither "overly nationalist nor anti-imperialist or emotional" but simply reflected Venezuela's economic dependence on oil (1974: 9–10). Simply stated, the country would not offer the companies any new tracts of land for drilling. Instead, it would attempt to ensure collection of taxes on preexisting grants and the honest calculation of federal revenues accruing from royalties (*Oil and Gas Journal*, 1945: 63). Leftist critics argued that AD's policy excluded smaller U.S. firms in favor of the three giants that already controlled the majority of proven oil reserves (de la Plaza, 1999: 99).

Since 1917 the state had become increasingly dependent on oil revenues. From 1917 to 1936 oil made up 29 percent of state revenues; from 1936 to 1945 it was 54 percent and from 1945 to 1958 71 percent (*Economic Bulletin for Latin America*, 1960: 1; Vallenilla, 1975: 62). These conditions, according to a National Security Council report, gave rise to a symbiotic relationship between the U.S. oil companies and the Venezuelan government, since anything that diminished the profits of the oil companies "also reduced the income of the sovereign."[12] One U.S. business publication went further, arguing that this purported "interdependence" diminished popular support for labor disputes, since such actions deprived the state of funds and negatively affected the status of the middle class (Taylor and Lindeman, 1955: 62).

The three large foreign companies continued to hold substantial tracts of land, most of which remained unexplored. Among these, the Standard affiliates held 65 percent of the industry's proven reserves.[13] In return for an increased share of revenues (16 2/3 percent of royalties) and the construction of refineries in Venezuela, the Petroleum Law of 1943 extended company concessions that would have expired in 1960 (Valero, 1993: 51). One company official estimated that it would take the companies upward of five years to develop the newly acquired tracts (*FRUS*, 1969–1987: 1948, p. 757). Even without any new oil concessions, production was expected to rise 20 percent over the next five years. According to one U.S. embassy official, the principal impediment to higher production was "the shortage of Venezuelan labor and the difficulty in obtaining steel pipe . . . not the policies or practices of the Venezuelan government." Despite public protestations to the contrary, AD's policy of no more concessions did not undermine the position of the large oil producers. Rather than open conflict, AD and the U.S. oil companies spent the next three years in a "truly cooperative—if arm's length—relationship" (*Fortune*, 1949a: 178). U.S. business, according to *Fortune*, found "allies among reformers who were given to calling themselves socialist" (1949b: 161).

For AD's leadership, Venezuela's dependence on oil precluded outright nationalization of the petroleum industry as Bolivia had done in 1937 and Mexico in 1938 (Philip, 1982: 57–58). Opponents of nationalization insisted that Venezuela lacked the refining capacity, an adequate tanker fleet for transportation, and a marketing network. As late as 1947, 94 percent of Venezuela's oil was still being exported as crude (Vallenilla, 1975: 81). One Standard analyst offered a different perspective: "We have to admit that the Latin American governments, at least one or two of them, have demonstrated that they can operate petroleum properties."[14] Intent on consolidating its hold on power, AD feared the sharp drop in production and the even sharper drop in revenues that would have followed nationalization. With a tenuous hold on power, it opted not to follow this course; it needed U.S. recognition to keep opponents at bay. Moreover, it desperately needed oil royalties to expand the state apparatus and develop a patronage system that linked the interests of the growing urban middle class with powerful oil workers. The U.S. ambassador offered the following assessment of Betancourt:

> [The president is] astute enough to realize hopes of putting into effect its [AD's] economic and social programs upon which its popular support relies depend upon oil revenues. There is every reason to expect that Betancourt appreciates Junta's basic interests are thus similar to those of the oil companies and that will treat them with kid gloves unless pressure from labor becomes too great. (*FRUS*, 1969–1987: 1945, vol. 9, p. 415)

In December 1945, however, the government decreed an end-of-year tax on oil to recoup profits, and in November 1948, it sought to put teeth into the 50/50 profit-sharing agreement initiated, in part, by the 1943 oil reform act. This policy of "wise nationalism" expressed the limits of government policy (Pérez Alfonzo, 1974: 57).

After Mexico's nationalization of oil, Venezuela acquired strategic political as well as economic importance for the United States and the oil companies (López Maya, 1996: 76). It was the world's largest exporter of oil and the only nation in Latin America that permitted "large-scale production . . . of oil by private companies" with "no restrictions on the outflow of dollars" (*Fortune*, 1949b: 101). Creole's investment in Venezuela, according to one business source, represented the largest overseas expenditure by a U.S. company in a single country. Furthermore, 48 percent of Standard Oil of New Jersey's dividend income from affiliates was derived from Creole profits (Taylor and Lindeman, 1955: 2; *Fortune*, 1949c: 180). In addition, opting not to deplete its own strategic reserves, the U.S. government considered Venezuela the "keystone" of its "petroleum war production needs outside of the United States in World War II."[15] Reserves in the Middle East and elsewhere in Latin America had not been fully developed. As a result, the U.S. government and the oil companies repeatedly promoted Venezuela as a model for Latin America and the Middle East. One State Department official even suggested the Venezuelan 50/50 oil arrangement as a possible solution to United Fruit Company's problems in Guatemala during the early 1950s (*FRUS*, 1969–1987: 1951, vol. 2, p. 1448).

During the Trienio, AD also invited foreign capital to participate in the nation's development and granted new nonpetroleum mineral concessions. Bethlehem and U.S. Steel procured rights to explore rich iron ore deposits in Guayana. The Venezuelan embassy in Washington began to publish an English-language *Venezuelan Newsletter* seeking to furnish "the business and financial sector of the United States public with accurate information regarding trade and investment prospects and benefits in Venezuela" (*Venezuelan Newsletter*, May 15, 1947). According to Sergio Aranda, U.S. investments, once limited to oil, began, under AD, to penetrate other important areas of Venezuela's economy (1977: 27).

Fear of Communists in the labor movement further encouraged cooperation between AD and the large oil companies. In its fight against the Gómez dictatorship, the Communist Party had gained considerable support among students, intellectuals, and labor. After Gómez's death, subsequent governments built up the state security apparatus to deal with challenges, real or imagined, from the left. For instance, to buttress internal security and "protect" the rural oil fields, the government created the National Guard in 1937. Throughout the oil fields, it quickly became known as la Guardia Petrolera, (the Petroleum Guard). In 1938 the Caracas government established a political-social bureau within the city's police force to deal with the increased political activism. Then in 1941 the Medina government authorized a national identification card, (*cedula de identidad*) a move widely applauded by the oil companies because it facilitated identification of their workers. Concerned about the left in 1947, the AD-controlled junta formed the Seguridad Nacional (National Security — SN) described by the U.S. State Department as an "FBI-type organization."[16] Despite these measures, U.S. government and business interests continued to express concern regarding the presence of Communists in the labor movement.[17] On one occasion in 1946, fifty U.S. businessmen in Caracas presented a petition to the U.S. ambassador urging the State Department to "combat the rising Communist influence in Venezuela" (*New York Times*, August 14, 1946; *Inter American*, 1946b). Publication of the letter by U.S. newspapers produced a storm of controversy in Venezuela. In Caracas, the Communist Party organized demonstrations against U.S. interference in Venezuela's internal affairs. Despite fueling nationalist sentiments, the episode, according to an observer, had one positive outcome: increasing the antipathy between AD and the Communists. In fact, U.S. Ambassador Corrigan reported to Washington that Betancourt had pledged that in the event of a war with Russia, "Venezuela would support the U.S. 100% and would imprison all militant communists" (cited in Consalvi, 1991: 94). Clashes between the two groups continued during the Trienio, and Betancourt pledged that as long as he was president, "there would be no Communists in the cabinet" (*Inter American*, 1946a; 1946b). In 1948 the Central Intelligence Agency (CIA) concluded that the Betancourt regime in its last months and the newly elected Gallegos administration had shown increasing concern over the Soviet threat and, as a result, Venezuelan policy had moved increasingly into "the orbit of the United States."[18]

Continued investments by U.S. oil companies reflected confidence in the basic framework of state and company relations. *Fortune* believed that the best indicator that Creole was not worried about the long-term Venezuelan future was a "matter of $500 million in capital expenditures to be invested in the country over the next four years" (1949c: 88–97). Construction by Shell and Creole of the "world's two most expensive refineries," at Punta Cardón and Amuay on the peninsula of Paraguaná in the state of Falcon continued without letup (*Oil and Gas Journal*, March 31, 1945: 161; *Fortune*, 1949c: 182). Each installation would be capable of refining over forty thousand barrels a day. Despite its aridity and heat, Paraguaná's proximity to Lake Maracaibo and the existence of "safe berth for deep-draft ocean tankers and a clear run to U.S. and European ports" made it an ideal site for the refineries. The Shell and Creole projects included major deep-sea ports, extensive tank farms for storage, electrical power plants, water distilling units, a 150-mile network of roads and a community to house over twelve thousand employees (*World Oil*, 1948: 222).

AD'S ELECTORAL DEMOCRACY

In December 1947, in the first free and direct presidential elections in the country's history, the esteemed novelist Rómulo Gallegos, AD's candidate, won with over 70 percent of the vote. During this period AD established a national apparatus that survived the Pérez Jiménez dictatorship. Wolfgang Hein described its policies as aimed at developing "close ties between the party and the labor movement on the one hand and between AD and the industrial bourgeoisie on the other" (1980: 236). AD's strategy did not go unnoticed. The newly organized Comité de Organización Política Electoral Independiente (Independent Political Electoral Organization Committee—COPEI) (Christian Democrat) and the Unión Republicana Democrática (Democratic Republican Union—URD) (center left) objected to its blatant use of the government apparatus to build a patronage system.

After the elections, Communist presence in labor became a frequent subject of discussion between AD, the United States, and the oil companies. In one meeting the new U.S. ambassador, Walter Donelly, informed President Gallegos about Communist influences in the industry, "giving him facts and figures on infiltration [by] Communist labor syndicates in strategic operations, including transportation ports, pipelines, power plants, and refineries." The ambassador complained that Communists had made inroads because AD labor leaders seldom visited rural oil camps. Gallegos promised to have AD labor leaders visit the interior of the country at once and have the army "remove dangerous communist elements from strategic points" (*FRUS*, 1969–1987: 1948, vol. 9, pp. 765–767). A CIA memorandum applauded AD's efforts, indicating that the party appeared "determined to remove Communists from the labor field and from the petroleum industry in particular."[19]

Political intrigue marked the Trienio and the subsequent democratic interval. In the words of Pedro Estrada, director of the SN, the Trienio was characterized by "never-ending conspiracies" (quoted in Blanco Muñoz, 1983: 97). Relations between the military and AD remained tenuous at best; neither side fully trusted the other. The U.S. army and naval attachés stationed at the embassy in Caracas had anticipated a coup as early as December 1947. The U.S. cooperated with Betancourt to find the possible conspirators. The FBI and the Justice Department investigated Venezuelan exiles in the United States and concluded that several Dominicans and U.S. citizens had participated in a plot to procure weapons illegally and overthrow the Venezuelan government. The U.S. government derailed several other attempts by limiting access to weapons but refrained from prosecuting those involved for fear that the publicity would be "detrimental to inter-American relations" (*FRUS*, 1969–1987: 1947, vol. 8, p. 1062; *Venezuelan Newsletter*, June 15, 1947).

U.S. support of AD did little to quell internal opposition to the government. Claiming that AD had sown dissension within its ranks, the military finally ended the democratic experiment in November 1948. Shortly after being toppled, AD blamed the United States and the oil companies for its overthrow. Playing to nationalist sentiments, Gallegos dispatched a letter to President Harry Truman condemning the presence of U.S. military attachés at the Caracas army barracks during the revolt (*U.S. Department of State Bulletin*, 1948: 777). Although little evidence existed to substantiate the charges, some in AD also accused the U.S. oil companies of having instigated the revolt against

Gallegos. Oil companies such as Creole had cultivated relations with AD and did not stand to gain by promoting a coup (*Fortune*, 1949c: 179). U.S. interests appeared satisfied with AD since, according to one business source, it had "stopped the Communist movement in its tracks" (*Fortune*, 1949b: 101). Rather, the military found allies among "conservatives and wealthy business men, industrialists, large landowners, some government employees, and professional men who feared change."[20] Despite AD's having received 70 percent of the popular vote in the recent election, according to the *New York Times*, there was "no popular opposition to the military's action" (November 25, 1948). After the coup, most political parties adopted a wait-and-see attitude while some openly cooperated with the military.

PÉREZ JIMÉNEZ, FOREIGN OIL, AND THE UNITED STATES

The rise of Pérez Jiménez coincided with a favorable international climate for Venezuelan oil, allowing the dictator to reap massive revenues from petroleum. During the 1950s U.S. demand for oil increased as the country sought to replenish the strategic reserves used during the war. The conflict in Korea, the nationalization of Iranian oil, and the Suez crisis all spurred demand for Venezuelan oil (Ewell, 1984: 110). Continued reliance on oil, however, caused concern in some international business circles. As early as 1941, Standard Oil of New Jersey projected various scenarios for Venezuela if Middle Eastern oil once again became available and a postwar depression materialized in the United States.[21] Other observers actually went further, underscoring the point that if Venezuela did not confront its dependence on oil the "country [would] be little more than a glorified filling station" (*United Nations World*, 1948: 30).

During the 1950s, and with the support of the U.S. government, the U.S. oil companies launched new explorations, reopened old fields, and located new deposits in Guatemala, Colombia, Ecuador, Peru, and Bolivia (*The Lamp*, Summer 1956: 2–5). Conditions were developing under which no single oil-exporting nation could hold a preferred position in the international trade (Pogue, 1949: 53). Increased competition from oil-producing countries in the Middle East compelled Venezuela to take a proactive role in defending its perceived interests. It had already dispatched a mission to Mexico and Canada "to bring about a closer understanding between Venezuela and other oil producing countries."[22] In a move that predates the founding of the Organization of Petroleum Exporting Countries (OPEC), in 1949 a Venezuelan delegation visited Iraq, Iran, Kuwait, and Saudi Arabia, initiating an unprecedented dialogue among oil-producing nations. The British ambassador in

Caracas indicated that the visit was intended to "gather information so that the Venezuelans could appraise the future impact of Middle East petroleum production on the markets for Venezuelan oil and encourage the Arab States to increase royalties and taxation so as to raise Middle East production costs and improve Venezuela's competitive position."[23] The U.S. and British companies failed to fully recognize the significance of the trip and actually provided some of the logistics for the Venezuelan delegation while in these countries.[24] Despite these actions, Venezuela slowly ceased being the world's leading exporter of oil, and its share of total world trade in petroleum declined from 46 percent in 1948 to 33 percent by 1958 (*Economic Bulletin for Latin America*, 1960: 25).

Relations between the Truman administration, big oil, and Pérez Jiménez quickly improved. When U.S. tariffs threatened the flow of Venezuelan oil, the two governments negotiated a new trade agreement. U.S. tariffs on Venezuelan oil remained linked to the price of Mexican oil, a rate of 10.5 cents a barrel. When the Mexican treaty with the United States expired in 1951, Venezuela was forced to pay 21 cents a barrel. Nelson Rockefeller and Creole's president, Arthur Proudfit, personally lobbied the U.S. administration for a new treaty (*FRUS*, 1969–1987: 1952–1954, vol. 4, p. 1593). In spite of criticism from Texas oil producers, the United States negotiated a new agreement with Venezuela ensuring continuation of the old tariff. In return Venezuela reduced duties on U.S. goods, including cars, radios, televisions, planes, and trucks, representing advantages to "practically every important group of U.S. exporters" (*U.S. Department of State Bulletin*, 1952: 92). As had occurred during the Trienio, the Pérez Jiménez administration continued to depend on oil profits and appeared willing to sacrifice internal markets in order to maintain existing revenue levels. Imported consumer goods from the United States reached an all-time high of $695.4 million in 1957, with an additional US$500 million being spent on freight, insurance, and other services (*Magazine of Wall Street and Business Analyst*, March 15, 1958: 742). Continued access to strategic petroleum reserves was only one consideration in U.S. support of the new treaty. The National Security Council (NSC) insisted that a new agreement with Venezuela was vital in that it "provided the basis for stabilizing relations between oil companies and other governments, particularly in the Middle East (*FRUS*, 1969–1987: 1952–1954, vol. 4, p. 1603). Internal Creole documents echoed these sentiments: "The Venezuelan example is, we hope, beginning to make an impression."[25] Peru, Colombia, Cuba, and Guatemala adopted oil laws that reflected the 50/50 formula (*Oil and Gas Journal*, 1948: 61). Implicit in this assessment was the belief that Venezuela would compensate for the higher tariffs by altering the 50/50 formula, precipitating new demands from other oil-producing nations, especially in the Middle East.

With the exception of 1956 and 1957, the Pérez Jiménez government largely followed the policy of no new concessions, and as before the arrangement posed no immediate threat to the three major companies. Arthur Proudfit summarized the effect of the policy as follows: "We are not concerned. . . . This policy contributes to the orderly exploration and development of the large concessions now held."[26] Even without new concessions, crude production in 1955 exceeded previous records; the companies produced 2,157,216 barrels a day, compared with 956,000 during the war years (*World Oil*, 1956: 247). Creole maintained its position as industry leader, operating 3,000 wells, employing more than 14,000 people, and pumping close to half the nation's output, 982,365 barrels a day. In 1954 it paid US$232 million in taxes and royalties to the government. Shell continued as the second-largest producer and Mene Grande remained third. Besides these principal corporations, a number of smaller companies began to expand or establish new operations in Venezuela. During the 1950s, companies such as Socony-Mobil, the Texas Company, Standard of California, Sinclair, Richmond, Pantepec, Phillips, and Atlantic increased their presence in the country. In addition, independent American drilling companies began to move into Venezuela in larger numbers (*Oil and Gas Journal*, 1958a: 76; *Petroleum Engineer*, 1958: 26). At times, the smaller firms found themselves at odds with the industry leaders.

Government oil profits collected from 1948 to 1957 totaled 25 billion bolivares, more than US$7 billion at prevailing exchange rates (*Economic Bulletin for Latin America*, 1960: 23). Government expenditures were invested in major population centers, where they would produce the most political effect. Oil profits physically transformed Caracas, as its population more than doubled, reaching 1.2 million inhabitants by 1957 (*World Oil*, 1957: 177). According to the Chase Manhattan Bank (1954–1958: 1958, p. 23), construction activity in Caracas reached record levels, with expenditures on public works from 1948 to 1953 amounting to US$1.3 billion. During the fiscal year 1957–1958 public investments reached $US685 million, providing ample opportunity for government corruption in the issuance of contracts.

Boom conditions continued well into the mid-1950s. Although government expenditures on public works reached new peaks, "a large budget surplus was turned in" (Chase Manhattan Bank, 1954–1958: 1958, p. 22). The excess funds acquired during 1956 were for the most part obtained from increased oil production extracted to compensate for the closure of the Suez Canal. For the first time since 1943, Pérez Jiménez opened new concessions to the oil companies, filling the administration's coffers. In one such sale the government awarded over 793,000 new acres to the companies, netting it $US668 million in revenues (*Oil and Gas Journal*, 1957: 97). Sale of new tracts occurred again in 1957.

By 1958 the reopening of the Suez Canal increased production from the Middle East, creating an oil glut on international markets (*Oil and Gas Journal*, 1957: 77; *Barron's*, 1958: 5). Standard Oil of New Jersey, for example, estimated that in the Western Hemisphere alone there was a "spare producing capacity of 4 million barrels a day" (*The Lamp*, Fall 1958: 1). While producing at record pace, companies like Standard had been able to diversify supply sources, lessening their reliance on Venezuelan oil (*The Lamp*, Spring 1960: 1). Since the early 1950s, analysts in the United States and the oil industry had foreseen this development. A 1950 State Department report predicted that the development of Near Eastern and western Canadian oil constituted a long-range threat to Venezuela's oil market (*FRUS*, 1969–1987: 1950, vol. 2, p. 1027). Diversification, however, did not hurt oil industry profits; on the contrary, they improved. Standard Oil of New Jersey reported that "as a result of diversification of operations, Standard's earnings are up, by 1959, 20% over equivalent months in 1958" (*The Lamp*, Summer 1960: 1). Venezuela, however, was not so fortunate. By 1957, as world oil supplies increased, *Barron's* reported that Venezuela's gusher was in "trouble" (*Barron's*, 1957: 3).

In the United States, independent oil producers, threatened by a world oil glut and a looming recession, increased pressure on the Eisenhower administration to impose quotas on imported oil (Rabe, 1982: 158). Hoping to stave off mandatory restrictions, U.S. companies in Venezuela adopted "voluntary" ones (*El Universal*, December 27, 1957). Venezuela regularly shipped 40 percent of its oil to the United States (*El Farol*, May–June 1960: 17). Shrinking markets in Europe and talk of oil quotas in the United States frightened the Venezuelan elite and Pérez Jiménez. Headlines in *El Universal* and other Caracas newspapers blasted the "Yanquis" and threatened retaliation if the United States adopted quotas (*El Universal*, December 27, 1957). With good reason the U.S. State Department worried about the "growth of anti-Americanism in Venezuela."[27] Officials in the Pérez Jiménez government and business leaders recommended scrapping trade agreements with the United States. Pérez Jiménez adamantly opposed the restrictions and threatened reprisals. *Barron's* reported that talk of restrictions by the United States might lead Venezuela to alter the 50/50 oil profit sharing arrangement: "The wrath of the Pérez Jiménez government may fall hardest on the very U.S. oil companies which, because they have producing wells in that country, have been seeking to protect Venezuelan interests" (1957: 3). Oil restrictions, in the words of the ambassador, would cause the United States to lose "the outstanding example of good oil company-government relations," and "forfeit its showroom for [the] USA system in Latin America" (*FRUS*, 1969–1987: 1955–1957, vol. 7, pp. 1120–1121). Plans by the Pérez Jiménez administration to construct an oil refinery also caused concern; the United States considered them a significant departure from "the government's stated policy of private industrial development."[28] Washington also disapproved of the government's efforts to purchase sophisticated weaponry from Italy, France, and England, and NSC documents reveal that it worried that Pérez Jiménez did not recognize the "great danger of allowing communists and ex-communists to control any labor activity."[29] In 1956 the NSC actually formulated a plan for the removal or isolation of purported Communist labor leaders in Venezuela and presented it to Pérez Jiménez.[30] The dictator's unpredictability was a matter of continuing concern.[31]

In 1957 Pérez Jiménez attempted to extend his rule by means of a plebiscite, and by midyear the opposition was openly calling for his removal. The fraudulent plebiscite served as a catalyst for the formation of the Junta Patriótica, composed of AD, COPEI, URD, and the Communist Party. The junta demanded adherence to the constitution, an end to presidential reelection, and the establishment of a democratic government that would respect civil liberties (*El Universal*, January 28, 1958). Important sectors of the military distanced themselves from Pérez Jiménez. By the late 1950s, promotional opportunities had declined for younger officers, and Pérez Jiménez had become identified with his old Andean counterparts (Gómez, López Contreras, and Medina Angarita). Winfield Burggraaff argues that "the problems of maintaining loyalty in the younger generations of academy graduates, unsolved by Medina, remained to plague Pérez Jiménez" (1972: 151). On January 22, 1958, a general strike called by the Junta Patriótica paralyzed the country. When Pérez Jiménez called out the military to crush the strike, they did not respond. The next day, the dictator hurriedly left the country.

U.S. BUSINESS AND THE OUSTER OF PÉREZ JIMÉNEZ

As the political tide in Venezuela turned against Pérez Jiménez, U.S. economic forecasters expressed a surprising lack of concern regarding the fate of foreign oil in the country. Not one major business publication expressed fear of impending disaster, nationalization, or expropriation. The oil companies were affected neither by the general strike that preceded the ouster of Pérez Jiménez nor by the political turmoil that ensued.

Conscious of the need to secure U.S. recognition, the new junta moved to reassure the foreign oil companies that the new regime would "protect investments"(*El Farol*, January–February, 1958: 1). According to Ambassador Charles Burrows, the leader of the interim government, Wolfgang Larrazábal, had sought the opinions of the United States on legalizing the Communist Party and requested support for a new "secret political investigative agency" that would focus on Communism (*FRUS*, 1969–1987: 1958–1960, vol. 5, microfiche supplement, February 12, 1958). Throughout January and February

1958, industry sources insisted that "conservatives" rather than revolutionaries dominated the new junta. The *Wall Street Journal* reflected the prevailing business mood: "Venezuela continues to be the brightest spot in the U.S. foreign investment picture in Latin America. Communism has nothing to do with its recent revolution and although it is now openly active, its role so far seems to be of little importance" (March 15, 1958). U.S. oil company investments in Venezuela reflected this confidence. In February, less than a month after Pérez Jiménez had been overthrown, Mobil Oil of Venezuela announced plans to invest $US28 million in the construction of a new refinery. Both Shell and Creole augmented the capacity of their refineries, while Richmond expanded its distillation units. Notwithstanding Pérez Jiménez's ouster, 1958 and 1959 were record years in the construction of new refinery facilities.

Prior to 1958, U.S. companies had made significant profits from their investments in Venezuelan oil. Unable to supply European sources with Middle Eastern oil because of the Suez crisis, U.S. companies sought to make up the difference by increasing production of Venezuelan oil (*El Farol*, May–June 1960: 17). The reopening of the Suez Canal in the latter part of 1957 had the inverse effect on Venezuelan oil. Production dropped but remained above 1955 levels. For Creole, increasing production to compensate for changing Venezuelan policies was consistent with its previous actions (*El Universal*, June 21, 1959).

The status of U.S. oil in Venezuela during 1958 and 1959 contrasted sharply with its fate in another Caribbean nation during the same period. Whereas Venezuelan insurgents had left oil installations untouched, Cubans had not. A month after the ouster of Fulgencio Batista, industry sources warned of a campaign by Cuban rebels to destroy oil installations on the island. Already, one Esso refinery (a subsidiary Standard Oil Company of New Jersey), had reportedly been bombed (*Oil and Gas Journal*, 1958b: 85). The radical program of the Cuban rebels struck a responsive chord in Venezuela, and Caracas newspapers closely followed events on the island (*El Universal*, February 11–15, 1958; *El Nacional*, January 25, 1959). As they had reacted to the Mexican nationalization in 1938, oil interests and the U.S. government now worried about the impact that the Cuban revolution might have on foreign investments in Latin America (*El Farol*, July–August 1962).

Despite initial concerns, foreign oil companies came to terms with the new Venezuelan government. Creole was among the first to affirm its faith in it. H. W. Haight, its president, asserted that "the petroleum industry would continue to contribute to the aggrandizement of the nation and its citizens." As the representative of all U.S. companies in Venezuela, he informed Larrazábal, "For our part, we wish to assure you that the Venezuelan oil industry will conduct its operations always cognizant of the important role that they play in the country, and will always cooperate fully with the government authorities in charge of the nation's oil wealth" (*El Farol*, January–February 1958). Shortly after the revolt, Creole replaced Haight as president of the company with Arthur Proudfit, who had been president of Creole during the Trienio and had extensive ties with the Venezuelan leaders who assumed power after 1958.

One month before the provisional junta turned over power to the newly elected president, Rómulo Betancourt, it unilaterally altered the 50/50 arrangement and increased the government's share to 60 percent of oil profits (*The Lamp*, Winter 1958: 24–25). As startling as this may seem, however, the decree did not represent a dramatic departure from existing practices. Momentum for a change in the law had been building for quite some time. In a 1958 memo to President Dwight Eisenhower, Brigadier General A. J. Goodpaster warned the administration that "strong pressure [was] rising in Venezuela for basic change in oil policy, including revision of 50-50 profit split."[32] Allen Dulles, director of the CIA, reported that Betancourt favored a formula closer to the 60/40 split rather than the 75/25 advocated by some nationalists.[33] The new 60/40 split appeared acceptable to U.S. officials, since, according to Dulles, by "application of all revenue and exchange measures Venezuela now receives about 56% of the net income of the oil industry."[34] A 1960 report by the Economic Commission for Latin America concurred with this assessment, indicating that the "total taxation paid by many companies . . . had in any case reached or exceeded 50 percent of assessable profits"(*Economic Bulletin for Latin America*, 1960: 32).

Betancourt assured the oil companies that future changes in the nation's oil policies would occur only through "careful discussions between the parties," with a view to Venezuelan oil maintaining its ability to compete normally with that of other countries (*World Petroleum*, July 1958: 46). In keeping with past policy, Betancourt urged the oil companies to consider the long-term profitability of aligning themselves with "responsible and democratic governments in Venezuela." Sustained profits, according to Betancourt, would offset temporary losses caused by modifications in oil taxation. Although they protested the increase, the oil companies did not stop investing in the country or reduce production levels in protest. The *Oil and Gas Journal* reported that 1962 had been a "record year for Venezuela's oil industry (1963: 78). Although the oil companies may have increased production to offset new taxes, their willingness to increase expenditures to augment output indicated their confidence in the political situation within Venezuela.

THE UNITED STATES

Five days after the new junta attained power, the United States recognized the new government of Venezuela (*U.S. Department of State Bulletin*, 1958a:

257). Assistant Secretary of State William McCombie expressed the government's view of the situation: "We are in a position to feel and do feel satisfaction and pleasure when people of any country determinedly choose the road to democracy and freedom" (*U.S. Department of State Bulletin*, 1958b). This swift recognition of the junta underscored U.S. confidence in the non-Communist Venezuelan parties, in particular AD and its leader Rómulo Betancourt. Following the ouster of Pérez Jiménez, politics in Venezuela became synonymous with Betancourt. His views became the litmus test for democracy in Venezuela, and debates in the State Department, Congress, and the popular press centered on his political beliefs. Fearing any reforms, cold warriors in the United States fiercely attacked Betancourt's record (Withrow, 1958: 8717). The State Department, however, had a different view: "Mr. Betancourt's political orientation may be best described as nationalistic, leftist, non-communist, and frequently outspokenly anti-Communist. . . . When in power he co-operated with the United States. . . . It is believed that he is basically friendly towards this country" (*FRUS*, 1969–1987: 1952–1954, vol. 4, pp. 1668–1669, 1672–1673). His leadership of AD and his tenure as president during the Trienio established him as an acceptable representative of Venezuelan democracy. Despite his early nationalist rhetoric, after 1948 Betancourt traveled in the United States and nurtured ties with AFL-CIO labor leaders, elected officials, the State Department, academics, the press, and business circles.[35] In a 1957 letter to Betancourt, the historian Edwin Lieuwen commented on the favorable review he had written of Betancourt's *Política y Petróleo* for the *Hispanic American Historical Review*, stressing that he considered it the "Bible" for understanding contemporary Venezuela.[36]

After 1958, stable relations with the U.S. government and the oil companies remained critical for ensuring the flow of revenues to the government and fueling the expansion of AD's patronage system. Invariably AD sought to increase revenues but left the basic structure of oil development by private companies untouched (*El Universal*, December 11, 1958). At no time did it promote the nationalization of foreign oil companies (Ellner, 1987: 13). Moreover, for the oil industry, AD's unions and political organizations served as an effective counterbalance to militant labor and leftist demands for nationalization. Still, political conditions remained volatile, and the United States worried about a rising tide of nationalism and the outcome of the elections scheduled for December 1958. A foreign polling company commissioned by U.S. and Venezuelan companies predicted that Wolfgang Larrazábal, the interim junta president, would win the presidency by a comfortable margin (*El Universal*, December 4, 1958). Larrazábal's national coalition, which included URD, independents, and the Communist Party, projected itself as a national unity ticket. Since its rhetoric appeared decidedly more radical than that of other parties, the United States did not want to see Larrazábal elected.[37]

Guardedly, the United States did what it could to support the election of Betancourt or, to a lesser extent, Caldera. The adoption of oil import restrictions by the United States loomed as the principal issue that might inflame anti-Americanism and force even the centrist parties to adopt a harder stance. U.S. policymakers soft-pedaled the issue and stressed consultation with Venezuelan officials rather than unilateral action. State Department officials led delegations to Venezuela to discuss the proposed restrictions (*El Universal*, March 14, 1958). The governor-elect of New York, Nelson Rockefeller, vacationing in Venezuela, reassured Betancourt and other political leaders (*El Universal*, December 4, 1958). Secretary of State John Foster Dulles repeatedly stressed that the United States no longer saw the need to adopt restrictive oil measures (*El Universal*, June 12, 1959). Despite these assurances, pressure mounted in the United States for a more restrictive oil policy. However, so as not to fuel anti-Americanism and possibly undermine the campaign of Betancourt or Caldera, the United States withheld public disclosure of a tentative cabinet committee recommendation that the "voluntary oil imports program" be revised until after the December 7 election. A State Department memo explained that the revelation of the recommendation would give the communists "an almost insuperable political advantage" and "would seriously undermine the campaigns of Admiral Larrazábal's two opponents for the presidency," either of whom was considered acceptable.[38] A month after Betancourt assumed office, the Eisenhower administration, citing national security concerns, announced the imposition of mandatory controls on oil imports, reducing earnings for the Venezuelan state.

CONCLUSION

Some scholars have traditionally sought to establish 1945 and 1958 as significant breaks in the construction of Venezuelan politics and the implementation of oil policy. Undoubtedly, changes occurred in 1945 and after 1958 that affected the structure of the state and the nature of political participation. However, the same cannot be said of the implementation of oil policy. Rather, relations between the large foreign oil companies and the Venezuelan government after 1935 reflect a gradual process of change, framed by the concerns of middle-class reformers to gain power and the convergence of geopolitical interests driven initially by fears of nationalism and subsequently by the determination to exclude the left. The oil companies were quick to recognize changing political conditions and position themselves to influence the outcomes, revising their labor and public relations policies and establishing links with labor and middle-class reformers to ensure that they could continue extracting Venezuela's oil.

Venezuela provides an important departure from the experiences of countries such as Guatemala and Chile, where the foreign companies actively destabilized reformist governments. The presence of a fiercely anti-Communist reformist party such as AD, with strong links to the labor movement, assuaged U.S. government and corporate concerns over potential radical social change. In the post-1958 period, AD party leaders proceeded cautiously with regard to policy, seeking to increase revenues but refraining from fundamentally restructuring the relationship that allowed foreign companies to operate freely in the country. This is the fundamental strategic relation that the foreign companies sought to preserve and that the reformers chose not alter.

Events in Venezuela underscore how dependence on oil shaped the views of middle-class reformers and labor leaders and highlight the limited capacity of nationalist discourse to alter the structures of power and inequality existing in the nation. Likewise, the U.S. government's embrace of the nationalist democratic left typified by AD reflected a long-term association based on the belief that these "reformists" would be the best antidote to Communism in Venezuela. After 1960 Venezuela became an important model for U.S. policy in the region, and the State Department described Betancourt as "in the vanguard of the Latin American forces of democratic, evolutionary economic and social reform."[39] As uneasiness over Cuba grew, Venezuela became a testing ground for new policy. The oil companies also recognized the advantages of stable relations with middle-class reformist or even nationalist governments. Intent on preventing another Mexico or another Cuba in the Western Hemisphere, the United States and the oil companies became exponents of the Venezuelan experience as a model for political and economic development throughout the Third World.

Oil policy in Venezuela since the election of Hugo Chávez represents a dramatic break from the past. Though the oil industry was formally nationalized in 1976, it continued to largely operate independently of the government while exercising tremendous control over the nation's purse strings. For many, this relationship proved reminiscent of the power that the foreign companies had exerted over the Venezuelan government throughout much of the twentieth century. After 2001 the Chávez government moved to assert state control of the industry and place its operation in line with its social and economic objectives. Profits from the oil company are now being used to fund a broad array of social programs aimed at the most disadvantaged sectors of society. Likewise, the government promoted new laws (Ley Orgánica de Hidrocarburos, 2001) that empowered it to renegotiate oil agreements that previous governments, intent on privatizing Venezuelan oil, had implemented in the 1990s in the framework of the program known as the Apertura Petrolera (Oil

Opening). These laws are also now being used to reassert PDVSA's control over heavy crude production in the Orinoco River basin area and have the potential of significantly increasing Venezuelan oil reserves (see Parker in this volume and Tinker Salas, 2005). The new policies thus undo a half century of strategies, relationships, and other forms of continuity in the oil industry. Indeed, a reassessment of Venezuelan oil policy during earlier periods of democracy and dictatorship provide the context with which to understand the current changes being implemented by the Chávez government.

NOTES

1. *Declassified Documents Quarterly* (hereafter DDQC), 1978, vol. 4 #(78) 60A, Report to the National Security Council, January 6, 1953, p. 5.

2. Manuel Egaña, personal archive. Manuel Egaña to Cristóbal L. Mendoza, November 24, 1937.

3. See DDQC, 1981, vol. 8 #(81), 231A September 15, 1967, Research Memorandum, Department of State, "The Armed Forces and Police in Venezuela," p. 3.

4. Standard Oil Company of New Jersey (hereafter SOCNJ), "Relations with Labor Organizations, Venezuela," Agenda of Coordination Committee, Miami, FL, February 8–13, 1946, p. 6.

5. Creole Petroleum Corporation, Caracas, Report of Technical Meeting, February 2–7, 1948.

6. SOCNJ, Agenda for Seaview Conference, Absecon, NJ, May 10, 1937.

7. SOCNJ, Topics for Seaview Conference, Absecon, NJ, May, 1940.

8. SOCNJ, "Legislation and the Latin American Oil Industry," Agenda of Coordination Committee Group, Miami, FL, February 8–13, 1946, p. 8.

9. Creole Petroleum Corporation, "Labor Developments in Venezuela," Report of the Technical Meeting, Caracas, February 2–7, 1948.

10. K. E. Cook, Creole Petroleum Corporation, "Creole's Public Relations Job," Coordination Committee Meeting, Caracas, February 19–21, 1951, p. 12.

11. Creole Petroleum Corporation, "Opening Address," A. T. Proudfit, Coordination Group Meeting, Caracas, February 19, 21, 1951.

12. DDQC, 1978 vol 4 #(78)59C, A report to the National Security Council, December 8, 1952.

13. SOCNJ, Agenda for the Seaview Conference, "Trends of World Demand and Supply over the Next 10 years and Influence of Venezuelan Crude Outlet," Absecon, NJ, May 12, 1941, p. 2.

14. SOCNJ, Coordinating Committee Group Meeting, "Legislation and the Latin American Oil Industry," Miami, FL, February 8–13, 1946.

15. DDQC, 1978 vol. 4, # (78)59c, "A Report to the NSC on National Security Problems Concerning Free World Petroleum Demands and Potential Supplies, December 8, 1952, p. 34.

16. DDQC, 1981 vol. 7 #(81) 231A, "Armed Forces and Police in Venezuela," Research Memorandum, U.S. Department of State, September 15, 1967.

17. DDQC, 1992, #2987, National Security Council, Operating Coordinating Board, Washington, DC, "Analysis of the Internal Security Situation in Venezuela and Recommended Action," June 13, 1956.

18. DDQC, 1977, #(6) R38B, "Vulnerability to Sabotage of Petroleum Installations in Venezuela, Aruba and Curacao," Central Intelligence Agency, May 14, 1948.

19. DDQC, 1977, #(6)R38A, "Vulnerability to Sabotage of Petroleum Installations in Venezuela, Aruba and Curacao," Central Intelligence Agency, May 14, 1948, p. 2–3.

20. DDQC, 1982, vol. 7, #002367, "Probable Development in Venezuela," July 24, 1952, p. 2.

21. SOCNJ, Agenda of the Seaview Conference, Absecom, NJ, May 12, 1941.

22. Public Records Office, London Foreign Office (hereafter PRO) FO 371/75117, British Legation, Teheran to Foreign Office, October 3, 1949.

23. PRO FO 371/75117, British Embassy, Caracas to Foreign Office, London, September 8, 1949.

24. PRO FO 371/75117, British Embassy Baghdad to Foreign Office, London, November 3, 1949.

25. K. E. Cook, Creole Petroleum Corporation, Coordination Group Meeting, Caracas, "Creole's Public Relations Job," February 19–21, 1951.

26. A. T. Proudfit, Creole Petroleum Corporation, Coordination Group Meeting, Caracas, "Opening Address," February 19, 21, 1951.

27. DDQC, 1983, Vol. 9, (2) #001244, Memo from Acting Secretary Christian Herter to Lewis Straus, Secretary of Commerce, November 21, 1958.

28. DDQC, 1987, vol. 12, #2351 "Venezuelan Oil Refinery," White House Staff Notes #82, March 11, 1957.

29. DDQC, 1981, vol. 7 #81(231A), "Armed Forces and Police in Venezuela," September 16, 1967, p. 29. Also *FRUS* (1969–1987: 1952–1954, vol. 4, p. 63, 238).

30. DDQC, 1992, #2987, National Security Council, Operating Coordinating Board, Washington, DC, "Analysis of the Internal Security Situation in Venezuela and Recommended Action," June 13, 1956.

31. See DDQC, 1978 vol. 4 (78)59C, National Security Council Report, December, 8, 1952, p. 42. This was not the first time that Pérez Jiménez had acted unpredictably. In 1952 when news of monopoly practices of the big U.S. oil companies surfaced, he had threatened reprisals.

32. DDCQ, 1987, vol. 13 # 001127, "White House Memo," Brigadier General A. J. Goodpaster to President, August 19, 1958.

33. DDCQ, 1984, vol. 10 #000794, Allen Dulles, "Profit Sharing Practices of the U.S. Firms Operating in Venezuela," CIA Memorandum for the President, December 19, 1958. Also see "Foster Dulles," *El Universal*, June 12, 1958, p. 10.

34. DDCQ, 1984, vol. 10 #00794, CIA Memorandum, Dulles to President, December 19, 1958, also Joseph E. Pogue (1949), who maintained that as early as 1949 Venezuela actually was deriving a much higher profit ratio from the 50/50 split. Also see *U.S. News & World Report* (1953: 82), where Pérez Jiménez is quoted as saying that the country was deriving 58% of the total profits of the oil industry.

35. Archivo Histórico de Miraflores, (hereafter AHM) 1848C, 1846C, and 1849C, 1952 through 1957; Letters from Betancourt to various U.S. personalities. Letters addressed to Betancourt while he resided in the U.S. appear to have been illegally intercepted by U.S. law enforcement agencies and subsequently delivered to the Pérez Jiménez government. Also see "Numerosas personalidades extranjeras invitadas por el Presidente Betancourt," *El Universal*, February 11, 1959, pp. 1–9. Present at Betancourt's inauguration were the AFL-CIO's George Meany, Congressman Charles O. Porter, Robert Alexander, and others.

36. AHM #1843-c, letter from Lieuwen to Betancourt at Stanford, July 15, 1957.

37. For U.S. views on nationalist governments see DDQC, 1981, vol. 7 #(335A), "NSC Report on Latin America," May 21, 1958, p. 30.

38. DDQC, 1983, vol. 9 (2) # 001244, Christian A. Herter, Acting Secretary to Lewis L. Straus, Secretary of Commerce, November 21, 1958.

39. DDQC, 1979, #323A, Position Paper on President Eisenhower's visit, Mr. Moskowitz, December 6, 1961.

REFERENCES

Alexander, Robert
    1964 *The Venezuelan Democratic Revolution.* New Brunswick NJ: Rutgers University Press.
    1982 *Rómulo Betancourt and the Transformation of Venezuela.* New York: Transaction.
Aranda, Sergio
    1977 *La economía venezolana.* Mexico City: Siglo Veintiuno.
Barron's
    1957 "Gusher in Trouble," December 30.
    1958 "Too Much Oil Supply," January 20.
Bautista Fuenmayor, Juan
    1981 *Historia de la Venezuela política contemporánea.* 8 vols. Caracas.
Blanco Muñoz, Agustín
    1983 *Pedro Estrada hablo.* Caracas: Universidad Central de Venezuela.
Burggraaff, Winfield
    1972 *The Venezuelan Armed Forces in Politics, 1935–1959.* Columbia: University of Missouri Press.
Carr, E. H.
    1961 *What Is History?* New York: St. Martin's.
Chase Manhattan Bank
    1954–1958 Latin American Highlights. Quarterly Reports.
Consalvi, Simón Alberto
    1991 *Auge y caida de Rómulo Gallegos.* Caracas: Monte Avila Editores.
de la Plaza, Salvador
    1999 *Petróleo y soberanía nacional.* Mérida: Universidad de los Andes.
Economic Bulletin for Latin America
    1960 "Economic Development in Venezuela since the 1950's." *Economic Bulletin for Latin America* 5.
Economic Commission for Latin America
    1960 "Economic Development in Venezuela in the 1950's." 5: 21–61.
Ellner, Steve
    1987 *The Venezuelan Petroleum Corporation and the Debate over Government policy in Basic Industry, 1960–1976.* Latin American Studies, University of Glasgow, Occasional Paper #47.
    1995 "Venezuelan Revisionist History, 1908–1958: New Motives and Criteria for Analyzing the Past." *Latin American Research Review*, 30 (1): 91–122.
Ewell, Judith
    1984 *Venezuela: A Century of Change.* Stanford, CA: Stanford University Press.
Fortune
    1949a "Creole Petroleum, Business Embassy." February.
    1949b "It's Hot in Venezuela." May.
    1949c "Creole in Operation," February.
FRUS (Foreign Relations of the United States; year following date in text is year of original document)
    1969–1987 Washington, DC: Government Printing Office.

Hein, Wolfgang
   1980 "Oil and the Venezuelan State," in Teresa Turner (ed.), *Oil and Class Struggle*. London: Zed.
Inter American
   1946a "Venezuela, Heady Freedom." April.
   1946b "Venezuela, Teapot Storm." October.
The Lamp
   1958 "Middle East." Fall 40 (3): 1.
   1959 "A Letter from the President." Summer 41 (2): 1.
   1960 "Strength through Diversity." Spring 42 (1): 1.
Lieuwen, Edwin
   1963 *Venezuela*. London: Oxford University Press.
López Maya, Margarita
   1996 *E.E.U.U. en Venezuela: 1945–1948*. Caracas: Universidad Central de Venezuela.
Marquez, Angel J. and Argelia Bravo
   1977 *El imperialismo petrolero y la revolución venezolana*. Caracas: Editorial Ruptura.
Martz, John
   1966 *Acción Democrática: Evolution of a Modern Political Party in Venezuela*. Princeton, NJ: Princeton University Press.
Oil and Gas Journal
   1945 "New Venezuelan Government to Respect Oil Laws." November 3.
   1948 "Peru Enacting Favorable Law." December 16.
   1957 "Venezuela Will Grant New Concessions." February 4.
   1958a "Looking at Venezuela for Opportunities." February 3.
   1958b "Rebels Boast of Refinery Fire." February 10.
   1963 "62 Was a Record Year for Venezuela's Oil Industry." February 4.
Pérez Alfonzo, Juan Pablo
   1974 *Petróleo y dependencia*. Caracas: Síntesis Dos Mil.
Petroleum Engineer
   1958 "An Independent Looks at Venezuelan Oil." January.
Philip, George
   1982 *Oil and Politics in Latin America*. London: Cambridge University Press.
Pogue, Joseph E.
   1949 "Oil in Venezuela," part 2, in *The Petroleum Engineer*, November.
Rabe, Stephen G.
   1982 *The Road to OPEC: United States Relations with Venezuela, 1919–1976*. Austin: University of Texas Press.
Singh, Kelvin
   1989 "Oil Politics during the López Contreras Administration, 1936–1941." *Journal of Latin American Studies* 21 (February): 89–104.
Taylor, Wayne C. and John Lindeman
   1955 *The Creole Petroleum Corporation in Venezuela*. Washington, DC: National Planning Association.
Tinker Salas, Miguel
   2005 "Fueling Concern: The Role of Oil in Venezuela." *Harvard International Review* 26, no. 4 (Winter): 54–60.
United Nations World
   1948 "Venezuela: Too Much Money." *United Nations World* (May), 2.
U.S. Department of State Bulletin

1948 December 19.
1952 January 21.
1958a February 17.
1958b March 13.
U.S. News and World Report
1953 Interview with Pérez Jiménez. June 26.
Valero, Jorge
1993 *¿Como llego Acción Democrática al poder en 1945?* Caracas: Editorial Tropykos.
2001 *La diplomacia internacional y el golpe de 1945.* Caracas: Monte Avila.
Vallenilla, Luis
1975 *Oil: The Making of a New Economic Order, Venezuela and OPEC.* New York: Mc-Graw-Hill.
Vivas Gallardo, Freddy
1993 *Venezuela–Estados Unidos, 1939–1945: la coyuntura decisiva.* Caracas: Universidad Central de Venezuela.
Withrow, Gardner
1958 *Congressional Record.* House, May 14, 1958.
World Oil
1948 "New Shell Refinery in Venezuela." March.
1956 "Venezuela . . . First Concession Granted in Twelve Years." August.
1957 "Wise Use of Oil Income Gives Venezuela Bright Outlook." July.

Chapter Four

Chávez and the Search for an Alternative to Neoliberalism

Dick Parker

The election of Hugo Chávez in 1998 broke a pattern of neoliberal hegemony in Latin America. During the 1990s all Latin American presidents embraced neoliberal formulas in which the state reduced its role in the economy, as demonstrated by the wave of privatization throughout the region. In Venezuela, even more than in Chile, Argentina, Mexico, and Brazil, state companies were sold off to foreign economic interests in strategic sectors such as telecommunications, steel, and airlines. Furthermore, the well-established political parties including Acción Democrática (AD), which had staunchly supported state intervention in the economy since its founding in the 1940s, endorsed the neoliberal economic program of President Rafael Caldera (1994–1999).

The triumph of Chávez with his antineoliberal discourse surprised many observers. Indeed, political scientist Luis Gómez Calcaño (2000: 3–4) asserted that, despite the widespread recognition of the existence of a political crisis,

> the only alternative discourse seemed to be that of 'modernization,' understood as the replacement of the parties by civil society, of ideology by pragmatism, of utopias by technocratic thinking, and of the state by the market. Very few thought that force capable of displacing [the dominant parties] AD and Copei would be Chavismo.

This virtual blindness underscored the overwhelming weight of neoliberal thinking in intellectual circles during the mid-1990s. It also reflected the conventional wisdom dating from the 1960s that Venezuela was different from the rest of Latin America and immune to the region's ongoing political and social turbulence. What became known as the "exceptionalism thesis" (see chapter 1) had been based on the smug assumption that Venezuela was a showcase for Latin America and that the abundance of oil resources had enabled the country's political leadership to discover the key to modernization. One basic positive feature was state-sponsored industrialization within the framework of democratic institutions. Another was a power-sharing arrangement between two multiclass parties that were increasingly difficult to differentiate ideologically, holding uniform positions on essential issues and investing substantial government resources to smooth over the social tensions inherent in rapid "modernization."

Of course, for most Venezuelans the exceptionalism thesis had a hollow ring. Oil abundance undermined industrial development not only in Venezuela, but also in most major oil-exporting countries (Karl, 1999). The non-oil component of the Venezuelan economy had stagnated since 1978, with only occasional, sluggish, and short-lived interludes of growth. By the 1990s, the evidence of growing impoverishment and increasing inequality contradicted the optimistic expectations of the 1960s and 1970s. The credibility of the basic democratic institutions had been progressively undermined since the forced devaluation of the local currency in 1983, and by the following decade the electoral influence of the traditional parties AD and COPEI began to decline. Indeed, by the late 1990s, the social, economic, and political crisis in Venezuela proved comparable with if not worse than those of other countries in the region.

The popular uprising in 1989 known as the *Caracazo* and the frustrated military coups in 1992 motivated Daniel Levine, one of the U.S. political scientists most identified with the exceptionalism thesis, to ask whether "exceptionalism" had not come to an end (1994). Despite the fact that the assumptions generated by the thesis have been largely discredited, the literature on Venezuela still bears the mark of its prolonged influence. Indeed, the uncritical acceptance of neoliberal thinking—with its tendency to pass over social differences and conflict—has tended to encourage, albeit momentarily, proponents of exceptionalism. A large majority of Venezuelan and U.S. academics in the social and political sciences are hostile to the antineoliberal Chávez, whose rise to power represented an implicit refutation of the exceptionalism thesis. These scholars have been unwilling to address the Bolivarian Revolution's declared goal of building an alternative to neoliberalism. Those who are skeptical can easily point out that the specific characteristics of this alternative have not been altogether clear. It is true that Chavismo shares with classical populist movements of the 1930s and 1940s the tendency to put greater emphasis on denouncing the inequalities of the prevailing system than on developing its own project. However, after seven years in power the regime has moved in the direction of sketching the contours of this alternative, thus opening the possibility of a debate over its feasibility.

NEOLIBERALISM IN VENEZUELA AND
THE IMPORTANCE OF OIL

For obvious reasons, any debate over neoliberalism and its alternatives in
Venezuela requires a discussion of oil and state energy policy. Indeed, the debate over neoliberalism in Venezuela has tended to underestimate the crucial
importance of the oil industry. After nationalization in 1976, the directors of
Petróleos de Venezuela (Petroleum of Venezuela—PDVSA), the state-owned
oil company, managed to keep the problem of company policy on the margin
of public debate. Until the early 1990s, it was widely assumed that the policies established in the legislation governing nationalization largely coincided
with national interests. PDVSA projected an image that differentiated it from
the rest of the public sector, that of an efficient corporation resembling the
private international oil giants. As a result, the political parties (including
those on the Left), largely lost interest in oil as a topic for debate and as a central feature of their programs. At the same time, Congress, which had closely
supervised the industry while it was in foreign hands, also lost interest. What
is more significant is that the national executive itself, and particularly the
Ministry of Energy and Mines, gradually lost its capacity to establish policy
and ended up as a mere rubber stamp for decisions made by the company
managers (Mommer, 2003).

The Venezuelan managers of PDVSA, who were kept on from the foreign
companies Exxon, Shell, and Gulf, resolutely pursued a policy of insulating
the company from government interference. They argued that by immunizing
PDVSA against the notorious clientelistic practices of the rest of the public
administration and preserving it as an efficient modern corporation, they were
serving the public interest. After 1982, when, to avert a devaluation, the Herrera Campins administration deprived PDVSA of U.S.$5.5 billion destined
for investment, the company directors adopted measures to limit government
interference. PDVSA officials directed resources abroad, including the purchase of the Citgo Petroleum Company and various refineries, on the pretext
that these acquisitions guaranteed a market for Venezuelan heavy crudes. It
was they and not the Venezuelan government who decided to transform the
company into an international conglomerate, and they pursued the strategy
without any major public debate. Venezuelan political organizations, including those that raised the urgent need for state reforms in the 1980s, largely ignored the oil industry.

Once the administration of Carlos Andrés Pérez (1989–1993) had opted to
open the economy, PDVSA began to push the internationalization policy with
greater audacity. The government's proposal to open the industry to foreign
investments proved controversial, since it clashed with the 1975 law governing nationalization and the nationalist principles that had inspired it. After

PDVSA won over the Supreme Court to a rather forced interpretation of that legislation, foreign investors returned to the oil industry initially for the exploitation of gas resources.

However, not until the Caldera administration in the 1990s, and under the direction of PDVSA's new president, Luis Giusti, did the company consolidate plans to encourage massive foreign investments. During Giusti's presidency the company pursued an ambitious plan to increase productive capacity, thus contradicting the Organization of Petroleum Exporting Countries (OPEC) policy of limiting production to maintain price levels. The policy was so well received in the United States that in 1998 Giusti was given the Petroleum Executive of the Year Award, the first to be granted to a Latin American or to the head of a state company. *The Oil Daily* explained that "Giusti was singled out for the leadership role he had played with a major reform of Venezuela's oil sector, including the reopening of oil and gas activities to private companies from home and abroad, as well as for the drive to double the country's production capacity to 6.4 million b/d by 2007" (May 22, 1998).

Local political figures including Hugo Chávez raised their voices in protest. They pointed to guarantees for foreign petroleum investors that proved extremely onerous for the Venezuelan state and to the fact that PDVSA's plans for expanding the nation's productive capacity implied a break with OPEC. Critics of PDVSA and its opening to foreign capital raised other points related to national politics. They accused the PDVSA executives of having contributed decisively to the state's financial crisis, pointing out that the company's fiscal contributions had fallen considerably over the previous two decades.

Once established as an international corporation, PDVSA assumed the attitude toward the state and its fiscal requirements typical of any large private corporation. Transfer-pricing limited its fiscal obligations. Furthermore, the profits generated by the increasingly abundant investments abroad were never repatriated to the parent company and thus contributed nothing to the state. In addition to these financial manipulations, PDVSA lobbied for a reduction of the prevailing taxation rates, arguing that they undermined the company's capacity to invest and operate competitively in an industry subject to continuous technological advances. Legislative reforms introduced in 1993 significantly reduced the tax burden. The result, according to Chávez's finance minister Tobías Nóbrega, was that "in 1991, fiscal income was equivalent to 16% of GNP but declined to less than 10% during the course of the decade, plummeting to less than 5% in 1998, before recovering to an average of 8.5% in 1999–2000" (Nóbrega, 2002).

PDVSA also came under attack for being less efficient than its carefully nurtured image suggested. Its critics were hampered by the company's policy of restricting the information on the industry available to the public and even to the government itself. Nevertheless, international business statistics suggested in 2000 that the internal problems of the firm were even more serious than its most outspoken critics had asserted. Estimates indicated that the labor productivity of Texaco generated an income of US$1.9 million per employee per year, that of Exxon US$1.8 million, that of Shell US$1.6 million, and that of BP-Amoco US$1.3 million; but the PDVSA employee produced no more than US$770,000 (Aharonian, 2003). These figures revealed the extent to which PDVSA had inflated its costs.

CHÁVEZ'S OIL REFORMS

The experience of seven years of the Chávez government in the areas of oil reform, social policy, and development models puts in evidence the broad outlines of an alternative to neoliberalism. From the beginning, the Chávez movement has linked its new development model to oil policy (Chávez, 1996). The Chávez government contributed to a rapid recovery of oil prices by strengthening OPEC. This achievement depended on one of the few aspects of oil policy that still remained firmly in the hands of the national executive, namely, intergovernment agreements. The revitalization of OPEC made possible the search for feasible social and economic alternatives in Venezuela.

Since the government considered a degree of macroeconomic stability a prerequisite for structural changes, it rejected the option of directly confronting the international financial institutions. Nonpayment of the foreign debt was ruled out, currency reserves were maintained high, and macroeconomic policy was designed to bring inflation under control. Indeed, it was precisely these "orthodox" aspects of economic policy that led some analysts to conclude that the balance was neoliberal (Vera, 2001). Other academics suggested that economic policy, far from responding to Chávez's antineoliberal rhetoric, simply retained the measures previously implemented under the recommendations of the international financial institutions, and on this basis they expressed fears that the regime might be heading in the same direction as Fujimori's and Menem's (Gómez Calcaño and Arenas, 2001: 108). These criticisms, however, failed to consider sufficiently the government's pressing immediate objectives. The fact is that during the first two years, the government's priority had to be increasing oil revenues to previous levels to avoid an economic disaster.

In addition to strengthening links to OPEC, the government immediately attempted to reestablish the role of the Energy and Mines Ministry in the formulation of oil policy. Under Alí Rodríguez Araque and his successors, the ministry began to prepare legislation designed to promote national interests.

The government was hardly reverting to previous policies. It is true that it honored contracts with foreign investors, despite their unfavorable terms, and continued to accept foreign investments in order to expand productive capacity, but it modified the terms under which foreign capital would be accepted in the future. At the same time, the plans for expanding production were reformulated not as an alternative to OPEC but to strengthen Venezuela's position during the periodical adjustments of the organization's member-nation quotas.

The administration designed a major legislative initiative to undermine PDVSA's capacity to manipulate its records to minimize fiscal contributions. The Organic Law of Hydrocarbons, promulgated as part of a controversial package of forty-nine laws in November 2001, reduced taxes and increased royalties because the latter were easier to calculate than the former. The law also mandated state possession of a majority of stocks in all mixed companies engaged in primary activity in the oil industry.

Initiating reforms within PDVSA proved much more difficult. The company executives inherited from the Giusti era had been invested with a "corporate spirit" and were accustomed to absolute control of the industry. The successive PDVSA presidents appointed by Chávez during the first three years of his administration did little to modify the company's functioning; its third president, General Guaicaipuro Lameda, actually became the spokesman for the executives who criticized the government's new Hydrocarbon Law. Indeed, the executives, organized as Gente de Petróleo, played a major role in the opposition's subsequent attempts to overthrow Chávez. They participated discreetly in the one-day strike called by the Federación Venezolana de Cámaras y Asociaciones de Comercio y Producción (Venezuelan Federation of Chambers and Associations of Commerce and Production—FEDECAMARAS) and the Confederación de Trabajadores de Venezuela (Venezuelan Workers' Confederation—CTV) on December 10, 2001, which set the stage for the work stoppage that preceded the coup in April 2002. They also played a central role in the December 2002 lockout, which resulted in the dismissal of eighteen thousand mainly white-collar employees. The relative ease with which production levels were restored after the two-month lockout suggested that the industry did, in fact, maintain an inflated labor force.

Once the government assumed control of the industry, new changes were introduced. PDVSA went ahead with plans to increase production and facilitate the participation of foreign capital. PDVSA's new president, Alí Rodríguez Araque, announced that the company would spend US$40 billion by 2007 to increase its potential output from three to five million barrels per day and that more than US$18 billion was expected from foreign investors. These plans were more modest than those proposed by Giusti. At the same time, the government stiffened the terms of foreign participation.

The government also revamped PDVSA's organization and introduced measures designed to favor local entrepreneurs, especially small and medium-sized firms. In the aftermath of the two-month lockout, workers' co-operatives and community organizations provided services in areas such as the distribution of gasoline, maintenance, and the supply of food and work clothes in order to generate employment beyond the confines of the oil industry. At the same time, PDVSA extended its social programs, particularly for neighborhood communities, and supported the missions dedicated to education, health, and endogenous development. The change has been dramatic. Between 1999 and 2003, PDVSA's average annual expenditure on social programs was US$48 million. In 2004, it was US$1.7 billion and in 2005, US$ 2.4 billion (www.venezuelatoday.org/05-05-31_es.htm). Nevertheless, it remains to be seen whether the government will be able to combine its ambitious investment plans with a surplus sufficient to finance its social agenda and whether it will resist the temptation to subject the industry to the clientelistic practices that opposition spokesmen have anticipated.

THE PROSPECTS OF AN
ALTERNATIVE TO NEOLIBERALISM

Critics of the government have argued that, far from embracing a policy favorable to local entrepreneurs and particularly to small and medium-sized firms as was promised, the government has adopted measures favorable to foreign capital. Thus, Carlos Blanco, a prominent opposition intellectual, argued that the government's "confrontation with the most conspicuous national business sectors led it to privilege foreign capital" (2002: 139). Similar arguments have been used to demonstrate that the government has pursued "neoliberal" policies. Inconsistencies in government policy, together with the tendency of local capital to play it safe when faced with risks or uncertainty, have encouraged this sector to transfer its profits abroad. According to one estimate, between 1999 and 2001 the net flight of capital amounted to US$26.2 billion, about 40 percent of oil earnings during the same period (Blanco, 2002: 375). Relations between the government and multinational corporations have undoubtedly been easier. This is not because of government preference, but rather because foreign capital has a longer time horizon and confidence that its diplomatic representation is capable of enforcing contracts.

Nevertheless, stated government policy emphasizes the need to regulate foreign capital and stimulate investment by local businessmen. One recent document of the Production and Trade Ministry describes its policy as follows (Ministerio de Producción y Comercio, 2003):

Public policy should concentrate on the creation of a competitive and stable environment and stimulate private initiatives as the motor of productive activity, without abandoning the role of State intervention in those cases in which the market proves deficient or where [such intervention] is justified by conflicts between private interests and social benefits. Furthermore, as the current dynamic of capitalism creates little employment, there is justification for import-substituting industrial policies in those sectors that generate substantial employment opportunities and are dedicated to meeting the needs of low-income groups.

The government's general policy, as in the case of PDVSA, is to look to the local market to provide the goods needed in the public sector. The government's preference for local over foreign capital is clearly revealed by its reaction to the Washington-promoted Free Trade Area of the Americas (FTAA). This position also reveals the Chávez government's views on the role of the state in the defense of national sovereignty. In the opinion of Vice Minister Víctor Álvarez (2003: 282),

The commitments and disciplines assumed under the Agreement will severely restrict the ability of countries to implement, as national interests warrant, many of [their] public policies in a sovereign and democratic manner. The implications of the following could be particularly devastating: restrictions on using government procurement to promote national development goals, the liberalization of all public services (which, in Venezuela's case, would make it difficult to comply with constitutional obligations to its citizens in critical areas of social policy and access to public services), and the issue of regulations being discussed in the context of liberalizing agriculture, which could also hinder Venezuela's ability to comply with the constitutional mandate to promote policies aimed at ensuring food security for the country.

After the failure of the World Trade Organization's Cancun meeting in September 2003, Latin American governments became more critical of U.S. proposals on hemispheric integration, thus encouraging Chávez to coordinate policies among various Latin American governments with the aim of opposing the FTAA and laying the basis for an alternative arrangement.

THE SOCIAL ECONOMY AND SOCIAL POLICY

Chávez's initial program, the Agenda Alternativa Bolivariana, included a vague proposal to stimulate what was defined as a "humanist self-managing economy" that was designed to promote cooperatives, small family businesses, and, in general, small and medium-sized firms as part of an effort to encourage "solidarity." At the same time, it argued that "while the neoliberal plans are based on the inhuman premise that 'the best social policy is a good economic policy,' the Agenda Alternativa Bolivariana is based on the principle that the best social policy is that which responds to the population's needs" (Chávez, 1996).

The Chávez government has applied measures to stimulate cooperatives and, as a result, their number has grown rapidly. The government has also granted considerable credits to small businesses. Neither cooperatives nor government-sponsored credits for the informal economy, however, are incompatible with neoliberalism. Indeed, similar programs inspired by proposals by the Peruvian Hernando de Soto (2000) have been incorporated into the mainstream of neoliberal policy for underdeveloped nations.

Nevertheless, the differences between Chávez's policy and the neoliberal approach are evident in the debate over the granting of property rights to squatters in slum areas. The opposition party Primero Justicia (Justice First— PJ) proposed legislation supporting recognition of property rights on the ground that they would provide the poorer sectors of the population with an opportunity to obtain credit (mortgaging their property) and thus stimulate the establishment of the small-scale enterprises envisioned by de Soto. At the same time, it proposed five-year jail sentences for future squatters. President Chávez ignored the proposal and issued a decree on February 4, 2002, that offered different solutions. To discourage future land invasions, the option of formalizing property rights was limited to those who had occupied land prior to the decree. There was no suggestion of new legal instruments to repress squatters. At the same time, instead of a simple property deed as proposed by PJ, the government established mechanisms to involve the respective communities in all decisions. Government policy not only addressed individual property rights but also promoted community participation in the policy decisions affecting public spaces and services. While individual property deeds obviously increased the possibilities of obtaining loans (as PJ proposed), the Chávez administration emphasized credit for cooperatives and neighborhood groups (Wilpert, 2004).

To discuss social policy, it is necessary to grasp the dimensions of the problem. The exceptionalism thesis explained Venezuela's political stability as a result both of the trickling down of oil revenues and of the conscious efforts of "responsible" political leaders to create the basis of a welfare state. However, by the 1990s little evidence of either existed. Indeed, since the early 1980s, the country had undergone accelerated impoverishment and deterioration of social services. According to the UN's Economic Commission on Latin America (ECLA), in 1990–1991 the proportion of the gross domestic product (GDP) dedicated to government social expenditure was below the average for Latin America (9 percent against 10.1 percent) and by 1996–1967 the contrast was even less favorable (8.4 percent against 12.4 percent). While all the other Latin American countries (except Honduras) had increased the proportion of GDP dedicated to social expenditure during the 1990s, Venezuela had reduced it. García Larralde (2000) reports that expenditures per capita in education and health fell from 1,100 bolívares (constant prices of 1984) in 1977–1982, to about one third of that amount during the Caldera administration (1994–1999). Expenditures on public education had fallen from almost 4 percent of the gross domestic product (GDP) to less than 2 percent in the same period and expenditures on health from almost 1 percent to 0.21 percent. Private health and education services had expanded to respond to the requirements of those capable of paying for them while the needs of the overwhelming majority of the population had been increasingly ignored.

On balance, the attempts of the Chávez administration to remedy this situation during the period 1999–2003 were relatively disappointing for its supporters and the promised social reforms were still not completely under way. Nevertheless, there were clear indications of its priorities. The progressive reduction of social expenditure was reversed. Between 1998 and 2001, these allocations as a proportion of GDP rose from 8.4 percent to 11.3 percent. Education expenditures increased from 3.2 percent to 4.3 percent and social security expenditure from 1.6 percent to 3.1 percent (Parra and Lacruz, 2003; Wilpert, 2004). The government prohibited enrollment fees for public schools and initiated a program of free meals. These measures contributed to the reincorporation of many children who had withdrawn from the system for economic reasons. Nevertheless, neither in education nor in social security were structural changes introduced during the first years of the administration. Indeed, during 2002 and early 2003, violent confrontation with the opposition forces (including the frustrated coup in April 2002 and the lockout in the oil industry from December 2002 to February 2003) stymied government initiatives in social policy.

Having survived the lockout, the Chávez government counterattacked and for the first time placed its social priorities in the forefront of its political strategy. Aided by buoyant oil prices, it increasingly assigned resources to the resolution of basic problems related to health and education. The government set up a series of "missions" financed largely from ministerial budgets and the state-owned enterprises (above all PDVSA) and carried out by parallel structures rather than the notoriously inefficient public administration.[1] While receiving some logistical support from the ministries, the missions also tapped the resources of the popular movement and organizations that had flourished in the wake of the coup attempt and the lockout. These missions contributed to a marked increase in support for the government. The emergency social measures introduced at the outset of the administration (Plan Bolívar, Fondo Único Social, etc.) had been conceived as stopgap measures that would last only until the promised structural changes occurred, but the programs were prolonged far beyond what had been anticipated. Even the current missions are emergency measures and, if successful, will eventually be integrated into a cohesive administrative structure.

Legislation laying the basis for a long-term identification of social priorities has been scarce. None of the forty-nine laws passed simultaneously in November 2001 addressed the problem and, at least until December 2002, there were no clear guidelines for overall policy. However, during the 2002–2003 lockout, the government promulgated the much-delayed Organic Law of the Social Security System, which is clearly antineoliberal. The new state-run system will be financed collectively and will provide universal coverage. The opposition dismisses the law as demagoguery because of its cost. Undoubtedly, the "renationalized" PDVSA will have to allocate substantial resources in order to make the system work. So far the necessary complementary legislation has not been forthcoming. What is nevertheless clear is that the law marks a radical rupture with the neoliberal model.

Some analysts have portrayed the government's social policies as a simple prolongation of the "focalized" approach typical of neoliberalism precisely because they are directed at the poor. But neoliberal social policies focused on the "critical poor," who could be identified as a minority left behind, or the unfortunate victims of the march toward progress. In contrast, the social policies of the Chávez government are directed toward the majority of the society that has been excluded from social citizenship that the welfare state had promised and that neoliberalism had systematically denied. In general, the Chávez presidency's basic aim is universal coverage for "basic social rights," as put in evidence by the mission programs, which are directed not toward minorities but toward the excluded majority.

Once the government consolidated its political position following the recall election in August 2004, it again took the initiative with measures that clearly contradicted neoliberal orthodoxy. Thus it launched a campaign under the slogan "War on the large landholdings," designed to accelerate distribution of lots to landless peasants. Until late 2004, the Lands Law of 2001 had resulted in the granting of about two million hectacres to an estimated one hundred thousand families, but mainly from state-owned property. In January 2005, the government issued a decree designed to increase the availability of privately owned landholdings. It appointed an "Intervention Commission" to review the legality of agricultural land deeds (often of dubious legality), thus posing a real threat to many large landowners. In several highly publicized cases, the government forced owners to negotiate the cession of part of their property to peasants. These initiatives clearly run counter to the policies recommended by the World Bank (Hernández Navarro, 2005).

Another important initiative affected those firms that had closed down during or after the lockout in early 2003. In some cases, the installations had been occupied by their workers and there was growing grass-roots pressure for the government to expropriate them. In cases in which the owners refused to negotiate with the government, the firm was expropriated and reopened on the basis of comanagement involving the workers and the state. Where the owners were willing to negotiate, the government offered them financial support in return for their acceptance of comanagement arrangements. In public companies, different experiments in comanagement have been put into practice, despite the reluctance on the part of most state managers to relinquish their traditional prerogatives (see the chapter by Steve Ellner in this volume). One of the striking features of the debate over the new forms of comanagement is the active participation of the Unión Nacional de Trabajadores (UNT), the pro-Chávez trade union confederation established after the 2003 lockout, which now takes in the majority of trade union members and has in many places displaced the widely discredited CTV.

Finally, in February 2005, during a period of marked economic recovery, the government created the Ministry of the Popular Economy with the expressed purpose of defining "the mechanisms for the participation of the public sector in the planning and implementation of programs related to the development of the popular economy" and "stimulating the role of cooperatives, savings banks, family enterprises, micro firms and other forms of cooperative associations . . . that are the result of popular initiatives" (Article 24 of the decree issued on February 10, 2005). At the same time, the ministry was responsible for promoting "Endogenous Development Units" consisting of small-scale producers as part of the general effort to lay the basis for an alternative development model.

CONCLUSION

Elsewhere (Parker, 2003) I have argued that within the current international context, there is room for initiatives designed to break with neoliberal hegemony. In this article I have attempted to demonstrate that, despite its inconsistencies and other shortcomings, the Chávez administration has finally moved decisively in the direction of alternatives that may be feasible. Furthermore, in doing so it has consolidated a firm base of popular support, reflected in the 58 percent of the voters who backed it in the recall election in August 2004, in the notable advances in the municipal and regional elections held two months later, and, finally, in the different surveys of voter intentions that unanimously predicted an overwhelming victory for those parties backing the government in the December 2005 legislative elections (before the opposition parties withdrew from the contests and left the National Assembly completely in the hands of government supporters).

Of course, the consistently high prices of oil on the world market after
2003 have facilitated an increase in the government's popularity. However, it
would be misleading to argue that simply by continuing to channel the abundant oil rent to support social programs or promote a popular economy the future of the Bolivarian project is assured. Karl (1999) has convincingly
demonstrated that oil rent has perverted the very basis of the social and political texture of the nation over an extended period of time. Although it appears
that the Chávez administration has established the political conditions for ad-
vancing toward a viable alternative to neoliberalism, this potential alternative
has by no means been consolidated and the radical changes that society still
requires will involve years of continuing struggle. Furthermore, the abundant
resources available due to the current level of oil prices have enabled the government to postpone two fundamental problems that will determine the long-
term viability of any alternative: first, how to combine the social priorities
with an adequate level of investment in the oil industry (Espinasa: 2006), and
second, how to create an autonomous capacity for accumulation on the basis
of the "endogenous" development model that is being offered as an alternative to neoliberalism.

What is clear, however, is that an eventual failure will lead to a return to
neoliberal formulas imposed without hesitation, as was made clear during the
short-lived Carmona regime and as is generally the case when an energetic
search for a popular alternative runs out of steam.

NOTE

1. The most important of these programs has been the round-the-clock primary medical attention in the slum areas, staffed with about fourteen thousand Cuban doctors (Misión Barrio
Adentro), the literacy campaign (Misión Robinson), and programs offering the completion of
secondary education for adults (Misión Ribas). Although academic research on the characteristics of the missions is scarce, there are three interesting discussions of the pioneering experiences that can be consulted: Alayón Monserat (2005), Antillano (2005), and Arconada Rodríguez (2005).

REFERENCES

Aharonian, Aran
    2003 "Venezuela: la re-nacionalización de Pdvsa." *ALAI. América Latina en movimiento*,
    January 6.
Alayón Monserat, Rubén
    2005 "Barrio Adentro: combatir la exclusión profundizando la democracia."*Revista Vene-
    zolana de Economía y Ciencias Sociales* 11 (September–December): 291–244. [www.revele
    .com.ve].

Álvarez, Víctor
2003 "Venezuela ante las negociaciones del ALCA. Documento presentado por la representación venezolana ante la XIII reunión del Comité de Negociaciones Comerciales del ALCA, Puebla, 8–11 de abril 2003." *Revista Venezolana de Economía y Ciencias Sociales* 9 (May–August): 279–286.

Antillano, Andrés
2005 "La lucha por el reconocimiento y la inclusión en los barrios populares: la experiencia de los Comités de Tierras Urbanas." *Revista Venezolana de Economía y Ciencias Sociales* 11 (September–December): 205–218.

Arconada Rodríguez, Santiago
2005 "Seis años después: Mesas Técnicas y Consejos Comunitarios de Aguas (Aportes para un balance de la experiencia desarrollada)." *Revista Venezolana de Economía y Ciencias Sociales* 11 (September–December): 187–204.

Blanco, Carlos
2002 *Revolución y desilusión: la Venezuela de Hugo Chávez*. Madrid: Catarata.

Chávez Frías, Hugo (Presentación)
1996 *Agenda Alternativa Bolivariana*. Caracas: (pamphlet).

de Soto, Hernando
2000 *Why Capitalism Triumphs in the West and Fails Everywhere Else*. London: Bantam Press.

Espinasa, Ramón
2006 "El auge y el colapso de PDVSA a los treinta años de la nacionalización." *Revista Venezolana de Economía y Ciencias Sociales* 12 (January–April): 151–186.

García Larralde, Humberto
2000 "Limitaciones de la política económica actual: la ideología económica en el deterioro del bienestar del venezolano." *Revista Venezolana de Economía y Ciencias Sociales* 6 (January–April): 83–143.

Gómez Calcaño, Luis
2000 "Sociedad civil y proceso constituyente en Venezuela: encuentros y rivalidades." Paper presented at the XXII International Congress of the Latin American Studies Association, Miami, March 16–18.

Gómez Calcaño, Luis and Nelly Arenas
2001 "¿Modernización autoritaria o actualización del populismo? La transición política en Venezuela." *Cuestiones Políticas* 26 (January–June): 85–126.

Hernández Navarro, Luis
2005 "Paradojas de una reforma agraria." *Masiosare* May 29. www.prensarural.org/venezuela20050529.htm.

Karl, Terry Lynn
1999 "The Perils of the Petro-State: Reflections on the Paradoxes of Plenty." *Journal of International Affairs* 59 (Fall): 31–46.

Levine, Daniel H.
1994 "Goodbye to Venezuelan Exceptionalism." *Journal of Interamerican Studies and World Affairs* 36 (Winter): 145–182.

Ministerio de Producción y Comercio
2003 *Declaración de Pozo de Rosas: principios rectores de la política industrial de la República Bolivariana de Venezuela*. April (mimeo).

Mommer, Bernard
2003 "Subversive Oil," pp. 131–145 in Steve Ellner and Daniel Hellinger (eds.), *Venezuelan Politics in the Chávez Era: Class, Polarization and Conflict*. Boulder, CO: Lynne Rienner.

Nóbrega, Tobías
2002 Seven articles on the oil problem, published in the weekly *Quinto Dia*, between the first week of March and the last of April. www.quintodia.com.ve/337/pages/economia3.php.
Parker, Dick
2003 "Representa Chávez una alternativa al neoliberalismo?" *Revista Venezolana de Economía y Ciencias Sociales* 9 (September–December): 83–110.
Parra, Matilde and Tito Lacruz
2003 *Seguimiento activo a los programas sociales en Venezuela: caso de los multihogares de cuidado diario; informe final.* Caracas: Centro de Investigaciones en Ciencias Sociales.
Vera, Leonardo
2001 "¡El balance es neoliberal!" *Venezuela Analítica*, July 23. www.analitica.com/va/economia/opinion/1338346.asp.
Wilpert, Gregory
2004 "La lucha de Venezuela contra la pobreza," *ALAI. América Latina en movimiento.* January 16. alainet.org/active/5300&lang=es.

Part III

LABOR AND RACE

Two of the central tenets of the Venezuelan exceptionalism model were the purported autonomous role of the organized labor movement and the relative absence of pronounced racial inequality in the country. An autonomous labor movement meant that workers were able to influence political developments and force the state to recognize their interests. The absence of virulent racism implied that the Venezuelan social landscape did not reflect the same fractured division evident in other countries in the region. The chapters in this section question these assumptions. Chapter 5 focuses on the challenges that the labor movement currently faces in establishing its autonomy in the context of a highly polarized political setting. Chapter 6 refutes the notion of Venezuela as a "racial democracy" and traces the historic and contemporary basis of racism in the country.

CHAPTERS 5 AND 6: LABOR AND RACE

Steve Ellner's chapter problematizes the proposition of trade union autonomy. He argues that rank-and-file support for autonomy has been evident in many of the decisions promoted by the Chavista labor leaders: the selection of Aristóbulo Istúriz as candidate for the Confederación de Trabajadores de Venezuela (Venezuelan Workers' Confederation—CTV) presidency, the exclusion of "Bolivariano" from the name of the new labor confederation, and the positions assumed by the Unión Nacional de Trabajadores (National Worker's Union—UNT) that were not shared by the Movimiento Quinta Republica (Fifth Republic Movement—MVR). The highly polarized and tense political environment in Venezuela, however, militates against trade union autonomy. Ellner ends his article by pointing to the relevance of the issue of autonomy within the exceptionalism thesis. Exceptionalism writers attributed the nation's longstanding stability to the strong presence of political parties in society, while failing to appreciate challenges to party control by trade unionists that placed worker interests ahead of political commitments and asserted the independence of organized labor. He shows that autonomy continues to be defended by some currents within the Chavista movement more than others, and in fact is at the center of internal divisions. He then calls on labor historians to reexamine Venezuelan history to document historical expressions of autonomy among trade unionists, research that would go a long way in debunking the myths associated with the exceptionalism thesis.

Jesús Herrera's chapter traces the evolution of racism in Venezuela and attributes its origins to the institution of slavery during the colonial period. He addresses how racism evolved, permeated social relations, and indelibly stamped the interactions between Venezuelans. He demonstrates the continuing prevalence of racism and the common differentiation made between an educated, civic minded, middle and upper strata (usually white or light skinned) and the popular masses often portrayed as an uncontrolled rabble (usually people of color). The myth of racial democracy in Venezuela found expression in the notion of "café con leche" (coffee and milk), which became the embodiment of the ideology of mestizaje (miscegenation, or racial mixing). Herrera's essay refutes this important tenet of the exceptionalism argument, namely that Venezuela over the years had been a veritable racial paradise. He shows that this claim became especially untenable beginning in the 1980s, when Afro-Caribbean immigrants were scapegoated for the nation's economic and even social ills. Moreover, it became indefensible when sectors of the opposition resorted to racism to attack Chávez and his supporters, while at the same time accusing the president of manipulating race to gain political advantages.

Chapter Five

Trade Union Autonomy and the Emergence of a New Labor Movement in Venezuela

Steve Ellner

For decades prior to Hugo Chávez's accession to power, Venezuelan labor leaders propagated the idea of the nation's workers movement as one happy family, a notion not entirely concocted. The family image stemmed from three historical tendencies that limited conflict. In the first place, the dominant party in organized labor, Acción Democrática (AD), displayed a certain "generosity" by including trade unionists representing diverse political parties, even ones with minimum worker influence, on the executive board of the Confederación de Trabajadores de Venezuela (CTV). In the second place, the members of the CTV's executive committee allegedly formulated policies on the basis of a "consensus." Every five years a united slate for the CTV's executive committee was ratified at its national congress. Indeed, when in 1985 and 1990 organized labor's second most influential party, COPEI, ran its own slate for the CTV's executive committee, it was penalized for its go-it-alone approach, losing the confederation's number-two position of secretary general.

Finally, the steady improvement in the general standard of living as a result of the stability of the international oil market instilled in Venezuelans a belief tantamount to the "American dream" that their children would live better than they did. The prevalent optimism militated against internecine labor conflicts and leftist control of the labor movement (Bergquist, 1986: 191–273; Ellner 1993: 100). Indeed, the CTV was lauded for engaging in "responsible" democratic trade unionism that contributed to the nation's political and social stability.

These tendencies contrasted with developments elsewhere in the continent, contributing to Venezuela's image as a stable and privileged Third-World country, a notion encapsulated in the term "Venezuelan exceptionalism." In contrast to the alleged unity and pluralism of organized labor in Venezuela, the workers' movements of Peru and Colombia were organizationally divided, while in Mexico and Argentina the largest political party completely

77

dominated the major labor confederation and limited the participation of other political forces (Murillo, 2001: 66–72). Furthermore, the sharp fluctuations in the world price of nitrates, copper, and tin facilitated leftist control of the labor movement in Chile and Bolivia and led to violent confrontations between labor and capital. Finally, labor unions in Argentina, Bolivia, Brazil, Chile, and Uruguay were held responsible for the unbridled "populism" that led to the military coups in the 1960s and 1970s.

Recent developments in the labor movement in Venezuela suggest that the applicability of the exceptionalism thesis, which implied social and political stability and credibility in democratic institutions, was exaggerated long before 1998. Thus class polarization under the Chávez government serves as a reminder that Venezuelan society was subject to acute social tensions over the previous two decades of economic stagnation. Furthermore, the CTV's much-touted pluralism was exposed in the confederation's elections of October 2001 when AD put together an electoral pact that included trade unionists of ideologically distinct parties, but reserved for itself the two top positions of president and secretary general. The turbulence of these electoral contests, which produced widespread accusations of fraud, recalled the unethical electoral practices that had enabled AD to dominate organized labor for decades. Finally, the alliance between the CTV and the business organization FEDE-CAMARAS, which led to four general strikes between 2001 and 2003 with the aim of ousting Chávez, drew attention to the fact that Venezuelan labor leaders had engaged in class collaboration politics and followed orders from their respective political parties over many years.

The depth of the reaction against the dependent status of labor unions was also put in evidence by the split within the Chavista movement between "moderates," who favored working within the existing union structure in order to undermine its party links, and "radicals" or "hard-liners," who called for the founding of new labor organizations in order to achieve a complete break with the past. This essay will show that in spite of their thorough critique of old-style trade unionism, the hard-liners ran the risk of creating new mechanisms of political dependence and parallel unionism. Some of the hard-liners also converged on several occasions with neoliberalism, which had its own reasons for attacking old-style trade unionism. During Chávez's first three years in office, the proposals of the hard-liners to overcome dependence by reorganizing the labor movement involved thorny issues. This complexity explains the vacillations among Chavista worker leaders, specifically with regard to certain reforms as well as relations with the CTV. Nevertheless, the greater polarization leading to attempts by the CTV leadership to force Chávez out of office limited options for the Chavistas, and helped justify their complete break with the confederation in 2003.

This chapter attempts to contribute to the discussion of Venezuelan exceptionalism by examining developments leading to the split from the CTV and the founding of the rival pro-Chavista Unión Nacional de Trabajadores (UNT). The essay is designed to determine whether the labor movement influenced by Chavismo has addressed the problem of organized labor's historical dependence on political structures, a relationship that tended to undermine the defense of class interests. A relatively autonomous labor movement would imply a degree of class identification and assertion of class interests, which most likely did not originate with Chávez's election, but rather dated back to at least the early 1980s with the beginning of economic contraction. In this sense, autonomy is at odds with the thesis of Venezuelan exceptionalism, which implies ongoing social harmony and low levels of class-consciousness.

In contrast, the pro-Chavista labor movement's reproduction of the tight union-party nexus of the past would indicate that the practices of the old trade unionism are deeply ingrained and hard to overcome, even under Chávez's "revolutionary" government. This second scenario has mixed implications for the exceptionalism thesis. A nonautonomous labor movement may be the result of healthy "institutionalization" in which political parties control civil society but represent popular interests at the national level and in the process guarantee social stability. This model accords with Venezuelan exceptionalism and explains why political scientists who defended that thesis viewed labor unions dominated by AD and COPEI as a key prop of the democratic system (Alexander, 1982: 666–667; Martz, 1966: 255; Levine, 1973: 214–223). On the other hand, a nonautonomous labor movement may be considered contrary to the exceptionalism thesis's optimistic evaluation of Venezuelan democracy in that it reinforces hierarchical decision-making, breeds clientelism and corruption, and dampens collective worker aspirations, thus undermining the credibility of the political system.

The assumption here is that the urgency with which autonomy and related issues have arisen during the Chávez period and the intensity of the struggle around them reflect the extent to which they have been matters of basic worker concern over an extended period of time. This assumption points to a major shortcoming of the exceptionalism thesis: its failure to recognize the dissension and discord that party domination of the labor movement produced over the years and its underestimation of the class-consciousness implicit in worker repudiation of dependence.

MISSED OPPORTUNITIES DURING THE CHÁVEZ GOVERNMENT'S EARLY YEARS, 1999–2001

For three decades following the opening of the modern democratic period in 1958, the CTV championed the model of import substitution and state intervention in the economy. In keeping with this line, the confederation called a one-day general strike on May 18, 1989, to protest the neoliberal program of President Carlos Andrés Pérez (1989–1993). Throughout the remainder of Pérez's presidency, labor leaders joined congressmen of AD and other parties in creating obstacles to, and delaying passage of, neoliberal-inspired legislation. In contrast, AD leaders entered into an unofficial alliance with President Rafael Caldera (1994–1999) in exchange for his pledge to refrain from mass layoffs of AD party militants in the public sector. In a blatant expression of trade union submission to party dictates, AD labor leaders participated in the drafting of neoliberal-inspired labor and social legislation promulgated in 1997.

During the 1998 presidential campaign, Chávez embraced a fervently antiparty discourse, at the same time that he attacked the established labor leadership as a "trade union mafia" that slavishly defended the positions of AD and COPEI. Thus Chávez's overwhelming victory in the 1998 presidential race and three elections held in 1999 over the new constitution and two more in 2000 placed CTV leaders on the defensive and opened a window of opportunity for Chavista labor leaders.

During Chávez's first three years in office, the Chavista movement debated between hard-line and moderate approaches. The moderates proposed dialogue and concessions in the face of an opposition that in 2001 became increasingly aggressive and began calling for Chávez's ouster. In contrast, the hard-liners called the opposition leaders "conspirators" and favored responding to their protests with mobilizations of their own. The split between the moderate and the hard-line approaches manifested itself within the labor movement, where one of the main points of contention was the issue of trade union autonomy, specifically the relations between organized labor and political society (the state and political parties). The hard-liners favored taking advantage of the Chavistas' upper hand, which included control of the national executive and congress, and the adversary's weakness in organized labor to deal the "trade union mafia" a fatal blow. The strategy thus compromised labor autonomy by relying on state power for the purpose of achieving far-reaching objectives, specifically the transformation of trade union structures that had allegedly bred class collaboration and corruption. The National Constituent Assembly in 1999–2000 and the National Assembly (the Congress) in 2000 considered several proposals. They included judicial proceedings against corrupt labor leaders, confiscation of trade union property, and the dissolution of the CTV in order to create a "united labor confederation" incorporating independent unions and the nation's small rival confederations.

By bypassing the existing CTV structure, the hard-line strategy ran the risk of promoting parallel unionism. This approach completely abandoned consensus politics, which had been a cornerstone of Venezuelan democracy since its outset in 1958. The consensus involving national actors such as the proestablishment leaders of political parties, organized labor, and business organizations was anathema to Chávez, who considered the process a form of elite decision-making. Thus, for example, he refused to convene the tripartite commissions of CTV, FEDECAMARAS, and state representatives to review minimum wage increases on an annual basis, as the Labor Law of 1990 (Article 167) required. In place of the neocorporatist tripartite commissions, the Chávez government promoted round-table discussions designed to incorporate emerging actors into discussions of policy and legislation.

A "moderate" current in the Chávez movement headed by Constituent Assembly President Luis Miquilena warned of the dangers of "parallel unionism" (whereby new labor organizations are created alongside already existing ones), which in the 1960s had condemned leftist trade unionists to isolation. The moderates were also concerned about the charges formulated by national and international actors such as the UN-affiliated International Labor Organization (ILO) that the Chavistas were seeking to establish an "official" trade-union movement. In 1999, Miquilena refused to proceed with a proposed resolution by a Constituent Assembly commission to abolish the CTV and schedule new elections to unify the labor movement. The following year, moderate Chavista congressmen modified the wording of a proposition for a national referendum (held in December 2000) that would have achieved the same objective. In addition, as a result of pressure from the ILO, the moderates shelved the proposed Ley de Garantías y Protección de las Libertades Sindicales, which implied a labor movement shakeup, and suddenly accepted round-table discussions with CTV leaders sponsored by the Labor Ministry on issues such as social security reform, unemployment, and the unification of the labor movement. The hard-liners reluctantly went along, but subsequently protested that the CTV leaders reneged on decisions reached concerning the reorganization of the labor movement.

During the 1990s, the hard-liners in the labor movement not only called for complete structural reorganization, but also questioned certain practices that, while strengthening organized labor, were conducive to corruption and other abuses. During the early years of the decade, the proleftist Causa R party (whose presidential candidate, ex-steel worker Andrés Velásquez, received 22 percent in the 1993 elections) and then the Chavistas represented the hard-line stand. Paradoxically, the position of the hard-liners and their attacks on the "trade union mafia" coincided with the posture assumed by probusiness defenders of neoliberalism. Indeed, some of the neoliberals, who were anxious to undermine political party control of organized labor, expressed sympathy for the Causa R's militant trade unionism that boldly challenged the pro-AD leadership of the CTV (Ellner, 1999: 117).

The Chavista labor leaders had mixed motives for promoting specific reforms. The changes were designed to expunge corruption and clientelism, but they also served to weaken the AD-dominated labor leadership and open up opportunities for the Chavistas. Thus, discussion over specific proposals did not involve definitively pro- or antilabor positions. One practice questioned by the Causa R and subsequently the Chavistas was the *costa contractual*, a company payment of certain union expenses, particularly those incurred in the collective-bargaining process. The payment created a relationship of dependence on management and often became a smokescreen for the bribery of union officials to moderate worker contractual demands. A second decades-old practice criticized by Chavista leaders and neoliberals alike that lent itself to corrupt dealings was the union hiring of 60 percent (formerly 80 percent) of all oil workers, an arrangement that also prevailed in the construction sector. After 1998, the Chavistas insisted that the hiring process be "democratized" by providing for community participation. The 2000 oil workers' contract eliminated union quotas altogether. The support of Chavista labor leaders for these efforts was undoubtedly intended to undermine the influence of AD oil trade unionists. A third practice riddled with abuses that some Chavistas (along with the neoliberals) criticized was job security (*inamovilidad*) and other benefits provided union officials, which often translated itself into an extended paid leave of absence. The Chavistas pointed to CTV leaders, as well as hundreds of local union delegates, who over a period of decades had become divorced from the workplace. As a corrective, some Chavistas insisted that all union officials be active members of the work force. The Chavista government at one point called into question two other worker and union benefits: the system of check-off of union dues, which in the case of public education sometimes involved simultaneous deductions for several labor organizations without the employee's consent; and absolute job security for oil workers, some of whom supported antigovernment work stoppages.

The convergence between neoliberals and some Chavistas became evident in 2000 when Chávez-appointed PDVSA president Héctor Ciavaldini drew up what he called a "modern contract" for oil workers that was designed to overhaul the industry. Nicolás Maduro and other Chavista labor leaders supported Ciavaldini's proposals in an attempt to displace the AD-controlled FEDEPETROL headed by Carlos Ortega. Ciavaldini's plans received a boost from the Constituent Assembly, which in March 2000 decreed a 180-day suspension of negotiations on the regular oil workers' contract. Indeed, the decree played into the hands of those who denied the proworker orientation of the Chávez government. Ciavaldini then drafted his own contract without consulting FEDEPETROL, which he accused of being corrupt and tied to political interests. The PDVSA president traveled throughout the country to recruit oil workers as "volunteers" to participate in discussions over the proposed "modern contract," whose main points were approved by a 55 percent vote in a referendum held in August. Ciavaldini called this new approach to collective bargaining the "New Labor Focus."

Ciavaldini's "modern contract" jeopardized basic worker gains in the name of making the industry more efficient. In the first place, it would have extended the collective bargaining agreement's two-year duration, which dated back to the first oil workers' contract in 1946, to three years. In the second place, Ciavaldini favored elimination of the system of *comisariatos* (company stores) on grounds that they privileged the 30 percent of the workforce that had access to them, and in their place proposed special purchasing cards for use in supermarkets. The proposal disregarded the argument of worker-elected delegates, including some Chavistas, that the quality of produce at the *comisariatos* should be improved rather than scrapping the system altogether. In the third place, Ciavaldini was in favor of excluding workers employed by PDVSA's contractors from the collective bargaining agreement for PDVSA employees, thus adding to the fragmentation of the oil workers' movement initiated with the neoliberal-inspired partial privatization (known as the *Apertura Petrolera*) in the 1990s.

Finally, Ciavaldini argued for sacrificing bonuses and other special payments in order to increase basic salary. According to Ciavaldini, the tradeoff would benefit the workers since salary determined retirement payments, whose purchasing power had declined over the years. The same argument on the need to sacrifice fringe benefits for the sake of increasing salaries was used by the neoliberals who drafted the labor reform of 1997, which modified the system of severance payments to the detriment of the workers.

Ciavaldini's strategy for undermining the position of FEDEPETROL president Carlos Ortega and "revolutionizing" the industry backfired. At the outset of the negotiations for the 2000 labor contract, Ortega (along with AD labor leaders as a whole) was on the defensive, and indeed he called off a proposed strike when the Constituent Assembly decreed the suspension of negotiations in March. However, he gained support by denouncing Ciavaldini's "new labor focus" as "neoliberal" on grounds that it bypassed existing worker organizations. Indeed, Labor Minister Lino Martínez (himself a leftist from the 1960s) shared the concern that Ciavaldini was declaring war on organized labor as a whole. According to Martínez, Ciavaldini violated the legal requirements that collective bargaining originate with a proposed contract submitted by union representatives to the Labor Ministry. Martínez also objected to the absence of both the Labor Ministry and the National Electoral Commission from the referendum held in August to ratify the "modern contract." Oil worker delegates who were elected by the rank and file also opposed the "modern contract," particularly Ciavaldini's disregard for the tradition of a single, two-year collective bargaining agreement for the entire industry. In effect, militant rank-and-file trade unionists including Chávez followers refused to go along with the approach of Nicolás Maduro and other progovernment labor leaders of parlaying influence at the executive level into organizational gains for the Chavista movement.

Ortega claimed that workers were intimidated into participating in the referendum in August. Shortly afterward, he called a strike, which obliged Ciavaldini to negotiate with FEDEPETROL. The resultant contract signed in October provided workers with substantial gains, facilitating Ortega's political recovery and leading to Ciavaldini's removal as PDVSA president. The experience of the 2000 collective-bargaining agreement impressed many independent trade unionists, including future FEDEPETROL president Rafael Rosales, with the need to maintain some distance from political parties and the state.

CTV ELECTIONS AND GENERAL STRIKE CALLS, 2001–2003

In spite of the polarization of the nation's political leadership after 1998, a group of important labor leaders assumed positions independent of their respective parties and soon broke with them as tensions reached new heights. These "independents" had originally belonged to CTV organizations and had opposed the creation of a parallel confederation. They changed and in some cases were radicalized as a result of the charges of fraud and the violent confrontations set off by the confederation's elections held in October 2001. Their subsequent opposition to the four politically motivated general strikes called by the CTV and FEDECAMARAS within one year further influenced their decision to leave the confederation. Thus, the trade union events in 2001 and 2002 help to explain the evolution of the "independents" in the direction of the Chavista camp.

The most prominent independent was Ramón Machuca, president of the Sindicato Unico de Trabajadores de la Industria Siderúrgica (SUTISS), one of the nation's largest unions, which represented the workers of the privatized steel company SIDOR. In May 2001, Machuca led a three-week strike against SIDOR that seriously affected the economy of the Ciudad Guayana region, where the company is located. In keeping with its militant tradition, SUTISS raised noneconomic demands along with economic ones. It insisted on reducing the number of workers considered "confidential" and by definition excluded from the labor contract, and also raised the issue of discriminatory treatment against Venezuelan employees. From the outset it was clear that Machuca's exclusive interest was in winning the conflict, and for this reason threatened to appeal to the six thousand workers in companies that purchase steel from SIDOR to join the strike. In contrast, CTV leaders such as future confederation president Carlos Ortega and Alfredo Ramos (of the Causa R party, which Machuca had recently distanced himself from) had a different agenda with political implications. Ramos's Causa R at first dismissed the strike as a lost cause, but then reversed itself and proposed that the CTV call a general strike in support of the SIDOR workers. Ortega raised the possibility that workers in key sectors whose contracts had expired follow the example of SUTISS by calling work stoppages. The Chavistas on the executive committee of SUTISS supported the strike (unlike the Chavista mayor of Ciudad Guayana where SIDOR is located) but opposed its escalation for political reasons. Had Chávez's followers at SIDOR or Chávez himself vehemently opposed the strike or confronted Machuca, the future convergence of Chavistas and "independents" would have been less likely. The strike was finally settled on terms favorable to the union, including a one-year moratorium on layoffs. President Chávez subsequently recognized that the strike had been successful and that both the government and the union leadership had learned from the experience (Díaz Rangel, 2002: 130–131).

Aware of their reputation of being an appendage of their party, AD trade unionists created the Frente Unitario de los Trabajadores (FUT), which took in antigovernment parties of diverse ideological backgrounds. The FUT included AD, COPEI, the "Bandera Roja" (which came out of the guerrilla movement), and the Unión para el Progreso (led by Chávez's former comrade in arms Francisco Arias Cárdenas). Despite the FUT's much touted diversity, the positions of president and secretary general on the slate went to Carlos Ortega and Manuel Cova, both of AD. Indeed, for the first time in thirty-five years, the top two CTV posts were to be simultaneously held by members of the same party. Given the limited trade-union influence of COPEI (which after 1998 lost most of its worker activists), the Bandera Roja, and the Unión, the FUT appeared simply to mask AD's bid for continued labor-movement hegemony.

The pro-Chávez trade unionists were originally grouped in the Frente Constituyente de Trabajadores, which was organically linked to the governing party Movimiento Quinta República (MVR). Some Chavista worker leaders resented the MVR's interference, including the practice of naming the Frente's regional coordinators rather than leaving the decision up to party trade unionists. Furthermore, during Chávez's first two years in office, the moderates headed by Luis Miquilena wielded considerable influence in the MVR and clashed with Chavista labor leaders over issues such as the systems of severance pay and social security. Subsequently, the Chavista worker leaders modified their relationship with the party by creating the Fuerza Bolivariana de Trabajadores (FBT), which lacked formal ties with the MVR and took in trade unionists belonging to other progovernment parties, including Patria Para Todos (PPT), the Communist Party, and the Liga Socialista. Chavista labor spokesmen hailed the new organization as an expression of authentic autonomy.

The FBT's decision to participate in the CTV elections represented a triumph for the MVR moderates, who were opposed to splitting off from the confederation. In another demonstration of flexibility, the Chavistas chose as their CTV presidential candidate Aristóbulo Istúriz of the PPT, which had had stormy relations with President Chávez, rather than MVR stalwart Nicolás Maduro, who also sought the nomination. The selection of Istúriz put in evidence the sensitivity of the Chavistas to the widespread concern among workers about the danger of an "official" labor movement, particularly in light of President Chávez's forceful defense of the positions of his trade-union followers. Nevertheless, the Chavistas stopped short of choosing Pablo Medina, also of the PPT, who campaigned actively for the nomination for the CTV's presidential candidacy and accused Istúriz of being too submissive to the government.

Upon receiving the nomination, Istúriz called for a broad front to defeat FEDEPETROL's president Carlos Ortega in his bid for reelection. As a result, FBT leaders discarded the policy of promoting parallel unionism, which had led to their transformation of an oil workers' union in the state of Monagas into a nationwide parallel union named SINUTRAPETROL to compete with FEDEPETROL. Istúriz insisted that the FBT switch its support from the president of an oil workers' union local with little support outside of eastern Venezuela to former COPEI member Rafael Rosales. This endorsement was a masterstroke in that it encouraged the emergence of a movement within the CTV of independents who in the months following the elections would ally themselves with the Chavistas.

The elections held in October 2001 for the CTV and its affiliates were characterized by widespread disturbances, accusations of fraud and other irregularities, and an abstention rate estimated at between 50 and 70 percent. Three weeks later the CTV's electoral commission proclaimed Ortega and Cova president and secretary general respectively and announced that the FUT had received 64 percent of the votes and the FBT slate 19 percent. At one point, Istúriz hinted that Ortega had received more votes than he, but that the FUT's percentages had been greatly inflated. Indeed, AD had good reason to distort the electoral results in this fashion: only with an overwhelming victory for the FUT would AD labor leaders have been able to maintain their dominant position in the CTV and at the same time guarantee their allies in the FUT representation on the confederation's executive committee.

The October electoral imbroglio pitted Ramón Machuca, Rafael Rosales, and other independents against the AD labor leadership and explains their exit from the CTV a year and a half later. In the case of Machuca, the incident also resulted in his definitive separation from the Causa R. Shortly after the elections, Causa R national leaders had protested against the incidents that occurred in the state of Bolívar, which included the burning of twenty sheets of official voting results and disturbances that left fifteen wounded. They had blamed the FUT for committing electoral fraud that gave its candidate a slight edge over Machuca for the presidency of that state's federation. At the time, they threatened to withdraw from the CTV electoral process in protest, but they then did a sudden turnabout. Machuca reportedly felt stabbed in the back by the Causa R due to its surprising reconciliation with the FUT both at the national and state levels.

The October 2001 elections produced an equally intense confrontation between Rafael Rosales and Carlos Ortega, who attempted to secure his reelection as FEDEPETROL president. Rosales's surprising victory was proclaimed by FEDEPETROL's electoral commission (although with nearly half of its members dissenting), but was not recognized by Ortega. For nearly a year, the FUT attempted without success to dispute the results, going so far as to take the case to the Supreme Court. The outcome was especially important because Rosales belonged to a faction of former COPEI members in the CTV headed by the confederation's ex–secretary general Carlos Navarro and including Franklin Rondón, president of the federation of public employees FEDEUNEP. The FUT also questioned Rondón's triumph as president of FEDEUNEP for some time after the elections.

Immediately after being declared CTV president, Ortega began to formalize an alliance with FEDECAMARAS that would produce four general strikes within one year with the aim of forcing Chávez out of power: that of December 2001, April 2002 (which led into the short-lived coup), October 2002, and December to February 2002–2003. The latter strike brought oil production to a near halt and resulted in widespread hardship for the general population. At first glance, the general strikes seemed to stand Marx on his head. In all four cases, worker and business organizations joined hands in calling for the ouster of the "revolutionary" President Hugo Chávez or immediate presidential elections. In fact, as Marx would have predicted, class largely determined the reaction of Venezuelans to the strikes. While downtown and poorer neighborhoods quickly returned to normalcy during the indefinite general strikes of April 2002 and December–February 2002–2003, the affluent areas of major cities avidly supported the work stoppage. Furthermore, during the two-day ousting of Chávez in April 2002, labor leaders such as Machuca and those of the FBT made plans to call a general strike in opposition to the new regime.

The independent labor leaders Rafael Rosales, Ramón Machuca, Franklin Rondón, and Francisco Torrealba (president of the subway workers) opposed the general strikes on two grounds. First, they argued against alliances with FEDECAMARAS, labor's traditional adversary. Second, they pointed out that Ortega and other national CTV leaders had failed to consult the rest of the confederation prior to announcing the strike call.

In the case of FEDEPETROL, Rosales clashed with the federation's secretary general Félix Jiménez, who argued at the time of the April 2002 strike that the government's violation of the merit system, and its attempt to fill professional positions in PDVSA with Chavistas, would subsequently be applied to blue-collar workers. The fact that in the aftermath of the April 2002 abortive coup there were no reprisals against high-level PDVSA employees, who nevertheless went on to make plans for the general strike in December, cast doubt on Jiménez's "institutional" argument. Rosales, who was hardly a hard-core "Chavista," indicated his willingness to consider support for the CTV's position prior to both the April and October general strikes. Most of FEDEPETROL's worker demands, however, were satisfied shortly before the October general strike as a result of the signing of a new collective bargaining agreement. Most important, the 2002 contract restored union hiring quotas and granted workers a 35 percent wage hike. Subsequently, Rosales pointed out that the general strikes had been politically motivated and constituted a veritable lockout.

Although the ten-week general strike of 2002–2003 did much to discredit the CTV, some trade unionists in the pro-Chávez camp continued to be reluctant to leave the confederation to form a rival one. Thus, for instance, the "La Jornada" oil workers' faction (which for ten years had participated in FEDEPETROL unions in the eastern part of the country) was divided over the issue. Some members of the group pointed out that the traditional leftist approach throughout the world of boring from within "majority unions," as opposed to forming small splinter groups, had proved to be the most effective strategy. They added that the error of leftist trade unionists in leaving the CTV in the 1960s had proved costly in that it had isolated them from the working class. Similarly, the pro-Communist Central Unitaria de Trabajadores de Venezuela (CUTV) warned that a split-off confederation would be perceived as progovernment, and instead advocated creating a national coordinating committee to prepare the ground for a new unified organization.

Several developments strengthened the position of those who favored a new confederation. In the first place, the CTV had been discredited as a result of the failure of the ten-week general strike, and the period immediately following that conflict was seen as the ideal moment to deliver the confederation a fatal blow. Some argued that should the Chavistas fail to completely break with the CTV, they themselves would lose the respect of the workers. In the second place, at the time of the April abortive coup, Luis Miquilena and his followers, who had been the staunchest defenders of the strategy of working within the CTV, had left the MVR. Finally, the CTV's electoral imbroglio in October 2001 and the subsequent general strikes had encouraged the emergence of a group of independent labor leaders who for the most part were disposed to break definitively with the confederation.

The shift in opinion during the conflict-ridden year 2002 of rank-and-file workers who were neither pro- nor anti-Chávez coincided with the deterioration of the CTV's image. The "independents" were perplexed and angered by the CTV's prolonged alliance with FEDECAMARAS. While the views of political independents (who constituted an estimated 40 to 50 percent of the population at large) went unrepresented in national politics, those of independent trade unionists were reflected by the positions taken by Machuca and other nationally prominent labor leaders (Ellner and Rosen, 2002: 15).

In the immediate aftermath of the ten-week strike, the leading independents including Machuca, Rosales, Torrealba, and Rondón traveled throughout Venezuela organizing support for a new workers' confederation. They insisted that the organization maintain a distance from the state. Machuca pointed to Chávez's public remarks—such as his statement during the CTV elections that if Aristóbulo Istúriz were elected president of the confederation he would "have a seat in Miraflores [the presidential palace]"—as placing labor movement autonomy in doubt. Machuca added that Chávez's trade-union adversaries took advantage of errors of this type (Harnecker, 2002–2003).

THE FOUNDING OF A NEW LABOR CONFEDERATION AND ITS EARLY YEARS

Machuca was convinced that the only way the new confederation could refute charges of being "official" was by naming one of the "independents" as president. Originally Machuca proposed Rondón, but then the independents agreed that Machuca himself should head the new organization. At the founding meeting of the Unión Nacional de Trabajadores (UNT) in April 2003, however, the Chavistas of the FBT proposed a "horizontal" structure with a twenty-one-member national coordinating committee and no president or secretary general. They argued that such a structure should prevail until UNT elections were held in order to avoid discontent over the naming of a president. The FBT Chavistas won over the independents to this structure, with the exception of Machuca, who refused to join the new confederation. Subsequently, Machuca met with UNT members and did not rule out the possibility of reconciliation. In one concession, the FBT leaders dropped their insistence on calling Venezuela's new confederation "Bolivariana" and accepted the UNT name, which was originally proposed by the independents.

The differences between Machuca's group of "independents" and the FBT centered on the issue of timing. The independents argued that only through a well-planned, protracted process of rank-and-file participation would a truly autonomous confederation be created. In contrast, the Chavistas of the FBT maintained that the political situation in the country, specifically the

imminence of another attempt to overthrow the government, required the immediate formation of a workers' confederation with mobilization capacity.
These differences in approach also characterized the proposals put forward
by the FBT and Machuca for the creation of a new hemispheric labor confederation to formulate positions on issues such as the foreign debt and the
Free Trade Area of the Americas. While the FBT favored promoting a pro-
leftist Latin American labor organization that would take in important confederations in Peru, Colombia, Brazil, Chile, and elsewhere, Machuca argued for reaching out to emerging social movements and following a
bottom-up approach. The FBT's plans ran the risk of alienating the independents, with their disparate ideological orientations.

The independent president of FEDEPETROL, Rafael Rosales, also favored
a gradual approach to building the UNT and a more tolerant and pluralistic attitude toward the CTV adversaries than did the Chavistas in the FBT. Ever
since FEDEPETROL's elections in October 2001, Rosales had maintained
cordial relations with AD oil worker leaders, who, unlike their party's political leadership, had recognized his electoral victory over incumbent president
Carlos Ortega. Trade unionists belonging to AD and other opposition parties,
however, participated in the general strike in 2002–2003 and were among the
eighteen thousand PDVSA employees who were discharged in the wake of
the conflict. The layoff of labor leaders weakened a number of FEDE-
PETROL locals. At first Rosales proposed the unification of the entire oil
workers' movement, but Nelson Nuñez, president of the pro-Chavista SINU-
TRAPETROL, rejected the proposition out of fear that the new organization
would be controlled by the much larger and independently led FEDE-
PETROL. Rosales, who along with Nuñez belonged to PDVSA's board of directors, used his influence in the company's human resources department to
favor the rehiring of anti-Chavistas. The reincorporation of opposition party
militants into the oil industry was intended to avoid the condemnation of
PDVSA by the International Labor Organization for discriminatory and an-
tiunion practices.

The hard-line Chavistas attacked Rosales's tolerant position on the grounds
that the purges and the formation of parallel unions were justified and politically necessary. They argued that, given the intensity of political conflict in
the nation, guaranteeing control of the strategic oil workers' movement was a
political imperative. They were particularly critical of Rosales's wait-and-see
attitude toward the building of the UNT and his failure to call worker assemblies in oil worker localities in order to establish unions affiliated with the
new confederation.

The UNT's founders insisted that the new confederation avoid the structures and practices that had bred corruption, political control, and class collaboration in the past. For this reason they supported the right of workers to

petition for a recall referendum against union officials. In addition, UNT leaders were determined to avoid the penetration of the new organization by labor bureaucrats who lacked ongoing ties with the rank and file. Therefore national deputies who claimed to represent labor but lacked a trade-union following became UNT "advisors," while all twenty-one coordinators were allegedly trade union activists. Some UNT leaders (particularly the independents led by Machuca) argued that trade-union leaders at all levels should be active workers, but no consensus was reached on the proposition.

The positions assumed by the UNT did not overlap with those of the MVR. Some of the differences reflected conflicting stands between the labor wing of the MVR and party politicians dating back to the beginning of Chávez's rule. Among the positions adopted by the UNT that were not officially backed by the MVR were: automatic salary indexation, the reestablishment of the old system of severance pay in accordance with the new constitution, formation of a "debtors bloc" among Latin American nations to present alternatives to payment of the foreign debt, promotion of an economic model based on a large internal market (as opposed to prioritizing export growth), and the prompt implementation of the Ley Orgánica del Sistema de Seguridad Social (LOSSS), passed in December 2002. The state-based social security system created by the LOSSS embodied the FBT's proposal on social security that was at odds with the privatization plan pushed by Miquilena's supporters and the "mixed" system advocated by Chávez's ministers in the area of social affairs.

Support for direct worker participation in company decision-making also represented a "vanguard" position within the Chávez movement. During the ten-week general strike, the FBT called on the government to allow interim worker management of the companies that had shut their doors. Following the strike, workers took over the Constructora Nacional de Válvulas (CNV), whose owner Andrés Sosa Pietri was a former PDVSA president, as well as hotels such as the Sheraton of Vargas, sugar mills, and other firms that had closed due to bankruptcy. At the UNT's founding congress, delegates chanted "empresa cerrada es empresa tomada!" ("a closed company is a company taken over!"). The new confederation supported worker control of companies that were in the hands of the state's Fondo de Garantías de Depósito (FOGADE) as a result of Venezuela's financial crisis of 1994. UNT labor leaders were undoubtedly encouraged by developments in Argentina, where workers had recently taken over two hundred workplaces in response to the nation's financial crisis. They also took note of events in PDVSA, where in the wake of the ten-week strike, Rafael Rosales and Nelson Nuñez were appointed to the company's board of directors as a step toward worker participation in decision-making. The selection of two oil worker federation presidents differed sharply from employee-participation arrangements decreed in 1966 in which worker representatives on company boards were invariably individuals who lacked work experience in that sector and thus played a limited role in decision-making.

During the two years following the general strike, the government refused to dislodge employees who had occupied plants, but also refrained from turning the companies over to worker management, and instead deferred to the courts on the matter. In some regions, judges and Labor Ministry inspectors were unsympathetic to the worker occupiers. Then, in January 2005, President Chávez expropriated the paper company VENEPAL in Morón, followed by several other occupied companies. The workers of two of these firms—the CNV, which produced high-pressure valves, and the tube company SIDEROCA in the state of Zulia—had called on PDVSA to make purchases from them. By the end of 2005, VENEPAL, which was run by the workers with minimum state participation, was the most commercially successful of the expropriated companies. In the same year, Chávez also announced a policy of taking over all companies that closed down. The government proceeded to study the cases of 139 failing companies and proposed to their owners worker comanagement arrangements in return for state aid as an alternative to expropriation. Chávez also committed himself to worker comanagement in state companies. UNT trade unionists, however, complained of resistance to the idea from "technocratic" executives, particularly those of PDVSA, who allegedly claimed that the oil industry should be excluded from these arrangements due to its strategic importance.

UNT leaders insisted that the economic hardships resulting from the ten-week strike be borne by the companies and not the workers. In contrast to this position, some CTV trade union leaders signed agreements recognizing the suspension of collective bargaining agreements, temporary worker layoffs, and the abandonment of fringe benefits corresponding to the duration of the strike. These concessions were intended to provide companies with breathing space in order to avoid bankruptcy during the difficult period following the strike. Some CTV leaders claimed that the rigid demands of the Chavista trade unionists were designed to force companies out of business to pave the way for worker control.

The ten-week general strike of 2002–2003 brought to the fore an issue that had been discussed within the Chavista labor movement from the outset of Chávez's presidency in 1998: the need to weed out unreliable employees from the public sector. After the general strike, the hard-line Chavistas insisted on the complete purge of the oil industry. Approximately eighteen thousand employees, mostly those of the white-collar staff who had supported the strike, were fired for allegedly having participated in a criminal paralysis of the industry including sabotage. The hard-liners warned that many employees who had supported the strike attempted to work their way back into the industry by seeking employment from contractor firms in distinct locations, a practice that PDVSA's new managers were not acting to prevent. The hard-liners held PDVSA president, Alí Rodríguez, and other "moderates" responsible for having been taken by surprise (in spite of warnings) and not having proceeded against anti-Chavista executives in the industry, who had engaged in political activity within PDVSA following the April coup. At the same time, the hard-liners raised the specter of another oil workers' strike. They argued that, given the threat of sabotage, support for the goals of the "revolutionary process" (though not necessarily for Chávez) should be a prerequisite for employment in the oil industry.

The hard-liners favored extending the purge of the oil industry to include blue-collar workers, a demand that was particularly significant because FEDEPETROL had been an AD stronghold for many years. They insisted that Chavistas who risked their lives during the 2002–2003 strike by forming civilian brigades to guarantee the security of oil installations should be given preference in the selection of personnel to replace those who had walked out in December. Undoubtedly, this demand was part of a trade union strategy of promoting Chavista influence in the oil workers' movement and FEDE-PETROL's breakaway from the CTV. The hard-liners also pointed to other sectors, such as public education and the state-run electricity company (CADAFE), in which adversaries such as the followers of Luis Miquilena held key positions and assumed a hostile attitude toward Chavista employees. A resolution passed at the UNT's founding congress called for the removal of all coup supporters from the public administration. The replacement of employees belonging to traditional parties by Chavistas, however, was conducive to political clientelism, a deeply rooted practice in Venezuela.

Hard-line labor leaders generally expressed skepticism regarding the viability of worker cooperatives formed by those outside of the formal economy with start-up capital from the Ministry of the Popular Economy (MINEP). Indeed, they made a distinction between the MINEP-promoted cooperatives and the comanagement arrangements in state industries in the Guayana region as well as companies that had previously closed down and were then taken over by the workers and expropriated. The UNT leaders were convinced of the far-reaching significance of worker participation in decision-making in these existing companies, which they viewed as the seeds of a revolutionary proletariat-led transformation. The UNT leadership, however, was less enthusiastic about the MINEP-promoted cooperatives because most of their members did not have a solid working-class formation and were lacking in skills and discipline. UNT leaders pointed out that the MINEP cooperatives would never be able to compete with large-scale capital and that, far from representing a viable economic model, they were mainly designed to alleviate social problems. The UNT trade unionists also expressed apprehension that the MINEP cooperatives, which were not subject to labor legislation, would lower general labor standards. As a corrective, Orlando Chirino, who belonged to a left-wing current within the UNT, insisted that cooperative members, in spite of their property-holding status, be represented by labor unions.

By 2005, three well-defined currents had emerged within the UNT. Ramón Machuca, Franklin Rondón, and others grouped in the "Revolutionary Workers Movement Alfredo Maneiro," which they claimed was independent of the Chavista political leadership. They favored opening the UNT elections to all workers of the formal economy and not just unionized ones. The two other currents represented what this work has called a "hard-line" within the UNT. One, which was headed by Orlando Chirino (who led a splinter Trotskyist group, "Voz de los Trabajadores"), called for the immediate transformation of the UNT into a regular labor confederation with elections for top leadership positions and the affiliation of as many unions as possible, even at the expense of fostering parallel unionism. Chirino and his followers were convinced that they would win the UNT elections and that for this reason the rival currents were holding back the process. In contrast to the Machuca group, Chirino's followers often favored creating new UNT unions over affiliating old ones in order to avoid the corrupt and clientelistic practices that were well rooted in the Venezuelan labor movement. Chirino was particularly supportive of worker occupations and government expropriation, even before Chávez decreed the state takeover of VENEPAL in 2005. The Chirino current preferred expropriation of companies that faced bankruptcy over agreements whereby the firm's owner accepted worker participation in management decision-making in return for state financial relief. A second "hard-line" current was closely tied to the Labor Ministry and the political parties of the ruling coalition and in some states was represented by the FBT.

In spite of the confrontation between the currents led by Chirino and Machuca, both shared a concern for defending the right to strike and maintaining union autonomy. This convergence was particularly evident in their positions toward labor conflicts in the public sector. The Chirino current insisted that the UNT target public-sector violations of labor legislation and collective bargaining agreements as well as the state's overreliance on temporary labor in order to ensure that a good example was set for the private sector. As head of the public employees, Rondón of the Machuca current held a similar position.

The rivalry between the three currents held back further advances for the UNT, particularly in the Guayana region. In both SIDOR and the state aluminum company ALCASA, UNT currents opposed to Machuca attempted to unseat him and his followers. In union elections at SIDOR in November 2005, Machuca's allies won the top two posts of president and secretary general but failed to maintain control of the union's executive committee. The UNT's division into various slates facilitated inroads by parties of the opposition grouped in "Slate 99." Unlike the Chavista trade unionists, Slate 99 opposed SIDOR's renationalization, which Chávez himself at one point had threatened to decree.

IMPLICATIONS FOR THE EXCEPTIONALISM THESIS

In glorifying Venezuelan democratic institutions over a period of decades, writers who defended the exceptionalism thesis singled out the nation's labor movement for special praise. They depicted the CTV as a pluralistic institution and a bulwark of democracy that acted responsibly by toning down demands at critical moments in order to maintain political and social stability (Alexander, 1982: 506). Nevertheless, the CTV's 2001 internal electoral debacle sheds light on the electoral manipulation and fraud that had enabled AD to maintain absolute control of the confederation over a period of decades. This unethical behavior is evidence that exceptionalism-thesis scholars overstated the case regarding the sense of pluralism of AD labor leaders and their "generosity" toward other political currents in the CTV.

The main issue of concern in this chapter is the labor movement's dependence on political parties and the state. The lack of autonomy was made blatantly evident in 1997 when AD labor leaders translated their party's political commitments to the proneoliberal Caldera administration into acceptance of the modifications of severance payment benefits that undid 60 years of steady improvement in the system. Of equal importance was the CTV's failure to restructure the labor movement to create national unions as the 1990 Labor Law permitted, thus keeping organized labor weak and subordinate to political parties and the state.

This chapter discussed the importance of the issue of autonomy among those trade unionists who challenged the leadership of the CTV and later formed the UNT. Most important, a group of independents from diverse political backgrounds defied polarization by raising the banner of trade union autonomy vis-à-vis political parties and the state. Some of them insisted on a more drawn-out process for the founding of the UNT in order to establish principles and procedures of rank-and-file participation that would make the confederation immune to political party and state interference. In addition, the MVR labor leaders, the FBT, and the UNT did not always coincide with the positions held by the MVR party leaders on issues ranging from social security legislation to worker takeovers of companies that had closed down.

Nevertheless, the emerging labor movement did not escape the danger of political control. While the independents placed a premium on autonomy, many Chavista worker leaders were largely concerned with the power struggle within organized labor. After 1998 they attempted to take advantage of the MVR's dominant position in the government and the weakness of the opposition by formulating a strategy of relying on executive and legislative power to wrest control of the labor movement from AD. The Chavistas precipitated the emergence of parallel structures by forming new unions (as in case of the oil workers' movement) that had little possibility at the time of displacing the established CTV labor organizations. Chavista labor leaders even supported initiatives that promised to help them make inroads into organized labor, but in the process converged with positions assumed by neoliberals (as in the case of the "modern contract" in the oil industry). After 2001, the need to defend the Chavista government in light of the deepening of polarization and political crisis also influenced the FBT to take political imperatives into account.

These developments explain why trade union autonomy was such a thorny issue and was discussed so ardently at the UNT's founding meeting in March 2003, and why Machuca decided not to join the confederation for the time being. Simple solutions to the issues that were under discussion hardly awaited the UNT trade unionists. The danger of sabotage in the oil industry, and the possibility of another CTV-led attempt to oust Chávez, convinced many UNT leaders that trade union struggles could not be divorced from political ones. At the same time, however, UNT leaders were determined to avoid repeating the CTV's historical errors of subordinating worker interests to political commitments and promoting clientelism.

Just as the electoral fraud of October 2001 and President Chávez's attacks on the "trade union mafia" point to the undemocratic and unethical practices of the CTV leadership over a period of decades, the call for trade union autonomy recalls worker struggles of the past that were not controlled by political parties or the state. Indeed, the positions assumed by Orlando Chirino, Ramón Machuca, and others designed to steer the UNT on an independent course did not emerge in an historical vacuum. Machuca, for instance, had formerly belonged to the Causa R Party, which was steeped in a tradition of worker independence dating back to the outset of the democratic period in the industrial region of Guayana (Buxton, 2001: 132–165). Throughout the decades, assertion of worker independence occurred at critical moments, although the enormous oil-derived resources at the disposal of the state and proestablishment political parties often allowed them to co-opt rebel leaders and rein them into the AD and COPEI folds (as in the case of trade unionists belonging to the Movimiento Electoral del Pueblo in the 1970s). In 1948, for instance, AD worker leaders' plans for a general strike to preempt a military coup were vetoed by party leaders, and in 1958–1960 labor leaders of all currents called for unity at a time when AD politicians attempted to marginalize the Communist Party and promoted polarization (Ellner, 1980: 140–141; 1993: 5–16).

The exceptionalism thesis disregarded class cleavages and maintained that the proestablishment political parties and their labor leaders guaranteed social stability and harmony (Martz, 1966: 286). Exceptionalism writers failed to recognize that corruption, clientelism. and electoral fraud explained in large part why AD worker leaders were able to retain control of the CTV for so long. Furthermore, exceptionalism writers played down challenges to party control and assertion of worker interests. The need for a reexamination of the labor past parallels President Chávez's call for a reexamination of Venezuela's entire history. Just as the nineteenth century was not the monotonous history of avaricious caudillos and sell-outs as many Venezuelans have been led to believe, the nation's labor history is not one of unwavering control by AD in the absence of assertions of independence and expressions of class-consciousness. Labor historians cannot ignore the pursuit of labor autonomy in the past, just as it cannot be ignored in the present. In this sense, debunking the exceptionalism thesis encourages the labor movement to face the challenges of today.

REFERENCES

Alexander, Robert Jackson
1964 *The Venezuelan Democratic Revolution: A Profile of the Regime of Romulo Betancourt.* New Brunswick, NJ: Rutgers University Press.
1982 *Rómulo Betancourt and the Transformation of Venezuela.* New Brunswick, NY: Transaction.

Bergquist, Charles
1986 *Labor in Latin America: Comparative Essays on Chile, Argentina, Venezuela, and Colombia.* Stanford, CA: Stanford University Press.

Buxton, Julia
2001 *The Failure of Political Reform in Venezuela.* Aldershot, UK: Ashgate.

Díaz Rangel, Eleazar
2002 *Todo Chávez: de sabaneta al golpe de abril.* Caracas: Planeta.

Ellner, Steve
1980 *Los partidos políticos y su disputa por el control del movimiento sindical en Venezuela, 1936–1948.* Caracas: Universidad Católica Andrés Bello.
1993 *Organized Labor in Venezuela, 1958–1991: Behavior and Concerns in a Democratic Setting.* Wilmington, DE: Scholarly Resources.
1999 "The Impact of Privatization on Labor in Venezuela: Radical Reorganization or Moderate Adjustment?" *Political Power and Social Theory* 13.

Ellner, Steve and Fred Rosen
2002 "Chavismo at the Crossroads: Hardliners, Moderates and a Regime under Attack." *NACLA: Report on the Americas* 36 (July/August): 9–15.

Harnecker, Marta
2002–2003 "Los trabajadores en el proceso bolivariano: entrevistas" [unpublished interviews] (October 2002–May 2003).

Levine, Daniel H.
1973 *Conflict and Political Change in Venezuela.* Princeton, NJ: Princeton University Press.

Steve Ellner

Martínez, Filiberto
    2003 Interview with FBT candidate for president of FetraAnzoátegui, August 5, Barcelona (Venezuela).
Martz, John D.
    1966 *Acción Democrática: Evolution of a Modern Political Party in Venezuela*. Princeton, NJ: Princeton University Press.
Murillo, María Victoria
    2001 *Labor Unions, Partisan Coalitions, and Market Reforms in Latin America*. Cambridge, UK: Cambridge University Press.

Chapter Six

Ethnicity and Revolution: The Political Economy of Racism in Venezuela

Jesús María Herrera Salas

Despite the prevailing myth of racial democracy that has traditionally pervaded Venezuelan culture and society, racism continues to be a serious problem in the country. The economic crisis that began with the decline in international petroleum prices and the subsequent devaluation of the bolivar in February 1983 (known popularly as "Black Friday") served to expose the existence of profound racism directed not only at Afro-Venezuelan and indigenous inhabitants of the country but also at broad sectors of the population. These groups are regularly berated by the upper and middle classes, who are opposed to the process of political change, as "vermin," "mixed breeds," "Indians," "barefoot," and "rabble." This political economy of racism reflects the historical continuation of the long process of conquest and slavery of the indigenous and Afro-Venezuelan populations that began with the arrival of the Spanish in 1496.

The current political struggles conducted by those opposed to the changes initiated by President Hugo Chávez and the Bolivarian revolutionary processes have exacerbated racism in the country. Spokespersons for the right stubbornly uphold the theory of Venezuela's exceptionalism with regard to racism. Hans Neumann, for example, argues that

> in Venezuela we complain about a lot of things that we think are wrong. But we have some things that should serve as an example to other countries. One is that race is not important in judging a person. In Venezuela racial discrimination is not a factor either in employment or in social or intellectual realms. . . . Prejudice against someone because of the color of his skin does not exist. This is not an obstacle here as it is in other places. (Neumann, 1997:1)

Racism in Venezuela, however, is alive and well. In fact, the publication of Jun Ishibashi's (University of Tokyo) 2003 essay "Toward an Opening of the

99

Debate on Racism in Venezuela," reinforces the work of Venezuelan social scientists who over the last several decades have attempted to debunk the myth of racial democracy in Venezuela. His article intensified the academic debate of a subject that traditionally had been addressed in a rather superficial manner. To examine the assertion that racism continues to be a factor in Venezuela, I have grouped the contents of this chapter into four sections. In the first, I provide a brief but essential reference to the historical roots of racism as an ideology of the slave system and of Spanish colonial society. In the second, I examine the fundamental assumption that has prevailed until recently: the ideology of egalitarian miscegenation and the supposed social and racial equality of "all" Venezuelans. Subsequently, I trace the gradual reemergence of racism in Venezuela dating back to the economic crisis beginning in 1983. I describe the rise of new political actors and social movements that struggled in an organized way against racial discrimination and critically review some of the principal academic studies on the subject during this period. I then examine the Bolivarian Revolution in 1998 and the gains that this process has produced for indigenous communities and Afro-Venezuelans. Lastly, I address the way racist and class reaction on the part of privileged sectors opposed to the process of change under Chávez has exacerbated racism in the country. This conservative reaction was most clearly expressed in the coup of April 2002.

HISTORICAL BACKGROUND OF THE PROBLEM

In analyzing racism in Venezuela it is essential to review, however briefly, its historical background. Almost all of the authors who have studied racism in Venezuela—among them Miguel Acosta Saignes, Federico Brito Figueroa, Michaelle Ascencio, Ligia Montañez, Rafael Marcial Ramos Guédez, Esteban Emilio Mosonyi, and Jesús Chucho García—agree that the study of the slave era is critical to an understanding of current phenomena, including racial discrimination, intolerance, and endoracism. In the case of Afro-Venezuelans, for example, Michaelle Ascencio affirms that "it is precisely [in this period] that the racist ideology against blacks was sown," also observing that "slavery, along with the violence of the corresponding mode of production, included racism as an essential ideological component" (Ascencio, 1984: 103).

Along this line, we must bear in mind that millions of African slaves were introduced into the Americas in the course of four centuries. Millions of human beings were torn from their lands, stripped of their families and ethnic and cultural references, and relocated in a new land where they suffered physical humiliation, economic exploitation, social exclusion, and sexual violence at the hands of the colonial sectors for whom the economic benefit justified the negation and extermination of a part of humanity. Trafficking in Africans, therefore, was a planned action within the framework of the "economic necessities" of the imperial metropolises. The importance of African slave trafficking to the European political economy has been evaluated by Gonzalo Aguirre Beltrán, Frederick Bowser, Michele Duchet, Manuel Moreno Fraginals, José Luciano Franco, Immanuel Wallerstein, and Joseph Inikori, among others.

In Venezuela, the formal African slave trade lasted until 1797. Over three centuries, some 100,000 Africans entered the country, by legal or illegal means, with the official figures distributed as follows: 6,595 in the sixteenth century; 10,147 in the seventeenth century; and 34,099 in the eighteenth century (Brito Figueroa, 1985: 180). In his famous book, *Of a Journey to the Equinoctial Region of the New Continent*, Baron Alexander von Humboldt provided a vivid description of the treatment of Africans in the country:

> The slaves offered for sale were young people between fifteen and twenty years of age. Every morning coconut oil was distributed among them to be rubbed on their bodies in order to give their skin a black shine. Buyers constantly appeared who determined the age and health of the slave by the condition of their teeth, forcing open their mouths, as is done in the markets with horses. (Humboldt, 1941 [1805]: 423)

Germán Arciniegas discusses the profound lack of humanity in the trade: "When the women go to market, where the slavers brought their merchandise out of their ships, they examine each slave touching him all over. Then, so as not to leave an impression of familiarity, they spit in his face" (Arciniegas, 1993 [1944]: 221). To legitimize their project, the Spaniards created a myth about the origin of Africans, conveniently taken from their own Holy Scripture. Through a complex argument combining "physical explanations" with "moral explanations" the theologians of the Spanish Empire determined that

> the Ethiopians, who we usually call blacks, find their origins in Ham, who was the world's first servant and slave, since his father, Noah, had cursed him and all his generation for his shamefulness, showing little reverence when he became drunk after eating some grapes . . . and for this Ham lost his nobility and even his freedom, causing him and his entire generation to become slaves; this was the first servitude introduced into the world. And being light-skinned by ancestry, he was born dark. And from there blacks were born, and we could even say that slaves too were born as if God blackened his children for coming from bad parents . . . those who have good ones, we say have light blood. (Sandoval 1987 [1627]: 74)

"Therefore," the theologians categorically concluded, "this stems directly from God's will" (Sandoval 1987 [1627]: 74).

Two centuries later, in the final stages of the colonial period, the white oligarchy reacted to the Royal Certificate of Special Dispensation of 1795 that allowed those of mixed race to purchase the classification of "white." The promulgation of this decree might even be considered a milestone in the interracial struggles in Venezuela:

> The enormous cacao plantations which represented the greatest source of wealth of many *criollos* during the colonial period could only be developed through their ownership of those lands and their advantages in acquiring slave labor and indigenous servitude. Cacao allowed a large number of white *criollos* to set themselves up as a predominant economic sector and, of course, to ennoble themselves, since they paid for almost all the titles of nobility known in the history of Venezuela with that product. The Cabildo (town council) of Caracas, which was the most active center of white *criollos* in Venezuela, always pressured, especially in the eighteenth century, to maintain and deepen those inequalities. From its core came forth vigorous opposition to the aspirations of social ascent of the racially mixed, against the determination perceived in them to become equal to whites. (López, 1988: 934)

The ideological influence of the theology of slavery, however, extended well beyond the colonial period in Venezuela, since the new dominant class of *criollos* preserved the system of slavery. The latter sought to retake effective control of the societies dismembered by the wars of independence and to reinvigorate the white sector of the population by uniting the opposing bands of royalists and patriots through the promotion of "white" immigration and the prohibition of "black" immigration. As Germán Carrera Damas indicates, "the nucleus of what would become the liberal treatment of the slavery question was formed in its three principal components very early on: preservation of the economic structure, reconciliation of the liberal principles of property, liberty, equality and fraternity, and the guarantee of white hegemony" (Carrera Damas, 1987: 44).

In analyzing the country's ills, Venezuelan leaders and their positivist ideologues pointed to the existence of a population "battered" by the constant mix of whites, Indians, and blacks. This was one of the motives that led the nineteenth-century ruler Antonio Guzmán Blanco to promote large-scale European immigration "for the improvement of the race." The form of the hegemonic political discourse changed, and new social theories replaced the traditional theological argument previously used to justify slavery (Herrera Salas, 2003). Its essence, however, remained intact; as "irrationals" or as "inferior races," Afro-Venezuelans and indigenous peoples continued to be the "cause" of the country's social ills. Purportedly based on an exhaustive knowledge of biology and physical anthropology, the first theories supporting racial discrimination arose along with this trend. This situation persisted in the twentieth century once Juan Vicente Gómez came to power. Thus, the majority of the intellectuals associated with his regime found the origin of Venezuela's troubles in the mixture of races (Vallenilla Lanz, 1984 [1930]: 139).

Although much has changed since the time of slavery, the population of African origin and the indigenous peoples continue to belong predominantly to the oppressed popular sectors. In this context, the Venezuelan psychologist Ligia Montañez has argued:

> We should not be surprised at the survival of numerous manifestations—subtle and not so subtle—of discrimination and rejection of persons with predominantly black physical features. . . . The idea of historical genesis has already been too widely developed in the area of human and social sciences for us to skip over it. The present is always an updating of the past, and it is most similar precisely to those aspects in which the essential part of the past has not been transformed, even though it may have experienced changes and taken on our vestments. (Montañez, 1993: 52)

Thus, the distortion of identities initiated by the Spaniards and continued by the republican *criollos* in the nineteenth and twentieth centuries is still present in Venezuela today.

THE IDEOLOGY OF MESTIZAJE AND THE MYTH OF RACIAL DEMOCRACY

As we have seen, the birth of the republic and even the abolition of slavery did not reduce the condition of servitude for the indigenous and Afro-Venezuelan communities. Racism endured in the social projects initiated by the dominant elites that replaced the colonizers. Though the formal legal chains were broken, new encumbrances were created. The appearance of the ideology of *mestizaje* (miscegenation), also known as the myth of democracy or racial equality, served to mask racial discrimination and the socioeconomic situation of the Afro-Venezuelan and indigenous communities. This ideology attempted to close the wounds produced by the clash of different cultures and hide the unequal relations of power between the different ethnic groups. In practice, however, it identified the white European as the civilizing agent, making Africans and the indigenous and their descendants largely invisible. With the aim of consolidating the processes of nation building, the Latin American elites tried to forge a national mestizo identity that excluded Indian and Afro-American ethnicity. "The ideology of *mestizaje* denies the existence of social classes and the possibility of incorporating Indians and Afro-Americans with their own identity into the national society" (Muratorio, 1981). In general terms this ideology asserted that as the biological and cultural mix progressed, society would move toward uniformity, thus eliminating the causes of racism. José Vasconcelos's proposal of a "cosmic race," ultimately mestizo, influenced many Latin American thinkers of this period.

Political and social integration did not appear enough; total cultural integration would be necessary. To achieve this objective, a homogeneous culture had to be created by means of the educational system that would be capable of erasing heterogeneity and thus of appealing to a single national specific tradition elevated over any foreign or universal one. However, the project of a homogeneous nation only existed in the imagination of its intelligentsia. The ideology of mestizo assimilation was put into practice by the Venezuelan state with the help of organic intellectuals. The best-known case of this is *indigenismo*, adopted by liberals as government policy from the beginning of the republic. Indigenous peoples were simply to be considered campesinos. Ignoring their specific ethnicity, they were "educated" in Spanish in order to assimilate them to the language and culture of the *criollos*.

Indigenismo was one of the main strategies implemented by the liberals to achieve the integration of the Latin American states into the hegemonic models of capitalist development. As the Mexican anthropologist Bonfil Batalla indicates, "the integrating mission expressed in Indianist policies evidently corresponds to the capitalist need to consolidate and expand the internal market. . . . The Indian does not fit in this enterprise" (Bonfil Batalla, 1992: 52). Elsewhere he has argued that "the goal of Indianism, crudely stated, consists of achieving the disappearance of the Indian" (Bonfil Batalla, 1970: 43). César Uzcátegui describes the economic interests that drove these policies:

> The liberal concept of the oligarchic elites sought, among other things, to reduce the population of Indians and incorporate them into a new model of economic and social development in which they lost their right to the land. The logic of this policy, geared towards consolidating the private nature of property, was aimed at legitimizing actions that allowed the Venezuelan state to expropriate large tracts of lands . . . broadening the property base of the landowner class which controlled the government. The destruction of the collective forms of communal property and the loss of all the elements that formed the material basis of their ways of life brought about their destabilization as historic societies, converting them in fact into a marginalized sector. Government policy implemented by political figures in the post-republican period produced similar outcomes; broad legal measures served to eliminate most indigenous lands. An early example of this policy was represented by the Act of April 1836 that ordered the distribution of the indigenous lands. This process created the bases of the economic structure and allowed the consolidation of property in the hands of an oligarchy. (Uzcátegui, 1995: 201)

As in the case of Indianism, the "whitening" project constituted the institutionalization of racism as official policy:

The relationship established in the legal mechanism between immigration and "colonization" is enlightening on this point. Immigration is imposed as one of the instruments of internal colonization, occupation, and appraisal of the national territory. For the state it is a question of clearing, occupying, homogenizing, and "civilizing" in order to occupy the land according to the well-known formula created by the Argentine Alberdi: "to govern is to populate." The state is called upon to play a predominant role in this process. (Martínez, 1997: 3)

The racist content of the "whitening" in Venezuela was eloquently summarized by Arturo Uslar Pietri, then director of the Office of Immigration and Colonization:

It was even more impossible to appreciate the Indian than the Spaniard. He had neither the capability nor the will for systematic work. The words "laziness" and "bad habits" constantly appear when the colonial chroniclers speak of the Indian. The arrival of blacks in America was a result of the incapacity of the Indian. Nor do blacks constitute a contribution that could benefit the race. The resulting mix has not improved on the original components. What we could call the current Venezuelan race, in general terms, is as incapable of a modern and dynamic conception of work and wealth as were its predecessors for building modern states. (Uslar Pietri, 1937: 6,943)

The ideology of *mestizaje*, or the supposed "harmonious" coexistence of three worlds, has been widely criticized as a legitimating discourse of societies with hierarchies based on class or ethnic groups. With its racism and implicit reverence for Western culture, it has been used, in effect, to justify policies of whitening or selective immigration. In Venezuela as in other countries of the region, the myth of racial democracy and the ideology of *mestizaje* have served to conceal racist structural practices that displace indigenous and Afro-Venezuelan cultures and strengthen institutional discrimination (see Bonfil Batalla, 1992; 1994 [on Mexico]; Stutzman, 1981; Ibarra, 1992; and Almeida, 1992 [on Ecuador]; Nascimento, 1978; and Hanchard, 1998 [on Brazil]; Pérez Sarduy and Stubbs, 1993, 2000 [on Cuba]). The special edition on *mestizaje* of the *Journal of Latin American Anthropology* edited by Charles E. Hale (1996) and an article by Lourdes Martínez-Echazabal (1998) are also important. These works serve to expose the myth of racial democracy and the ideology of *mestizaje*, demonstrating in each case their racist consequences.

THE ECONOMIC CRISIS OF 1983 AND THE RETURN OF VISIBLE RACISM

The enormous petroleum income that Venezuela generated with the rise in the price of crude oil after the Arab-Israeli War of 1973 and the ensuing Arab oil boycott reduced the visibility of racism, but in the initial stages of the economic crisis of 1983, the upper and middle sectors blamed the country's problems on Afro-Caribbean and indigenous immigrants who had come to Venezuela in search of opportunity. In this racist and xenophobic discourse it was not that Venezuelans had squandered a large portion of their petroleum income but rather that "those blacks from Colombia, the Dominican Republic, and Haiti" as well as "the Indians of Peru and Ecuador," all "that rabble," had "made the country falter" (Suárez, 2000). Soon, however, the comments and racist attitudes were extended to include Afro-Venezuelan and indigenous inhabitants and members of the popular sectors in general. Montañez has correctly pointed to the link between racial discrimination and social and economic discrimination in a political economy of racism: "The direct and indirect descendants of the old slaves and free blacks of the colony continue to belong predominately to the popular, oppressed sectors, holding less qualified, lower-paid jobs that require greater physical strength and sharing . . . scarce benefits" (Montañez, 1993: 51; Wright, 1990; López Sanz, 1993).

In response to this visible increase in racism and discrimination, there was an increase in the number of organized social movements and Afro-Venezuelan and indigenous organizations pursuing "more autonomous logics of social dynamic and less instrumental forms of political practice" (García, 2002: 134). As these organizations emerged, left intellectuals began to revalue traditional culture "in order to vindicate the national culture" (Ishibashi, 2001:12). The convergence of these various forces fueled a movement of cultural resistance and helped foreground the issue of national identity. The main actors in this movement in the Afro-Venezuelan community have been the Union of Black Women and the Afro-America Foundation, led by Jesús Chucho García, which joined with other regional grassroots organizations to form the Network of Afro-Venezuelan Organizations in 2000. The indigenous movement in Venezuela coalesced around the Consejo Nacional Indio de Venezuela (National Indian Council of Venezuela—CONIVE), established in August 1989. CONIVE brought together some sixty indigenous organizations, and its Interethnic Council includes representatives of the country's thirty-two indigenous peoples. It promotes the participation of indigenous communities in the improvement of their socioeconomic conditions and at the same time strengthens their cultural identity.

THE BOLIVARIAN REVOLUTION

By 1998 the bipartisan model of liberal representative democracy in Venezuela had been exhausted. The pauperization of 70 percent of the population as a result of fifteen years of neoliberal policies, as well as the growing deterioration and loss of legitimacy of the traditional Acción Democrática and COPEI parties opened a space for new political and social forces. It is in this context that the political movement led by President Hugo Chávez emerged. The movement is characterized by participative and protagonist democracy and is popularly known as the Bolivarian Revolution. I will limit myself to highlighting the gains derived from this process by indigenous and Afro-Venezuelan groups. I will also address the racist and classist reaction that these political and social changes have generated among the elites and middle-class sectors that constitute the core of the political opposition.

The new policies and forms of participation promoted by the Bolivarian Revolution can be seen from the very beginning of the process in the call for a national constituent assembly. The direct participation of grassroots indigenous organizations as well as regional and national organizations (such as CONIVE) in the process was completely novel in the history of the country. As the director of the Venezuelan National Foundation for Indigenous Studies, Domingo Sánchez, underscored,

> with the democratic elections of 1998 Venezuela's social, political, and economic relations experienced a profound change. A national constituent assembly was convoked by democratic means, and it drafted a new constitution that not only changed the correlation of social forces but also . . . entailed a profound transformation in the relationships between criollo society and indigenous peoples. (Sánchez, 2002: 3)

Article 121 of the Bolivarian Constitution underscores this new reality:

> Indigenous peoples have the right to maintain and develop their ethnic and cultural entity, worldview, values, spirituality, and sacred places of worship. The state shall promote the appreciation and dissemination of the cultural manifestations of the indigenous peoples, who have the right to their own education, and an education system of an intercultural and bilingual nature, taking into account their special social and cultural characteristics, values, and traditions.

In addition, the National Assembly ratified the International Labor Organization's Convention 169 on Indigenous and Tribal Peoples, and the government launched an important series of development projects that vindicate the rights and cultures of twenty-eight native communities. The indigenous organizations' rejection of the April 2002 coup, which threatened their new rights, underscored their awareness of the revolutionary process. In a public declaration issued immediately after the coup CONIVE stated:

> In the spirit of our ancestors and heroes of the indigenous resistance and in the face of the painful events of April 11, in the city of Caracas . . . we condemn the coup launched against the constitutional president of the Bolivarian Republic of

Venezuela Hugo Rafael Chávez Frías led by Pedro Carmona . . . joined by the country's major media and supported by forces foreign to the interests of our nation. We steadfastly condemn the attempt by the de facto government to eliminate the Constitution of the Bolivarian Republic of Venezuela, in which the rights of the indigenous peoples are hallowed, and which is recognized as one of the most advanced in the world in terms of indigenous rights, a product of the struggles and resistance by more than 30 indigenous peoples living in this country for 500 years. (CONIVE, 2002: 1)

For the first time in the history of the country, indigenous people have occupied high-level posts in the government. The most notable case is that of Noelí Pocaterra, a Wayuu who has been vice president of the National Assembly. The Chávez government has indicated its intent to reverse the Eurocentric form of teaching Venezuela's history and has changed the official name for October 12, previously called "Day of the Discovery" or "the Day of the Encounter" to the more historically accurate "the Day of Indigenous Resistance."

With respect to the Afro-Venezuelan groups, Jesús Chucho García points out that although not all the proposals for vindication brought before the constituent assembly by the Union of Black Women and other organizations were adopted,

The struggle continues on the basis of the preamble of the new constitution, which highlights "the re-founding of the Republic through profound transformations designed to establish a democratic, sovereign, responsible, multi-ethnic and multicultural society made up of equal men and women and children . . . in accord with the values of . . . national identity." We are in an era of social transformations and globalization, and the Afro-Venezuelan organizations have understood this process and have been active participants in the process of change. The legal-political transformations underway in Latin American nations have been utilized by the Afro-Venezuelan movements to make legislative proposals, and this is one of the central elements in our organization in the quest for public space, thanks to the awareness that we have gained in recent times. (García, 2001: 55)

Evidence of the possibility for change that Afro-Venezuelan groups see in the Bolivarian Revolution is made clear in the report in the *San Francisco Bay View* (September 25, 2002) regarding the reaction of this movement to the coup:

This month, for the first time in history, Venezuelan people of African descent have total control of their historic Black university, the Instituto Universitario Barlovento. . . . Another topic on their minds and hearts is the fate of President Hugo Chávez. He is Venezuela's first multiracial president and is called "Negro" (black) by his detractors because of his African-Indigenous features. Behind the enemies of Venezuela and Hugo Chávez are very large sums of money being spent to destroy the dreams of the people who historically have been discriminated against because of race, economic ideas, etc. Africans and people of African descent are beginning to tell our own story.

THE OPPOSITION'S RACISM

From the 1998 electoral campaign to the present, the political opposition has utilized a great number of adjectives for the purpose of berating Hugo Chávez. As Heiber Barreto Sánchez has pointed out:

"Indian, monkey and thick-lipped" have been some of the more illustrative expressions of this racial contempt that the opposition has displayed when describing Chávez. What it has forgotten is that the majority of us Venezuelans carry at least one of these features and by attempting to discredit them politically in this manner they are attacking the sentiments of a large part of the population. . . . An unprecedented classism can be added to this visceral racism: for years the middle and upper levels of our society have been referring to the people of the lower strata as "vermin and crass," revealing through this the lack of manners, taste, and customs characteristic of those who consider and project themselves as "educated, refined and polite." (Barreto Sánchez, 2002: 1)

Although the official spokespersons of the opposition have categorically denied the presence of this racism, the opposite claim has been made by a wide range of sectors at both the national and international levels. A few examples will suffice. William Lara, former president of the National Assembly, has asked,

How much racism is there in the rabid opposition that calls Hugo Chávez "mixed breed" with fierce contempt? The answer might be a great deal if we were to consider the racist attitudes and behavior that run under the surface in certain sectors of Venezuelan society. Certainly a minority, they nevertheless possess significant economic power and are fighting to recover their de facto political control from the time of the Fourth Republic. The spokespersons of those sectors openly exude their racist venom against the leader from Barinas [Chávez], ridiculing the color of his skin and his features. (Lara, 2002: 1)

Former Foreign Minister Chaderton formalized these accusations of racism before the Thirty-third General Assembly of the Organization of American States:

Our media show hidden or open signs of racism. In Venezuela you will not find newscasters or opinion show hosts who are black or mestizo. . . . I wonder if the fact that private media, when referring to brown or black-skinned high

Venezuelan officials, openly call them monkeys, macaques, or chimpanzees, does not warrant at least a minimum of attention.

Among other Afro-Venezuelan members of the Bolivarian cabinet, Chaderton spoke of the way in which some journalists have characterized the speech patterns of the president and of Education Minister Aristóbulo Istúriz. Lina Ron, one of the best-known grassroots leaders supporting the process of change, points to the

> outrageous discrimination towards the have-nots, towards those whose skin is dark, towards the poor, those who live in shacks on the hillside, towards those who identify with the revolutionary process. This is a tremendous class and race hatred, expressed in an abhorrent way. (Quoted in Murieta, 2003: 94)

The Bolivarian Circles, themselves frequently considered "rabble," have been particularly active in denouncing the opposition's racism. For example, Fabio Carboni, of the *17 de Marzo* Bolivarian Circle, says,

> Much of the Venezuelan opposition concentrates all of its criticism of Chávez on insignificant things. That Chávez is ugly, that Chávez is black, that they can't stand Chávez when he talks . . . not only do they expose their racism but they also try to hide what is essential. Let's start considering ourselves proud Latin Americans and stop believing that we are Europeans who by mistake or divine curse were born in Latin America. (Carboni, 2002: 1)

Similar remarks may be found on Bolivarian Circle websites.

Álvaro Agudelo points to the importance of racism in the ranks of the opposition:

> I've thought about the issue many times, seeking explanations for the repulsion towards Chávez observed in some sectors. What drives it? The disproportionate attitude of certain social groups has to do with a deeply-rooted class concept, riding on the white lie that in Venezuela there is social equality. Ours is a society that very carefully hides a racism and a discrimination that flourishes and shows its teeth in times of crisis. It's not true that our country is egalitarian. On the contrary, it's a country with profound social differences and a barely controlled racism. With Chávez the story is repeated: child of a humble home, rustic—campesino, actually—as he refers to himself, with a cultural formation different from that of the upper classes and, above all, with a dark skin color and hair, whose typology signifies a cleaning rag for these unforgiving posh sectors. I've heard many ask how is it that a monkey like Chávez could be in Miraflores? [the presidential palace]. The cause of so much hatred towards Chávez is, as we can see, very plain but unmentionable. (Agudelo, 2002: 3)

Alejandro López de Haro summarizes what is readily perceived in Venezuela: "Anyone who moves in middle-class circles will see how they openly speak with contempt about the rabble and the imperative of toppling the government by whatever means possible" (López de Haro, 2002: 1). In this context it seems important to highlight the abundance of racist political graffiti (e.g., "Out with the vermin" and "Death to the monkey Chávez") on the walls of the upper- and middle-class neighborhoods. Charges of intense racism toward the president and the popular sectors that support him have also been made by recognized international journalists, notably Ignacio Ramonet (2002), editor of *Le Monde Diplomatique* and one of the organizers of the Porto Alegre World Social Forum, and the British journalist and historian and former editor of *The Guardian*, Richard Gott (2002: 3).

One of the settings in which racism in Venezuela is most clearly visible is, in fact, that of the media, whose proprietors are currently leading the business and the upper- and middle-class organizations opposed to the revolutionary process. Ishibashi's research, financed by the Rockefeller Foundation, focused on advertising practices, soap operas, and modeling, and demonstrated stereotyped exclusion and inclusion in the representation of blacks. To estimate the extent of exclusion of blacks he counted the number of "black" people appearing in commercials, soap operas, and beauty contests and studied the roles assigned to "black" characters and the contexts in which they appeared. He concluded that the participation of "blacks" in the Venezuelan media studied was very limited and that they were stereotyped in a negative way (Ishibashi, 2003: 7, 13).

During a visit to Caracas to attend a poetry event in July of 2004, Ernesto Cardenal left his impressions in writing:

> Those media are always caricaturizing Chávez with a new racism that has arisen in Venezuela. They ridicule him about his features and skin color. Since some of his supporters call him "Mi Comandante" (My Commander), the right has nicknamed him Mico Mandante ("Monkey-in-charge") because he is mestizo or mulatto or perhaps both and because of his somewhat copper-colored skin. (Cardenal, 2004: 3)

The media's racism goes beyond the borders of Venezuela. As the BBC pointed out in March 2004, six African countries (Algeria, Egypt, Libya, Nigeria, Western Sahara, and South Africa) accused the television chain Globovisión of racism over a parody of Robert Mugabe, the president of Zimbabwe. In a joint statement they accused the station of a "crude and indecent spectacle, filled with vulgar effects, scornful comments, and endless mockery and overtures with undeniably racist content that offended African peoples and human dignity" (BBC, 2004: 1).[2]

Racism and classism are also found in the print media. As Mariadela Linares reports, one offensive editorial stated that for a march to be held on Sunday October 13, pro-government forces had brought in from the countryside "the same lumpen as always, which had become the perpetual bus riders, with a bread roll and a flask of rum" (Linares, 2002). Pressured by numerous nongovernmental organizations and other sectors of society, the newspaper's editorial office extended its apologies the next day. The racism of the opposition against the revolutionary process has been openly acknowledged by some of its members. Oscar Lucien, director of the Central University's Institute of Communications Research and an important advisor to the opposition, publicly admitted in a 2004 interview with Humberto Márquez that "the president's 'mixed-breed' status bothered one sector of the middle class" (H. Márquez, 2004).

The presence of racism in Venezuela's current political scene has also been publicly recognized by a representative of the most significant neoliberal academic institution in the country. In a collection recently published by the Institute of Advanced Administration Studies, Patricia Márquez begins her article by stating:

> Beyond the political sphere, a great deal of the debate that Hugo Chávez has created since he began to rise in the 1998 electoral opinion polls centered on his social status, his color and personal style. . . . The president, a native of Barinas, lower-middle class, dark in color . . . is the epitome of the Venezuelan from the masses that rose to the height of power. His image bothers the posh ladies of Caurimare and other parts of the country, while for the lowly, he symbolizes "one of them" who has attained the Presidency of the Republic understanding their problems and fulfilling promises not fulfilled by the parties of the past. (2004: 31)

Márquez continues:

> Everyday practices and expressions demonstrate that color differences *do* matter. In Venezuela there is a colorism (to use anthropologist Roger Lancaster's 1992 term), which manifests itself in an insidious and destructive way in the fabric of social relations. Skin color is a mark which, depending on the shade of café con leche, (coffee with milk), hinders or facilitates social mobility, just as it opens or closes windows of opportunity. (2004: 32)

In her opinion, however, it is President Chávez who has "stirred up the beehive of social harmony" (2004: 31). That "social harmony," however, did not include the Amparo Massacre, the Caracazo, poverty at 70 percent, and the structural violence characteristic of the Venezuela that President Chávez inherited when elected by a majority of Venezuelans in 1998. With the assertions that "the equilibrium has been broken" and "the acceptance of order in Venezuelan society has crumbled, with perhaps grave consequences," Márquez contradicts her own research.

The figure of President Chávez represents an important obstacle to the classism and racism of the opposition. The fact that he expressly identifies himself as "Indian," "black," or "mixed-breed" transforms these supposed insults into positive qualities of which one may feel proud. When publicly called "rabble" along with his followers, he answers "Yes, we are the same 'rabble' that followed Bolivar." The names that the president's followers have given to the Bolivarian Circles include those of indigenous leaders that resisted the Spanish Conquest and Afro-Venezuelan rebels such as José Leonardo Chirino and el "Negro" Felipe. It is evident, therefore, that his political discourse and the symbolic and cultural practices of the Bolivarian Revolution have emphasized so-called national values, significantly reducing the occurrence of ethnic shame and endoracism in the popular sectors.

It is important to remember that Venezuela has one of the world's highest levels of concentration of land and a scandalously unequal income distribution. Over 70 percent of the population lives in poverty. The 2001 Lands Act, in contrast to the failed "agrarian reform" of the 1960s, established the bases for holistic and sustainable rural development,

> understanding this to be the fundamental means of human development and economic growth for the agrarian sector within a just distribution of wealth and strategic, democratic and participatory planning, eliminating the latifundio as a system opposed to justice, the common interest, and social peace in the countryside.

Both the frequency and the intensity of the racist attacks on the president and his followers increased exponentially, reflecting the classist attitudes of the opposition, when it became evident that the so-called vermin were to receive land. It was, in effect, the passage of the Lands Act that catapulted the top echelon of FEDECAMARAS into leadership of the political opposition. Within a short time, they had engineered a coup, and the president of FEDECAMARAS declared himself president of the republic.

As the analyst Antonio Guillermo García points out,

> The intention to establish the bases for rural development through the granting of property titles to the dispossessed classes and the elimination of the latifundio contained in the very new Lands Act corresponds to a development strategy similar to the "wealth-sharing" mechanism successfully implemented by southeast Asian countries, which, in contrast to the models of development of Latin America and Africa, allowed for the "miracle" of an economic growth and sustained development that positively affected the quality of life of its citizens. (García, 2001: 1)

Evidently the Venezuelan economic elite did not share these concerns for social justice and redistribution of wealth. It was precisely at the moment when the government of Chávez demonstrated its determination to carry out changes in the distribution of wealth with the passage of this law that the majority of big businessmen not only withdrew all support from the president but began to conspire against him.

The violent opposition to the Lands Act—the creation of the so-called extermination groups organized and financed by the largest landowners of the country—has left a trail of death and desolation among union leaders and campesino and indigenous movements considered "invaders" by this rural paramilitary. This is why I have insisted throughout this essay on the existence of a political economy of racism. As an ideology and a practice, racism is closely linked to economic and social inequalities. As Robert Archer points out,

> As a general rule, racism and discrimination serve to protect the political and economic interests of those who discriminate. . . . Racial discrimination impoverishes and socially dispossesses those who suffer it. It denies them access (or access in equality of conditions) to land, employment, education, health and family planning services, and housing. Poverty and social marginalization, in turn, are cited as "proof" to confirm and justify racial prejudices and discriminatory practices of the dominant group. (Archer, 2000: 18)

Venezuela is no exception in the context of Latin America and the Caribbean. From the colonial era to the present a pyramid of social division can be perceived in which the variables of race, class, and power have always been closely interrelated. In general terms, economic and political power remain predominantly in the hands of the "white" sector, while the indigenous and Afro-Venezuelan populations, as well as the majority of their descendants, for the most part still find themselves in the lowest socioeconomic strata. The social and racially inclusive policies of the Bolivarian Revolution have, as we have seen, caused a reaction by the upper and middle classes of today's Venezuela as racist and as classist as those provoked among the ruling oligarchy by the Royal Certificate of Special Dispensation in the eighteenth century. As María Martha Mijares Pacheco has argued, "Denying the existence of racism in the country obstructs attempts to confront it openly and hinders the introduction of proposals for possible solutions" (Mijares Pacheco, 2003: 67).

NOTES

1. Any reader wishing to confirm these claims may examine the major websites of the opposition. See, for example, veedores.org; queremoselegir.org; Acuerdonacional.com; asambleaciudadanos.com; ciudadaniaactiva.com; Coordinadorademocratica.org; Mujeresporlibertad.org; gusanodeluz.com; www.11deabril.com.

2. See BBCMundo.com at news.bbc.co.uk/hi/spanish/latin_america/newsid_3588000/3588237.stm.

REFERENCES

Agudelo, Alvaro
2002 "Racismo habemus." *El Mundo*, Wednesday, March 6, 2002. www.elmundo.com.ve/ediciones/2002/03/06/p1-4s7.htm.

Almeida, José
1992 "El mestizaje como problema ideológico," pp. 125–139 in: José Sánchez Parga (ed.), *Identidades y sociedad*. Quito: Centro de Estudios Latinoamericanos.

Archer, Robert
2000 *La persistencia y mutación del racismo*. Versoix, Suiza: Consejo Internacional para Estudios de Derechos Humanos, 2000. www.ichrp.org/ac/excerpts/3.pdf.

Arciniegas, Germán
1993 [1944] *Biografía del Caribe*. México, Editorial Porrúa.

Asamblea Popular Revolucionaria Luis Morillo Báez
2002 "El racismo subterráneo sale a flote," *Aporrea*, December 30, 2002. www.aporrea.org/dameletra.php?docid=169.

Ascencio, Michaelle
1984 *Del nombre de los esclavos y otros ensayos afroamericanos*. Caracas: Universidad Central de Venezuela.

Barreto Sánchez, Heiber
2002 "Lo que se le olvida a la oposición política: raza y clase en la V república."*América Latina en Movimiento*, December 16. alainet.org/active/show_text.php3?key=2945.

BBC
2004 "Venezuela: marcha, televisión e impuestos," Wednesday, March 31. BBCMundo.com. news.bbc.co.uk/hi/spanish/latin_america/newsid_3588000/3588237.stm.

Bonfil Batalla, Guillermo
1970 "Del indigenismo de la revolución a la antropología crítica," in Arturo Warman et al. (eds.), *De eso que llaman antropología mexicana*. México, Nuestro Tiempo.
1992 *Identidad y pluralismo cultural en América Latina*. Buenos Aires, R. Argentina, and San Juan, PR: Fondo Editorial del CEHASS and Editorial de la Universidad de Puerto Rico.
1994 *México profundo: una civilización negada*. México, Grijalbo,

Brito Figueroa, Federico
1985 *El problema tierra y esclavos en la historia de Venezuela*. Caracas: Universidad Central de Venezuela.

Carboni, Fabio
2002 "Venezuela, ver lo Esencial," Círculo Bolivariano 17 de Marzo (website) August 27, 2002. www.angelfire.com/nb/17m/movimiento/veresencial.html.

Cardenal, Ernesto
2004 "Venezuela: Una nueva Revolución en América Latina,"August 1, 2004. www.americas.org/item_15476.

Carrera Damas, Germán
1987 "Huída y Enfrentamiento," pp. 34–52 in *Africa en América Latina*. Paris: UNESCO.

Chaderton, Roy
2003 *Discurso ante la XXXIII Asamblea General de la OEA*, June 2003. www.aporrea.org/dameletra.php?docid=3448.

Circulo Bolivariano Enlace
espanol.geocities.com/enlacevenezuela/Elfracasoesunexito.htm.

Círculo Bolivariano Venezuela
groups.msn.com/CirculoBolivarianoVenezuela.

CONIVE (Consejo Nacional Indio de Venezuela)
2002 *Declaración del Consejo Nacional Indio de Venezuela, Abril 2002.* www.memoria.com
.mx/160/Declaracion.htm.

García, Antonio Guillermo
2001 "Ley de Tierras: compartiendo la riqueza y conciliando el desarrollo." *Venezuela Analítica*, Thursday, December 6, 2001. www.analitica.com/va/economia/opinion/5768269 .asp.

García, Illia
2002 "Representaciones de identidad y organizaciones sociales afrovenezolanas," pp. 133–144 in Daniel Mato (coord.), *Estudios y otras prácticas intelectuales latinoamericanas en cultura y poder.* Caracas: CLACSO-FACES-UCV. www.globalcult.org.ve/Illia%20Garc %EDa.pdf.

García, Jesús Chucho
2001 "Comunidades afroamericanas y transformaciones sociales," in Daniel Mato (comp.), *Estudios latinoamericanos sobre cultura y transformaciones sociales en tiempos de globalización.* Buenos Aires: CLACSO. June 2001. www.clacso.edu.ar/~libros/mato/garcía.pdf.

Gott, Richard
2002 "Entrevista por Maurício Hashizume." *La Insignia Agencia Carta Maior*, Brazil, July 2002. www.lainsignia.org/2002/julio/ibe_068.htm.

Hale, Charles E. (guest ed.)
1996 "Mestizaje," *Journal of Latin American Anthropology* 2, no. 1. Waltham, MA: Women's Studies Program, Brandeis University.

Hanchard, Michael
1998 *Orpheus and Power: The Movimento Negro of Rio de Janeiro and São Paulo, Brazil 1945–1988.* Princeton, NJ: Princeton University Press.

Herrera Salas, Jesús María
2003 *El negro Miguel y la primera revolución venezolana.* Caracas: Vadell Hermanos Editores.

Humboldt, Alexander von
1941 [1805] *Viajes a las regiones equinocciales del nuevo continente (1799–1804).* 5 vols. Translated by Lisandro Alvarado. Caracas: Biblioteca Venezolana de Cultura.

Ibarra, Hernán
1992 "El laberinto del mestizaje," pp. 95–123 in José Sánchez Parga (comp.), *Identidades y sociedad.* Quito: Centro de Estudios Latinoamericanos.

Ishibashi, Jun
2001 "La 'nueva canción' en Venezuela: experimento político-cultural para el pueblo durante los años 1970 y su 'conversión' posterior." *Paper presented at the 23rd Congress of Latin American Studies Association*, Washington, DC, September 6–8, 2001.
2003 "Hacia una apertura del debate sobre el racismo en Venezuela: exclusión e inclusión estereotipada de personas 'negras en los medios de comunicación," in Daniel Mato (coord.), *Políticas de identidades y diferencias sociales en tiempos de globalización.* Caracas: FACES-Universidad Central de Venezuela. www.globalcult.org.ve/Rocky/Libro1/Rocky1.htm.

Lancaster, R.
1992 *Life Is Hard: Machismo, Power and the Danger of Intimacy in Nicaragua.* Berkeley: University of California Press.

Lara, William
2002 "El Racismo de los Golpistas." *El Mundo*, Caracas, September 16, 2002. www .elmundo.com.ve/ediciones/2002/09/16/p1-4s2.htm.

Linares, Mariadela
2002 "El lumpen de siempre." *Ultimas Noticias*, October 19, 2003.

López, José Eliseo
1988 "Criollos," in *Diccionario de Historia de Venezuela*. Caracas: Fundación Polar.
López de Haro, Alejandro
2002 "La Entropía en Venezuela." *Venezuela Analítica*, November 11, 2002. www.analitica .com/va/politica/opinion/3952071.asp.
López Sanz, Rafael
1993 *Parentesco, etnia y clase social en la sociedad venezolana*. Caracas: Universidad Central de Venezuela, Consejo de Desarrollo Científico y Humanístico.
Márquez, Humberto
2004 "Venezuela: racismo en reino del café con leche." Interpress Service News Agency (IPS). www.choike.org/nuevo/informes/1528.html.
Márquez, Patricia
2004 "Vacas flacas y odios gordos: la polarización en Venezuela," pp. 31–46 in Patricia Márquez and Ramón Piñango (eds.), *Realidades y nuevos caminos en esta Venezuela*. Caracas: Ediciones del Instituto de Estudios Superiores de Administración.
Martínez, Frédéric
1997 "Apogeo y decadencia del ideal de la inmigración europea en Colombia, siglo XIX." *Boletín Cultural y Bibliográfico* 34, no. 44. Bogotá: Banco de la República.
Martínez-Echazabal, Lourdes
1998 "Mestizaje and the Discourse of the National/Cultural." *Latin American Perspectives* 25, no. 3 (May).
Mijares Pacheco, María Martha
2003 "Reflexiones para enfrentar el racismo en Venezuela," in Daniel Mato (coord.), *Políticas de identidades y diferencias sociales en tiempos de globalización*. Caracas: FACES-Universidad Central de Venezuela.
Montañez, Ligia
1993 *El racismo oculto en una sociedad no racista*. Caracas: Fondo Editorial Tropykos.
Muratorio, Blanca
1981 *Etnicidad, evangelización y protesta en el Ecuador: Una perspectiva antropológica*. Quito: CIESE.
Murieta, Joaquín
2003 *Lina ron habla*. Caracas: Fuentes.
Nascimento, Abdias do
1978 *O genocídio do negro brasileiro: processo de um racismo mascarado*. Río de Janeiro: Paz e Terra.
Neumann, Hans
1997 "El racismo." *El Universal*, Caracas, Wednesday, February 5, 1997.
Pérez Sarduy, Pedro and Jean Stubbs
1993 *Afrocuba: An Anthology of Cuban Writing on Race, Politics and Culture*. New York: Ocean Press.
2000 *Afro-Cuban Voices: On Race and Identity in Contemporary Cuba*. University Press of Florida.
Ramonet, Ignacio
2002 "Ecos de la resistencia: la conspiración contra Chávez." *El País*, April 17, 2002. www.resistencia.org/ecos/venezuela_conspiration_contra_chavez.htm.
Sánchez, Domingo
2002 "A New Reality for Venezuela's Indigenous Peoples." Venezuela National Foundation for Indigenous Studies. www.centrelink.org/SanchezEnglish.html.
Sandoval, Alonso de
1987 [1627] *Un tratado sobre la esclavitud*. Madrid: Alianza Editorial.

Stutzman, Ronald
    1981 "El Mestizaje: An All Inclusive Ideology of Exclusion," pp. 45–94 in Norman Whitten (ed.), *Cultural Transformations and Ethnicity in Modern Ecuador*. Urbana: University of Illinois Press.
Suárez, Gitanjali
    2000 *Diagnóstico sobre las migraciones caribeñas hacia Venezuela*. Buenos Aires: Organización Internacional para las Migraciones.
Uslar Pietri, Arturo
    1937 "Venezuela necesita inmigración." *Boletín de la Cámara de Comercio de Caracas*, Caracas, July 1937.
Uzcátegui, César
    1995 "Aproximación al estudio de la política indigenista venezolana del siglo XIX." *Revista Montalbán*, Universidad Católica Andrés Bello, Caracas, No. 28, pp. 195–207.
Vallenilla Lanz, Laureano
    1984 [1930] *Disgregación e integración publicación*. Caracas: Centro de Investigaciones Históricas, Universidad Santa María.
Wright, Winthrop R.
    1990 *Café con Leche: Race, Class and National Image in Venezuela*. Austin, University of Texas Press.

Part IV

SOCIAL MOVEMENTS

Widespread mobilization by government partisans as well as those of the opposition is a salient feature of the Chávez phenomenon. Chapter 7 demonstrates that the rank-and-file members of the Chavista movement come from a wide variety of backgrounds but are united in their commitment to transformation, and it thus counteracts stereotypes regarding the relationship between Chávez and his followers as one of caudillo and "masses." Chapter 8 examines the social biases and occasional undemocratic behavior of the social movements aligned with the opposition in an attempt to refute the traditional view that indiscriminately glorifies all aspects of civil society.

CHAPTERS 7 AND 8: SOCIAL MOVEMENTS

Cristóbal Valencia's chapter explores the composition of the Círculos Bolivarianos (Bolivarian Circles) that support the Chávez presidency and the broader process of social change underway in Venezuela. To assess the condition in which the state is an ally of progressive social movement, Valencia provides an alternative reading of the concept of hegemony. He proposes that the Bolivarian Revolution can be thought of as a gradual process of "changing hegemony through the overthrow of the traditional dominant bloc by the Chávez administration and Chavista civil mobilization." Furthermore, he challenges the depiction of the members of the Círculos as uniformly poor, uninformed, and illiterate masses easily manipulated by a charismatic president who is tantamount to a caudillo. Círculo members represent people from all walks of life: skilled technicians, social workers, university students, and community organizers. Equally important, he disputes the widespread view of Círculo members as armed shock troops at the beck and call of the government. He also attempts to refute the notion that the Círculos are state-financed organizations that would disappear without government support. Employing a case-study approach, he reveals that many members of the Círculos Bolivarianos have a long history of political activism and maintain a degree of autonomy from the Chávez party and government.

María Pilar García-Guadilla's chapter examines the upsurge in social mobilization since the election of Hugo Chávez, focusing on opposition organizations. Her work counters traditional glorification of Venezuelan democracy by demonstrating that social movements have been class-biased. In doing so, she breaks from the traditional conception of social movements as autonomous entities that exist above class differences. Within the context of a growing polarization she examines the redefinition of values and interests among opposition social organizations and their defense of class interests. She points to the dilemma of the private versus collective interests of social organizations identified with the Venezuelan opposition and shows how the political crisis and the inclusion of certain rights in the Bolivarian Constitution have affected the practices of opposition organizations. Her realistic view on the class commitments of civil society challenges the exceptionalism thesis with its glorification of "civic culture and society, which it considered the pillars of [Venezuelan] democracy."

Chapter Seven

Venezuela's Bolivarian Revolution: Who Are the Chavistas?

Cristóbal Valencia Ramírez

The increasingly decisive electoral victories of the Chávez presidency call into question easy characterizations of his supporters as "the poor" or the "popular masses" and attendant notions of spontaneous, uninformed political actors. Since 1998, voters have elected Hugo Chávez to the presidency three times, and on August 15, 2004, voters returned to the polls to decide whether to remove him from office. Fifty-nine percent of voters affirmed the president's mandate and defeated the recall initiative. Chávez is also poised to win a new term in office in the December 2006 presidential elections. Several years earlier, on April 14, 2002, in a remarkable turn of events, Chávez was returned to power through civil society mobilization just forty-eight hours after being overthrown by a coup. In 1998, during his initial presidential bid, he won 56.2 percent of the total vote; in 2000 he won 59.76 percent of the total vote, and in 2004 he won 59 percent again, this time with 70 percent of voters participating (Consejo Nacional Electoral, 2004; Carter Center, 2004). Support for Chávez has come through the activism and mobilization of members of civil society who continue to turn out in increasing numbers to support the Bolivarian Revolution.

Following the 1998 election many of the organizations that made up the electoral coalition that elected Chávez (the Polo Patriótico) enjoyed the support of the state. These organizations were often examined by researchers and the media and increasingly identified as Chavistas and their projects as Chavismo. In addition, film documentaries and news reports of the April 2002 mobilization to restore Chávez to power focused on his supporters' spontaneity, depicting them as members of the popular masses organized solely around Chávez himself. This has had the effect of homogenizing supporters and personalizing the Bolivarian Revolution. However, many of these groups and their actions were not directly organized by the Venezuelan state or Hugo Chávez. Instead, many are to varying degrees autonomous from each other and the state, and some of them predate Chávez's appearance on the political scene.

This study examines civil support for Chávez through an analysis of the origins, aims, actions, and trajectory of a variety of Chavista organizations and the values and experiences of individual Chavistas. It also raises questions about our understanding of hegemony and resistance or counterhegemony. I argue that the Chavistas have been mischaracterized by the media, the opposition, and some academic analysts as the poor and popular masses. Rather, they are a mostly peaceful and autonomous counterhegemonic social movement that is allied with the state. Furthermore, I maintain that Chavistas are organized on various social and economic levels and their organizations are not solely dedicated to ensuring that Chávez remains in office but also to carrying out important social work. Finally, I show that many Chavistas have a long history of organizing, considerable political sophistication, a definite ideological overview, and goals that go beyond protecting the Chávez presidency.

THE SHAPE OF HEGEMONY IN VENEZUELA

Hegemony most often favors the state, elites, the high-ranking military, big business, and the church. In the Venezuelan context, hegemony and resistance (counterhegemony) take on new meanings. Their conceptual meanings do not change; hegemony is still the process by which one social group gains supremacy or domination over others, sometimes by armed force (Gramsci, 1971). However, in the Venezuelan case the state is no longer the sector that hegemony favors, and those favored by hegemony—the dominant bloc—do not control the formal apparatus of the state. This is a major departure from Gramscian notions of hegemony in which the state is the target of mobilization and struggle. Locating the state outside of the dominant bloc also has profound implications—still to be determined—about the shape and course of the counterhegemonic movement.

The traditional political parties, some high-ranking military officers, the hierarchy of the Catholic Church, the longstanding Confederación de Trabajadores de Venezuela (Confederation of Venezuelan Workers—CTV), the national and international private media, organized big business (the Federación Venezolana de Cámaras y Asociaciones de Comercio y Producción—FEDECAMARAS), and the former executives and upper management of the state-owned oil company (Petróleos de Venezuela—PDVSA) are the dominant bloc against which the Chavistas and the Venezuelan state are allied in struggle. The opposition bloc also has international ties and support including

U.S. policymakers. It has traditionally been the dominant force in negotiating hegemony but now in some instances finds itself, for the first time, outside the governmental power structure (the state). Nevertheless, its various factions continue to wield immense power, employing their material resources against the Chávez government and the Bolivarian Revolution.

In practice the Bolivarian Revolution can be thought of as a process of changing hegemony through the overthrow of the traditional dominant bloc minus the state, by the Chávez administration and Chavista civil mobilization. These efforts include street demonstrations, the development of economic cooperatives and small business associations, the provision of health care and education, and organization at the smallest of scales to expand participatory democracy through the extension of public powers to civil society. These efforts are designed to prioritize the poor, nonwhite ethnic groups, women, and the middle classes—all of them sectors that have traditionally been marginalized by Venezuelan politics. They also seek to change international power relationships through participation with international solidarity groups and the creation of an anti-imperialist bloc of Latin American countries. These actions and efforts form part of the counterhegemonic struggle embodied by the participants and supporters of the Bolivarian Revolution (see Valencia Ramírez, 2006, for a further analysis of the Bolivarian Revolution).

THE MISCHARACTERIZATION OF THE CHAVISTAS

Very little has been written about the identity, ideological formation, or mobilization of the Chavistas. When Chavistas have been analyzed they have typically been depicted by the opposition, media, and some academics as young, poor, politically unsophisticated, antidemocratic masses that prefer political violence to democratic and constitutional processes. Damarys Canache (2002: 148) exemplifies this analysis: "Chávez did build his base of mass support by appealing to Venezuela's most politically disaffected citizens: the young, the poor, and the uneducated." She argues that Chávez's presidential victory in 1998 was due to voters' indifference toward democracy. Furthermore, she asserts that Chávez supporters' indifference toward democracy amounts to a preference for or acceptance of political violence. Canache concludes that Chávez's election poses a threat to the very survival of democracy in Venezuela, aiming a pointed jab at the president himself: "an elected authoritarian is, after all, still an authoritarian" (2002: 150).

Additionally, Chavistas have been portrayed as state-controlled, statefunded, and state-armed thugs. Philip Oxhorn (2003: 13) has described the Chavista Círculos Bolivarianos as "sometimes armed community organizations loyal directly to the president," and Mark Ungar (2003: 32) has called them "armed pro-Chávez neighborhood groups." The international press has painted a similar picture of the Chavistas as poor, blind messianic supporters of a populist leader. In the hours after the 2002 coup Juan Tamayo, foreign correspondent for the *Miami Herald* (April 14, 2002), wrote:

> Thousands of pro-Chávez demonstrators lingered around the palace late Saturday. Army troops shouting pro-Chávez slogans and waving Venezuelan flags were seen cheering the protesters from the roof of the White Palace. . . . There were unconfirmed reports that at least nine people were killed in demonstrations throughout the day. The uncertainty over Chávez's resignation and the outrage over Carmona's draconian steps helped fuel the anger of Chávez backers who staged violent protests around the country Saturday.

Alex Bello of the *London Guardian* (April 15, 2002) described Chávez's return after the coup as follows:

> For a deeply religious man . . . it was deliciously apt that [Venezuela's] President Hugo Chávez was deposed on a Friday only to return in a miraculous political resurrection on Sunday. . . . But he returns to lead a deeply divided country. His popularity has dwindled from 80 percent to 30 percent, and he has managed to alienate almost every sector of Venezuelan society. His only support remains with the poor, although they have seen little improvement in their lives.

Bello suggests that the poor continue to support Chávez in the absence of any clear benefit or reason other than they are poor. Unfortunately, since the coup much of the media coverage has conveyed the same idea.

Academics have used populist analysis and theories of democratic breakdown to explain current Venezuelan political culture. These analyses may help us to understand the climate that led to Chávez's actions against the government in 1992, his landslide presidential victory in the 1998 election, and the events of 2002, but they are less useful in contributing to an understanding of the Chavistas. Ernesto Laclau (2004) explains that populist analysis should concentrate on a style of leadership rather than on the character of the leader's support base. In the case of Venezuela, however, populist analyses often represent the Chavistas as informal or community-based and therefore difficult to organize (e.g., Roberts, 2003; and Weyland, 2003). The poorest of them have been described as vengeful, volatile, and attracted to Chávez for reasons ranging from his prioritization of easing social inequalities to his penchant for playing baseball.

Kirk Hawkins (2003: 1137–1140) writes that populist leadership uses a "people versus the elite" discourse and that its inevitable consequence has been the adoption of an "anything goes" attitude by the Chavistas, legitimating the employment of violence against the opposition. To this date, however, little evidence exists of Chavista-perpetrated violence against the opposition.

In another instance, David Hansen and Hawkins (2006) argue that the populist attributes of the Chavistas, particularly the Bolívarian Circles, undermine the movement's democratic potential. They argue that clientelistic ties between the Chavistas and the state impair their ability to become institutionalized and fully democratic, making them dependent on Chávez's remaining in power. The authors acknowledge the "mixture of formality and informality" in the Círculos' organizational structure; dividing them into political (direct support of Chávez) and "not normally or necessarily political" participation in the delivery of social services and other activities (2006: 108–109). In addition, they use a survey to determine that Círculo members had strong clientelistic ties to the government and to Chávez.

Populist analyses point to the peculiarities of the Chavistas' relationship to the state, but their top-down approach is limited. Most important, these analysts fail to recognize the Chavistas' political expertise, their political backgrounds, organizational design, strategic use of the state as an ally in counterhegemony, influence on the state's social and political agenda, and the processes of power negotiation among Chavista organizations. Overall, populist analyses tie the Bolívarian Revolution and the Chavistas to the Venezuelan state's democratic and economic performance and to Chávez's enduring charisma (see Valencia Ramírez, 2006, for a more complete critique of populist analysis).

David Myers (2003) calls the Chávez government an incomplete democracy operating in a transitional paradigm following the demise of the traditional parties Accíon Democrática (Democratic Action—AD) and the Comité de Organización Política Electoral Independiente (Committee of Independent Electoral Political Organization—COPEI). He describes it as concentrating power in the executive office and allowing for little dissent, implying that it is more like a dictatorship than a democracy. This analysis is often extended to Chavistas as individuals and organizations, arguing that they are supporters of an undemocratic regime and therefore not constructive political actors. In short, many in the media and some in the academy argue that the Chavistas represent a threat to democracy.

Until the December 2005 elections that were boycotted by the opposition, Chávez's Movimiento Quinta República (Fifth Republic Movement—MVR) did not have a majority in the National Assembly and therefore contested policymaking was possible. The multiparty Consejo Nacional Electoral (National Electoral Council—CNE) established the guidelines for the August recall, and the process was observed and deemed fair by the Organization of American States and the Carter Center. Gregory Wilpert (2003: 102) argues that the image of a totalitarian Venezuela under Chávez is the creation of the round-the-clock attacks by the private mass media, and instead he describes the political climate in Venezuela as follows: "Citizens enjoy nearly total freedom of assembly: demonstrations blocking important installations or freeways are treated far more leniently than under most U.S. city governments. Congress meets freely, the opposition speaks openly, parties and movements organize actively." Margarita López Maya (2003) points out that the new constitution contains more checks and balances than the pre-Chávez constitution. These two viewpoints suggest that the Chávez government is in fact more democratic than previous ones.

While some academic analyses have obscured the complexity of the Chavistas, the opposition's and media's mischaracterization of them may have contributed to their persecution. The Ezequiel Zamora National Farmers' Coordinator estimates that fifty Chavista leaders involved in the land-reform process were assassinated in 2002–2003 (Wilpert, 2003). The high-profile Chávez-initiated literacy and health campaigns Plan Robinson and Barrio Adentro have also been the targets of attacks (*Últimas Noticias*, June 29, 2003, and July 2 and 5, 2003).

CHAVISTA ORGANIZATIONS

Chavista organizations exist at various levels from the neighborhood to the international. They may be spontaneous or well organized, ephemeral or long-lasting, poor or rich. My research identified a variety of mostly non-state-financed Chavista organizations with a long history of political participation and organizational structure. These organizations were nonviolent and not limited to safeguarding the Chávez presidency. They were organized on various levels with diverse aims. They were involved in such activities as consciousness raising and political education, increasing civil political participation and economic production, directing groups and individuals to resources available from the state, and planning and implementing social policy programs. These efforts push the boundaries of conventional politics. While social in nature, they also have a political function—furthering the Bolivarian Revolution.

Enrique González, a Spanish human rights investigator working in Venezuela since 1995, has constructed a taxonomy of Chavista organizations. In addition to the highly publicized and stereotyped popular masses already mentioned, he has identified organizations and sectors of the "classic left" (the Communist Party, the progressive church, student organizations) and the "alternative left" (women's organizations, gay/lesbian organizations) that have aligned themselves with the struggle. These groups participate directly in government ministries and community-based service-oriented Chavista organizations, support Chavista initiatives by organizing and participating in civil mobilizations, and provide electoral support for Chávez. This left sector includes people from the popular classes as well as the middle classes and the university-educated. Whereas the left struggles for radical change, the middle-class sectors hope to end the traditional clientelistic relationships and according to González are fundamentally interested in quotas of power. González considers the organized middle class the least recognized source of support for Chávez. Up until the April 2002 coup its support was concealed by the private media, which portrayed the middle class as a homogeneous anti-Chávez sector. There is also a heterogeneous sector in the military that has ties to the popular and middle classes that support the revolution. Another sector that is more difficult to account for is the mobilized groups that may or may not be armed but have engaged in street battles with the opposition and with the police (interviews, Caracas, June 23, 2003). This list is exemplary of the diversity of the support that exists for the movement. Some of these organizations are described below.

Círculos Bolivarianos

The Círculos Bolivarianos (Bolivarian Circles) provide an example of the basic unit of Chavista organizations. They are patterned after the clandestine units organized inside the armed forces and between the armed forces and the civilian left during the late 1970s (see Garrido, 2000: 7). They are designed to disseminate Bolivarian ideology and promote the exchange of accurate information and discussion. The main differences are that they are public, may be entirely civilian, and promote additional aims. The Círculos that I studied did not engage in violence and received no funding from the state. In some instances they were structured along class lines that coincided with neighborhood boundaries. Less commonly, they were organized across class lines in areas such as the workplace. López Maya (2003: 80) explains that in 1992 they served as the primary organizational base of the clandestine military left organization the Movimiento Bolivariano Revolucionario (Bolivarian Revolutionary Movement—MBR–200) in its efforts to become a national political organization:

> For this purpose, they traveled throughout the country and began establishing organizational structures and internal procedures to differentiate themselves from the establishment parties and to avoid sliding toward rigidity or authoritarianism. They did have as a peculiarity . . . the requirement that those who wished to join the groups had to make a "Bolivarian" commitment, specifically an oath to be "hard working, honest, and humble, and exercise solidarity."

Following the 2002 coup, the structure and aims of the Círculos changed. They opened up to even greater civil participation with new, more active responsibilities defending the revolution and the revolutionary ideology. Officially they consist of seven to eleven persons and are encouraged to register with the national directorate, and members are required to share a belief in the teachings of Simón Bolívar and the 1999 Constitution. However, I found that they have many informal as well as formal participants, do not strictly limit their numbers, and are not always registered. The Círculos may be thought of as cells that participate in larger organizations. For instance, members of neighborhood Círculos may participate in a Chavista workplace, university, or labor organization. A Círculo may also be a stand-alone organization, and not every Chavista organization is made up of Círculo members (interviews, Caracas, Rodrigo Cháves, Douglas Borges, and "Papín," June 24, 2003).

The text of a Bolivarian educational and organizational pamphlet entitled *Temas de organización y política para revolucionarios* states that the mandate of the Círculos is to organize civil society, raise political consciousness to safeguard and widen the process of change, encourage the participation of all communities in government, and mobilize the community to confront the opposition and to facilitate the meeting of social needs (García Ponce, 2001). Círculos are asked not to provide social services but to aid in the planning and implementation of such services in their communities. They act as a kind of planning, information, and referral center for state programs serving both to empower and to mobilize civil society. This includes not only involvement in community planning and decision-making but also assistance to community members in applying for and receiving services. Hansen and Hawkins (2006: 109) consider these activities "not normally or necessarily political," although I would argue that separating the "political" and "nonpolitical" in this context is often artificial.

While I was interviewing regional and national Círculos coordinators, several neighborhood-level Círculo representatives came into the national coordination offices at the Palacio Blanco to inquire about programs, acquire medicines needed by individual members, gather information on the release of state funds, learn about new state programs, and present the demands of the local organizations and communities. The Zulia state coordinator, Pedro Castillo, told me that the Círculos in his region had decided to concentrate on increasing health services at the local level and securing pension payments for their elderly members (interview, Caracas, June 24, 2003).

When asked why the Círculos had increased in popularity after the coup, the coordinators responded that no local or national organization had existed prior to the coup that could direct people to the myriad of services available through the government for self and community development and the Círculos had filled that gap. The Círculos had the capacity to encourage direct civil participation by the poorest sectors in the planning and delivery of services and the recognition of the state and were a direct link to the national government and Chávez himself (interview, Caracas, Rodrigo Cháves, June 24, 2003). Before the Círculos, many Venezuelans were not being served by the existing network of social services, which had little to do with the planning and supervision of services. From the perspective of the government the Círculos provide it a ready support base. For Chavistas, the Círculos' ability to arrange for the provision of appropriate social services as determined by community members is a political action that serves the goal of increasing participatory democracy.

I found no evidence that the Círculos were armed or had developed armed strategies. All the participants I interviewed denied receiving state funding. Coordinators were unpaid and members met in existing community gathering spaces. Rodrigo Cháves pointed to the small office with a computer, a telephone, and three cubicles in the basement of the Palacio Blanco as the only direct material support the government provided. Additionally, the coordinators and members stressed that participation in the Círculos and supporting Chávez were contingent on the government's continued expansion of resources for previously excluded sectors, a major component of the Bolivarian Movement (interviews, Caracas, Rodrigo Cháves, Douglas Borges, Pedro Castillo, and "Papín," June 24, 2003).

Trabajo y Tierra

Just outside of the Bellas Artes metro station in downtown Caracas is a garden cooperative called Trabajo y Tierra (Work and Land). The large terraced garden produces food for participants and local sale; organizers hope to open a restaurant in which they would use its produce. The cooperative is a Chavista association and is organized around local development issues and funded through neighborhood development associations. It has marched in support of Chávez's reforms. One of the project's coordinators, Nora Lee Verenzuela, said that the idea for the project had come from a local neighborhood assembly that, with the help of a Círculo, had taken it to the parish assembly of San Agustín, which had moved it through the municipal assembly. The project had received technical assistance from the military and two months of monetary assistance from the municipal assembly. Verenzuela stated that the goals of the neighborhood assembly in which the project originated were to generate a self-sustainable food supply, reclaim unused or misused areas in the parish, generate employment, and use the profits to fund development such as a restaurant (interview, Caracas, July 8, 2003).

Verenzuela commented that participants in the project had mobilized in support of Chávez on several occasions, especially when the opposition tactics became particularly ugly. They had marched both as a cooperative and as members of various other organizations to which individuals belonged. Because Trabajo y Tierra is a highly visible Chavista organization, it has been the target of opposition sabotage. Verenzuela recounted an incident in which two goats were put into the garden at night. When one of the coordinators arrived the next morning and found them, they had done little damage to the garden. She surmised that goats eat only during the daylight hours and the saboteurs did not know this. The workers at the cooperative killed and cooked the goats (interview, Caracas, July 8, 2003).

Fuerza Bolivariana de Trabajadores

The Fuerza Bolivariana de Trabajadores (Bolivarian Workers' Force—FBT) is a national organization that coordinates the actions and demands of unions around the country and is part of the Unión Nacional de Trabajadores (National Workers' Union—UNT). It was founded in September 2000, three years before the UNT, and is a Chavista organization. Its goals are consistent with the Bolivarian Revolution; it seeks to decentralize power and end representative democracy for the few by increasing the participation of workers in the political process. It receives no funding from the state, and its members represent workers from various economic classes, industries, and political affiliations.

One of the national coordinators of the FBT, Eduardo Piñate (interview, Caracas, June 29, 2003), estimated that the organization represents approximately 455 unions nationwide. Union coordination exists at the local, regional, and national levels. The national coordinators come from the MVR and other pro-Chavista parties as well as independent political associations; support for the Bolivarian Revolution is a requirement for member unions. Piñate stated that the primary reason for forming the FBT was to break with the practices of the national labor confederation, the CTV, which is closely linked with AD and has supported its neoliberal privatization measures. The CTV has been the dominant national representative of labor in Venezuela since 1936 (Ellner, 2003). The international organization Hands Off Venezuela (2004) has described the CTV as "extremely undemocratic" and claimed that its leadership "openly collaborated with the employers to prevent the struggle of the workers." The FBT provides services to workers in the informal sector (the underemployed) and the unemployed and constitutes an institutional structure for political education and consciousness raising among participants. Individual union delegates, rank-and-file workers, and the unemployed meet weekly to discuss the revolutionary process and the challenges it presents to workers. The FBT's goal is to educate members about the process and the politics of the Bolivarian Revolution while simultaneously strategizing to increase social benefits for all workers and potential workers (interview, Caracas, Eduardo Piñate, June 29, 2003).

Piñate described how on many occasions the FBT had mobilized in support of particular issues such as protesting the fraud that occurred during the 2001 national elections for the leadership of the CTV and member unions. The FBT had run candidates in these first-ever labor representation elections, and according to Piñate the FBT candidates had received 40 percent of the votes but had gone underrepresented on the CTV national committee. Indeed, Hands Off Venezuela (2004) reported that the elections "were marked by widespread fraud in which thousands of votes (the records for 9,000 polling stations) went 'missing' during their transport or in 'mysterious accidents.'" Additionally, the CNE never verified the election results. In the course of the protest the FBT had clashed with the opposition-controlled metropolitan police. During the so-called petroleum strike (more a management-led lockout than a strike) in the days leading up to the coup of 2002 the FBT had mobilized to warn workers about the opposition's intention to use the work stoppage to create shortages and civil unrest. It had also mobilized in support of restoring Chávez to power during the coup. During the national strike called by the CTV in late 2002, the FBT again promoted worker mobilizations and called on its members not to support the action. After the petroleum industry lockout, the failed coup, and the failed national strike, the FBT leaders participated in meetings with the Carter Center in which they called for trade union electoral reforms and an end to the CTV's monopoly on labor.

Assembly of Employees of the Instituto Venezolano de Investigaciones Científicas

At the Instituto Venezolano de Investigaciones Cientificas (Venezuelan Institute of Scientific Investigations—IVIC), researchers and blue-collar workers formed a Chavista group called the "Assembly of IVIC Employees." The group evolved quickly from an informal to an active mobilized organization supporting the ideals of the Bolivarian Revolution. It receives no support from the institute or the state, and membership is open to all employees. The Assembly had its origin in the events leading up to the failed April 2002 coup. Alberto Albornoz, a member of the Assembly, described the workplace organization in its initial phase as a space for researchers and other workers to discuss whether to participate in the opposition-led general strike and how to protect those forced to strike, to exchange information, and to analyze misleading information provided by the media. Following the coup, the group actively supported Chávez. Albornoz remembers the turning point as being the announced visit to the plant by the Miranda state governor Enrique Mendoza, who was himself a coup leader. In response the Assembly mobilized to protest his visit, forcing the plant and the governor to cancel the event (interview, Caracas, June 26, 2003). The Assembly now included more than one hundred employees, and in the following year it expanded further. Today its focus is on raising consciousness and providing support for the Bolivarian Revolution

within the IVIC. The organization is part of the Red Bolivariana de Trabajadores (Network of Bolivarian Workers). Individuals participate formally
and informally for extended or limited periods. Some members of the group
also participate in off-site Círculos that are unrelated to the Assembly, and
others are involved in organizing new Círculos.

El Banco de Desarrollo de la Mujer

The Banco de Desarrollo de la Mujer (Women's Development Bank—BDM)
was founded in September 2001 by order of President Chávez and is part of
the Bolivarian Network of Social Organizations. Besides providing loans, it
also educates its members about the ideals of the Bolivarian Revolution and
attemps to increase economic productivity. The BDM is the only Chavista organization I studied that received direct funding from the state; however, it
provided services to Venezuelans of diverse political affiliations including
those of the opposition. It was designed in part to provide loans to low-
income individuals and previously ineligible or excluded small organizations.
Many of its clients are referred to the bank by the Círculos. It easily competes
with the similar microfinance institutions established by NGOs; it does not
require any sort of collateral for loans and charges lower interest than these
institutions, making funds available for applicants previously denied loans. It
does, however, require that the recipient participate with its *promotoras* or organizers.

The work of these promotoras is very important in understanding the dual
role of the bank. Its primary aim is to provide economic resources; a secondary aim is to increase economic and political participation of recipients
through education programs. The bank's resources are accessed in person or
through formal written proposals. In both cases recipients request instruction in particular topics, among the options being reproductive health, nu-
trition, cooperative and small business management, participatory democracy, and interpreting the 1999 Venezuelan Constitution. Lidice Navas, the
BDM's public relations representative, summed up the promotoras' work as
helping to create a collective Bolivarian consciousness among the loan recipients (interview, Caracas, July 3, 2003). Many of the recipients, identifying themselves as Bolivarian cooperatives or small business associations,
have coordinated group actions in support of the president. Navas commented that the promotoras' localized instruction and regular personal communication with the cooperatives and associations were probably instrumental in these mobilizations, but there was no direct evidence that they had
organized specific political actions. Lidice agreed that the BDM was a
Chavista organization but stressed that she was unaware of which employees or customers participated in Círculos and which did not. She stressed

that the BDM was committed to providing loans and educating recipients about their political rights regardless of their political affiliation. Loans were based on applicants' proposals and their inability to secure funding elsewhere rather than on their willingness to participate in political mobilization. With only a single branch in Caracas, the bank has approximately twenty-seven thousand clients.

INDIVIDUAL CHAVISTA EXPERIENCES AND VALUES

The Venezuelan opposition's stereotype of the individual Chavista is contained in the "Plan comunitario defensa activa" (Community Plan for Defensive Action), which recommends that members not be "too trusting of domestic help, especially those that are day hires. Remember that many of them have been manipulated and some are beginning to see us as the enemy" (2003: 17) (see chapter by García-Guadilla in this volume). The plan was written in response to reports in the Venezuelan media that the Círculos Bolivarianos planned to attack middle-class neighborhoods and homes. It reinforces the stereotype of the Chavista as a poor, misled, and violent individual. On an individual level, however, many Chavistas are seasoned supporters of a larger revolutionary process that values the expansion of direct participatory democracy, the extension of public powers to civil society, and the development of social policies that prioritize the poor with the goal of changing traditional power relationships in Venezuela and internationally—values that have been incorporated into the 1999 Constitution. In short, Chavistas have personal values consistent with a counterhegemonic movement and exhibit a commitment to a political doctrine and a political sophistication that have developed over time out of their own experiences, including participation in multiple civic and political organizations. Furthermore, Chavistas are of diverse classes, and their commitment to the revolutionary process began before the election of Hugo Chávez and extends well beyond his term of office.

EXPERIENCED ACTIVISTS

Many Chavistas have participated in multiple organizations. Lidice Navas had had previous organizing experience with Christian base communities in El Salvador and considered this experience useful in her work at the bank. She was also a participant in a Pan-Latino civil movement called ANFITRIONA that supported the creation of an economic union between Latin America and the Caribbean in response to U.S. imperialism in the region (interview, Caracas, July 3, 2003). Participation in both of these organizations was compatible with the Bolivarian Revolution's ideals of expansion of democracy, extension of public powers to civil society, and the creation of an anti-imperialist union of Latin American countries. Eduardo Daza, the international relations representative for the MVR, had spent many years as a member of other political parties looking for an opportunity to promote the agenda of the Venezuelan left and indicated that many of his colleagues in the MVR had done something similar (interview, Caracas, July 7, 2003). The FBT coordinator Eduardo Piñate, had been involved in union coordination for over twenty-five years, much of it struggling against the CTV's failure to represent the interests of workers (interview, Caracas, June 29, 2003). Piñate and Daza in the past had participated in the Communist Party, the Socialist League, COPEI, and AD. Alberto Albornoz of the Assembly of IVIC Employees was a member of the Red Bolivariana de Trabajadores, a national workers' organization that supports the revolution, and also belonged to several Círculos and was the only person other than Daza to make reference to his membership in the MVR (interview, Caracas, June 26, 2003). This fact is important to dispel the notion that all Chavistas are devout militants of the supposedly violent and immature MVR.

Other respondents felt no need to highlight their affiliation with the MVR and responded ambiguously to questions about their participation in it; it was difficult to determine whether they were members or occasional participants. Membership in the MVR did not seem to be the primary reason for supporting Chávez, nor did the Chavistas seem to be blind followers of the party or the president's orders. Many of the interviewees indicated that they were supporters of *el proceso* (the revolutionary process) first and that Chávez was leading only by the will of the people. Many were uninterested in, uncertain about, or distrustful of the MVR's role. Nora Lee Verenzuela of Trabajo y Tierra described a long history of involvement with local neighborhood organizations including the Asamblea de Vecinos de San Agustín, the Junta Parroquial de San Agustín, the Coordinadora Simón Bolívar of the 23 de Enero neighborhood, and the local Círculo Bolivariano. She had become involved in the Bolivarian Movement and her local Círculo in part because the Minister of Education under Chávez, Aristóbulo Istúriz, was someone from her parish with whom she had previously worked. She was pleased that not only someone she knew personally but an Afro-Venezuelan had been appointed to a post in the Chávez government (interview, Caracas, July 8, 2003).

Conscious Participants

Individuals were brought into the movement for different reasons and by different contacts, but their reasons for continued participation were very similar and tied together by the values and ideals of the Bolivarian Revolution.

Navas said that she was involved in the movement because of its commitment to the ideals of a united Latin America (interview, Caracas, July 3, 2003). Daza said that he was involved because he saw the Chávez presidency as part of the overall revolutionary process of the Venezuelan left. Participation increased following the events of April 2002, and the heterogeneity of the movement was overshadowed by the common aim of maintaining an ally—Chávez—in the presidency. The common rationale for continued participation was the increasingly intense attacks on Chávez and the counterhegemonic movement. Many Chavistas said that the actions of the opposition had helped bring Chavistas with diverse interests together. Corina Fumero, a social worker with the Chávez-created Instituto Nacional de la Mujer (National Women's Institute—INAMUJER), told me how she and her husband, a Chilean, had left graduate school at the University of California, Berkeley, after Chávez was elected and the opposition began to sabotage his presidency. For her, the historic moment represented by Chávez's election to the presidency and the successes of the left demanded her efforts and presence at home in her native Venezuela (interview, Caracas, July 8, 2003). Albornoz was drawn to the movement for similar reasons; he had become more involved in the Asamblea when it looked as if the revolutionary process of the left was in danger of being derailed by the opposition (interview, Caracas, June 26, 2003). In her study Margarita López Maya concluded that middle-class participation increased after the petroleum lockout, the April coup, and the national strike (López Maya, 2003; 2002). Although participants in the movement had different goals and received different benefits from their participation, supporting Chávez and his government became a common preoccupation after the coup, but was not the main reason for their continued involvement.

Beyond the Chávez Presidency

Chavistas described themselves first as supporters of the Bolivarian Revolution and secondly as supporters of President Chávez. Rodrigo Cháves explained that for him Chávez occupied the "historically unique position of president and leader of the movement at an opportune time" (interview, Caracas, June 24, 2003). Guillermo García Ponce (2001) reiterates the uniqueness of Chávez's relationship to the movement: "Today Chávez's leadership is widely accepted as a principal course of action, whereas before the leadership was a source of permanent conflict." The tremendous importance of Hugo Chávez to the movement was obvious in the comments of individual Chavistas during interviews, but support for him was always contingent on his active commitment to the ideals of the Bolivarian Revolution. Albornoz commented, "The revolutionary process is more important than Chávez" (interview, Caracas, June 26, 2003).

When I asked participants what would happen to the movement if Chávez were to be overthrown or recalled, the responses were mixed. Navas felt that the BDM would be closed because of its successes, its role in educating previously excluded sectors of Venezuelan society, its focus on the poor, and its state funding (interview, Caracas, July 3, 2003). Verenzuela responded similarly, fearing that the hydroponic garden project would be closed down because it was a very visible symbol of Chávez's support for the Bolivarian Movement and its emphasis on providing development resources for the poor (interview, Caracas, July 3, 2003). Piñate was sure that a violent overthrow of Chávez would unleash repression and force the participants and leadership of the FBT to go underground and continue the struggle clandestinely. This response seems to reflect his long history of involvement on the left. However, he added, "In this revolution there is more than just one course of action," meaning that the movement did not depend entirely on Chávez's remaining in power (interview, Caracas, June 29, 2003). Albornoz echoed Piñate's concerns about the fate of the movement without Chávez. He was convinced that the Chavistas would continue struggling for change in Venezuela and that the revolutionary process that his presidency had brought to the forefront would not be obliterated. He felt confident that the victory of the Chavistas in the coup and the intense organizing and education done in its wake could not be extinguished simply by removing Chávez from office (interview, Caracas, June 26, 2003). Rodrigo Cháves's comments reflected this confidence; "Chávez is the current leader," he said, and "the historical memory of the excluded [Chavistas] will not disappear and neither will the Círculos Bolivarianos" (interview, Caracas, June 24, 2003).

Breaking the Stereotype

The Chavistas I interviewed and spent time with during the summer of 2003 were diverse in their aims, actions, and backgrounds. Albornoz was a scientific researcher and member of the middle class who spent much of his time organizing and working for various Círculos in poor neighborhoods. Piñate and Daza were both professors with years of experience organizing within the Venezuelan political system, and they also spent much of their time working with communities of which they were not members. However, all three pointed out that their roles were subordinate to the community organizations' leadership. Verenzuela pointed to the irony that her formal schooling and degree in tourism had little to do with her role in the movement. Fumero's career as a Berkeley graduate student also took second place to her commitment to the revolutionary process. She had no plans to return to the United States as long as Venezuela was in the midst of the Bolivarian Revolution. Along with Navas, these women felt that their own personal experiences and values were consistent with the claims of the Bolivarian Revolution, and that women, nonwhite ethnic groups, the poor, and the middle classes had been marginalized by traditional Venezuelan politics.

The characterization of Chavistas as politically immature is not sustained by this research. The individual Chavistas interviewed here had diverse reasons for their personal involvement but exhibit an ideological orientation consistent with the main goals of the Bolivarian Revolution. They participate in multiple organizations and their involvement in the revolutionary process dates back many years and is based on a long-term commitment to a specific set of values and not solely to Hugo Chávez. Hansen and Hawkins (2006: 124–125) correctly point out that the sharp decline of the Círculos has been accompanied by the reinsertion of their members in other Chavista organizational efforts. The personal values and larger organizational goals of the Chavistas are compatible because of a common commitment based on counterhegemonic political and social objectives as well as historical experiences and social consciousness. These ideals and ideas are disseminated by the Chavistas themselves, who are the intellectual base of the Bolivarian Revolution. Furthermore, they vary widely in age, sex, class, and education; they clearly cannot be characterized as young, unruly, and poor.

THE STATE AND HEGEMONY

The peculiar shape of hegemony in Venezuela—the state's alliance with the Chavistas—raises questions about who is in control of the revolution: The Chavistas, the state, or Hugo Chávez? Gramsci defines the state as "the entire complex of practical and theoretical activities with which the ruling class not only justifies and maintains its dominance, but manages to win the active consent of those over whom it rules" (1971: 244). Clearly, he did not envision a state that was outside of the ruling class or part of a counterhegemonic movement. The Venezuelan case should lead us to consider that the state can in fact be a force allied with resistance movements. Chavistas individually and collectively have proven their strength and willingness to support the current state in a joint project of reshaping hegemony. Likewise, the Chávez government has shown that it recognizes and supports this civil movement, capitalizing on its growing strength.

This alliance requires that we consider a second process of hegemony at work within the counterhegemonic movement itself. In Venezuela this line of thought would lead us to consider whether the Bolivarian Revolution is being dominated by the state. Chavista efforts in defining participatory democracy, creating new forms of politics, and the post referendum initiatives to deepen the process of change indicate a path of negotiating hegemony with the state. It is beyond the scope of this chapter to determine which trend is dominant in this process.

CONCLUSION

This study of Venezuelan political culture was originally prompted by the absence of studies of the Chavistas and their widespread characterization as young, poor, violent, and politically unsophisticated state-controlled masses. Analysts have focused on Hugo Chávez himself, attempting to discredit him as undemocratic and ascribing similar characteristics to his supporters. These analyses tell us little about the nature of the Chavistas, their strength as civil society, their success in reversing the coup, or their efforts at furthering the ideals of the Bolivarian Revolution. I have argued that when one explores the origins, aims, and actions of Chavista organizations and Chavista personal values and experiences it becomes clear that many Chavistas are politically experienced and relatively autonomous components of a complex counterhegemonic social movement that shares a political overview and is allied with the state. It is my hope that the analysis presented here will serve as a tool for better understanding the movement taking place in Venezuela and help shift the focus to the richness of the individual participants in these movements— their knowledge, sophistication, and commitment to democratic change.

NOTE

I would like to thank Raúl Madrid and Charles Hale for advice throughout the research and analysis stage of this project and Vivian Newdick and Fanny Suárez for editing and translation assistance. I would also like to acknowledge the support of the Advanced Seminar in Chicano Research and the Chicano Latino Association of Autonomous Anthropology.

REFERENCES

Canache, Damarys
  2002 *Venezuela: Public Opinion and Protest in a Fragile Democracy*. Miami: North and South Center Press/Lynne Rienner.
Carter Center
  2004 "Venezuela Elections: Analysis of the Carter Center's Second Audit."
  www.cartercenter.org/doc1690.htm (accessed September 21, 2004).
Consejo Nacional Electoral
  2004 "Resultados referendum presidencial 2004." www.cne.gov.ve/ (accessed September 21, 2004).
Ellner, Steve
  2003 "Organized Labor and the Challenge of Chavismo," pp. 161–178 in Steve Ellner and Daniel Hellinger (eds.), *Venezuelan Politics in the Chávez Era: Class, Polarization, and Conflict*. Boulder: Lynne Rienner.
García Ponce, Guillermo
  2001 *Temas de organización y política para revolucionarios*. Caracas: Asamblea de Trabajadores de IVIC.

Garrido, Alberto
  2000 *La historia secreta de la Revolución Bolivariana*. Mérida: Editorial Venezolana.
Gramsci, Antonio
  1971 *Selections from the Prison Notebooks*. Edited by Quintin Hoare and Geoffrey Nowell Smith. New York: International Publishers.
Hands Off Venezuela
  2004 "The Trade Union Situation in Venezuela: Recognizing the UNT as the Union Organizing the Majority of Workers." www.marxist.com/Latinam/trade_union_situation_venezuela.html (accessed July 30, 2004).
Hansen, David R. and Kirk A. Hawkins
  2006 "Dependent Civil Society: The Círculos Bolivarianos in Venezuela." *Latin American Research Review* 41(1).
Hawkins, Kirk
  2003 "Populism in Venezuela: The Rise of Chavismo." *Third World Quarterly* 24 (6): 1137–1160.
Laclau, Ernesto
  2004 "Populism: What's in a Name?" MS, Center for Theoretical Studies in the Humanities and Social Sciences, University of Essex. www.essex.ac.uk/centres/TheoStud/ (accessed August 7, 2004).
  2005 *On Populist Reason*. London: Verso.
López Maya, Margarita
  2002 *Protesta y cultura en Venezuela*. Buenos Aires: CLACSO.
  2003 "Hugo Chávez Frías: His Movement and His Presidency," pp. 73–92 in Steve Ellner and Daniel Hellinger (eds.), *Venezuelan Politics in the Chávez Era: Class, Polarization, and Conflict*. Boulder, CO: Lynne Rienner.
Myers, David
  2003 "Why Representative Democracy Unraveled in Venezuela: Perspectives from the Events of April 11–13." Paper presented at the 24th International Congress of the Latin American Studies Association, Dallas, TX.
Oxhorn, Philip
  2003 "From Allende to Lula: Assessing the Legacy." *NACLA Report on the Americas*, July/August, 9–13.
"Plan comunitario defensa activa"
  2003 MS. www.segured.com/ (accessed March 30, 2003).
Roberts, Kenneth
  2003 "Social Polarization and the Populist Resurgence in Venezuela," pp. 55–72 in Steve Ellner and Daniel Hellinger (eds.), *Venezuelan Politics in the Chávez Era: Class, Polarization, and Conflict*. Boulder, CO: Lynne Rienner.
Ungar, Mark
  2003 "Contested Battlefields: Policing in Caracas and La Paz." *NACLA Report on the Americas*, September/October, 30–36.
Valencia Ramírez, Cristóbal
  2006 "Venezuela in the Eye of the Hurricane: Landing an Analysis of the Bolivarian Revolution." *Journal of Latin American Anthropology* 11 (1): 173–186.
Weyland, Kurt
  2003 "Economic Voting Reconsidered: Crisis and Charisma in the Election of Hugo Chávez." *Comparative Political Studies* 36 (7): 822–848.
Wilpert, Gregory
  2003 "Collision in Venezuela." *New Left Review* 21: 101–116.

Chapter Eight

Social Movements in a Polarized Setting: Myths of Venezuelan Civil Society

María Pilar García-Guadilla

Venezuelan democracy has been considered to be one of the most mature and long-lasting in Latin America because of the continuity of formally democratic governments since 1958. An additional factor is the existence of active social organizations that since the 1970s have mobilized their members in favor of the deepening of democracy and the incorporation of their values and identities in the political system. Since the 1980s, a number of proposals have been made for state reform to resolve the nation's political crisis, and in 1999, under President Hugo Chávez, a new constitution was approved that promoted "participatory democracy" and included many of the social organizations' demands. This article will analyze the impact of the nation's political and economic crisis, and the approval of the new constitution on the identities and practices of the social organizations identified with the political opposition.[1]

The neoconservative and liberal theoretical traditions have pitted organized society against the state, considering both as independent of one another and civil society as a conveyor of ethical values that are above the state.[2] Some writers emphasize that one of the defining characteristics of social organizations and movements is that they do not defy the logic of the democratic system, one of their purposes being to construct democracy (Melucci, 1995; Restrepo, 1998). This school of thought also asserts, sometimes without sufficient evidence, that civil society is multiclass and an interlocutor of the collective interests that permeate all social classes in their confrontation with the state. Writers such as Lander (1995) and Bresser Pereira and Cunill (1998) have argued, however, that it is misleading to assign a democratic logic and positive values a priori to social organizations that act in favor of private and not collective interests. As Restrepo (1998) indicates, participation opens political spaces but can promote only specific values. The notion of the collective interests for the whole of civil society ignores the disintegrating force exerted by the market, which creates social inequalities and accentuates exclusion. The liberal position also overlooks the fact that in societies with high levels of inequality and poverty, civil society identifies more with the interests of the middle and upper class than with those of the poor. Indeed, the critique of the liberal approach reflected in these arguments calls into question the inherently democratic nature of the middle class.

For this reason, questions will be raised here about the private versus the collective interests of Venezuelan social organizations identified with the opposition—whether they promote greater inclusion in the Bolivarian project of President Chávez (considered by some analysts as shunting aside the middle and upper classes), or whether they defend their own values, projects, and private interests, which may include maintenance of class hegemony. The chapter will also explore the increasing social, political, economic, and ideological polarization of the nation and the concomitant redefinition of the values and interests of the social organizations of the opposition and their defense of class interests.

The defense of private interests can lead to political alliances that threaten the autonomy of civil society. One of the risks that civil society faces in its relationship with the state, according to Habermas (1984), is the authoritarian politicization, interventionism, and quasi-totalitarian corporatism arising from both the state and the market. This chapter applies these observations to the relationship between the social organizations identified with the Venezuelan opposition, on the one hand, and the state, political parties, and other economic and social actors, on the other. It will also attempt to determine whether social organizations have maintained their autonomy vis-à-vis the market and actors such as the mass media, or whether, on the contrary, their identities have been submerged or even sacrificed as a result of political conflicts.

As a consequence of the measures against social organizations taken by authoritarian regimes in Latin America between the 1960s and the 1980s, and the search for more participatory forms of democracy in the 1990s, civil society came to be associated with antiauthoritarianism. This association does not, however, accord with the recent emergence of antidemocratic and exclusionary behavior on the part of some social organizations, including coalitions involving the military and other sectors of society to overthrow democratically elected governments.

The gaps that exist between theory and reality with respect to social organizations lead to an appreciation of the complexity of the relations between civil society and the state. Critical views of civil society are few, but

Rabotnikof (2001), for instance, emphasizes the need to develop a richer, more differentiated and complex characterization of the concept of civil society that takes into account the historical complexity of Latin American societies. This chapter represents an effort along these lines.

RUPTURES AND CONTINUITIES:
A CRITICAL READING OF VENEZUELAN CIVIL SOCIETY

From the 1960s to the 1990s:
Myth and Reality of Exceptionalism

During the period beginning with the Constitution of 1961, political literature minimized the class differences in Venezuela, the exacerbation of social inequalities, the increase in poverty, the shortcomings of the democratic political culture, and the differences of democratic visions of state and society. Venezuela (along with Colombia, Costa Rica, and, to a certain extent, Mexico) was considered to be a case of democratic exceptionalism in the region because of the economic stability made possible by the petroleum economy; the tacit agreements and pacts involving the principal political, economic, military, and even religious actors; and the increasing mobilization of social organizations and movements in favor of democratic reform.

A great deal has been written on the democratizing potential and the role played by social movements and organizations in Venezuela throughout the last thirty years (Santana, 1988; Gómez Calcaño 1997; García-Guadilla, 2003). Much of this literature views Venezuelan democracy over the past fifty years as atypical with regard to the stability and consolidation of its political system, the maturity of its institutions and civil culture, and the strength of its social organizations. Political analysts point, for instance, to the effective mobilizations of social organizations whose members belonged to different social classes, but supposedly shared a vision of democracy and a desire for political reforms to stimulate greater participation.

Indeed, these mobilizations did exert pressure in favor of political decentralization, which was initiated by the presidential decree that created the Commission of State Reform in 1984 and the state and electoral reforms passed five years later (Silva, 1999). The mobilizations and struggles of social movements during the period 1984 to 1999 aimed at opening the political system to participation and gaining recognition of new identities and rights did contribute to the strengthening of democracy (García-Guadilla and Roa, 1996). Further evidence of the exceptionalism of Venezuelan civil society was its apparent lack of acute conflict, including class conflict. The social organizations and movements allegedly subordinated class interests to the joint pursuit of participatory democracy as a means to achieve political inclusion.

A more careful reading of political developments suggests, however, that civil society was not as homogeneous, pluralist, mature, or autonomous as was believed.[3] Beginning in the late 1970s, civil society was fragmented by conflicting projects and interpretations of democracy. The mobilizations of social organizations were characterized by social, economic, political, ideological, and even territorial polarization (Roberts, 2003), which became increasingly pronounced as the inability of the nation's representative democracy to resolve pressing problems became evident. The appropriation and privatization of public spaces and the resultant territorialization of sociopolitical conflicts began with the establishment of democracy in 1958, but the process intensified in the late 1970s as poverty and social inequality increased. While the crisis forced the political system to offer opportunities for participation and incorporate new societal goals through the deepening of democracy, the demands of the poor for social justice contributed to the politicization of class differences.

Social scientists failed to anticipate this process because their explanations focused on the prevalence of pluralism and consensus in civil society, and on a liberal view of citizenship, overlooking sociopolitical conflicts and their impact on divergent interests, values, and societal projects. Furthermore, political scientists who stressed institutional factors such as political parties failed to anticipate the new conflictive sociopolitical setting. In the face of social inequality, social and political polarization, and the frustration of class expectations, Venezuelan social organizations tended to differentiate themselves ideologically and socially and develop practices of exclusion and negation of the "other." This process had important implications for the concept of democracy, and specifically participatory democracy as embodied in the constitution of 1999.

Beginning in the 1970s social organizations emerged that exalted participation and a direct relationship with the state. They stressed the deepening of democracy and were part of civil society in that they did not enter into political pacts with the state. They did not, however, defend uniform interests, values, and projects of society, and in some cases they incorporated private interests associated with a particular social class. Thus, popular organizations defended a project of radical democracy emphasizing social justice and equality, while neighborhood associations connected with the middle and upper classes put forward a project of liberal democracy based on economic freedom and the defense of private property (Lander, 1995; García-Guadilla and Roa, 1997; Ellner, 1999). With some exceptions, analysts overlooked these differences, in part because the organizations acted together in promoting the deepening of democracy.

The 1990s: The Debunking of the Myth of a United Civil Society

The economic and political crisis of the 1980s, which found expression in the widespread violence and looting of February 1989 known as the *Caracazo*, forced social conflict to the surface. Although the violence was unplanned, it served as a warning about the capacity of the poorest sectors of the population to foment chaos and appropriate material goods if the challenges of poverty and inequality were not met. The middle-class fear that the *Caracazo*, referred to as "the day the Caracas poor came down from the hills," might repeat itself provoked class resentment. The *Caracazo* also accentuated territorial conflicts associated with socioeconomic and class differences, as the middle and upper classes sought shelter from the "other" in areas protected by gates, guard houses, and security systems (García-Guadilla, 1998).

President Hugo Chávez's assumption of power in 1998 and the ratification of the new constitution in 1999 contributed to the reformulation of the concept of civil society. His promotion of a new "Bolivarian" model of society, which differed substantially from the neoliberal project and was based on the "people" considered as "sovereigns," reinforced the existing division of society into two possibly antagonistic subjects: the "people" (the poor) and "civil society" (the middle and upper classes).[4] His attempts to achieve a hegemony that would displace the liberal project of the middle and upper classes and his class discourse simply politicized social differences and made them more visible.[5]

The constituent assembly that drafted the constitution of 1999 incorporated the demands of social organizations in favor of greater participation and recognized the rights, values, and identities promoted by social movements (García-Guadilla, 2002). Nevertheless, the acute economic crisis that aggravated social inequalities and poverty, and the political crisis that undermined the role of political parties as the principal democratic actors, led the Chávez government to seek new societal interlocutors. In doing so, it spurned middle and upper-class actors that had politically appropriated the term "civil society."

From 2000 to 2003: The Breakdown of Alliances

When the social organizations achieved a certain success in the deepening of democracy in 1999, they failed to formulate any overarching objectives with sufficient symbolic value to keep them united and integrated. Indeed, distinct conceptions of democracy including strategic differences regarding the defense of rights led to the rupture of existing alliances.

Increasing poverty and social inequality led the state to prioritize the demands of the popular sectors. For the first time since 1958, the national political project embraced by the president had greater affinity with radical democracy than with liberal democracy. Under the Chávez presidency, the middle and upper classes feared that respect for the individual values of freedom of expression and private property that they considered the cornerstone of democracy were being threatened, while the popular sectors were optimistic about the possibility of redistribution of wealth and social justice. After the approval of the new constitution, progovernment and antigovernment social organizations continued to mobilize to defend their values and interests, but new organizations and networks emerged on both sides of the political divide. These organizations were united not around values and projects of society but around their support for or opposition to the president.[6]

Interviews with representatives of Venezuelan social organizations show that at least two ideologically distinct proposals were formulated for society and democracy. One was intended to improve the quality of democracy, increasing competition in the marketplace, and stimulate the exercise of individual liberty—that is, to defend values consonant with liberal democracy. The other aimed to transform the values of society and redefine democracy in terms of social equality and justice. Social organizations also differed over concepts of democracy. Opposition social organizations tended to consider participatory democracy a mere complement of representative democracy, whereas progovernment organizations viewed it as an alternative. The clash between pro-Chavista and anti-Chavista social organizations on this issue manifested itself during the discussion in the National Assembly in 2002 and 2003 on the Organic Law of Citizen Participation.

The discourse of the Chávez government denigrates the market and gives preference to values such as justice and social redistribution over private property and even individual freedom. As a result, the liberal projects for society and democracy have little chance of becoming hegemonic. Social organizations with a neoliberal orientation have therefore adopted new strategies, including confrontation and open conflict with the state and alliances with political parties and corporatist bodies that oppose President Chávez. This new orientation has in some cases led to co-optation of these organizations and their loss of autonomy, as well as antidemocratic and exclusionary practices.

SOCIAL REPRESENTATIONS OF
EXCLUSION AND POLITICAL TERRITORIES

The conflicts arising from civil society perhaps find their greatest expression on the streets. In Caracas and other large cities, struggles have manifested themselves in spatial form, transforming the ambience of streets, plazas, and highways. The end result is a spatially and socially segregated city, loss of freedom to move about given the high risk of being identified with the "other," deterioration of services and quality of life, and emergence of areas generating fear and violence. In short, the "right" to the city has been sacrificed, and the result is exclusion and the erosion of democracy.

Beginning in the 1960s, Caracas and other large Venezuelan cities have been increasingly characterized by residential segregation. Since the ratification of the new constitution of 1999, the polarization of social organizations has been spatially reflected in Caracas, with Chavistas on one side and the opposition on the other. Indeed, the territory of the city has been transformed into political fiefdoms. The polarization is not only geographic but also class related. The Chavista territories are the slums, where the levels of urban violence are the highest largely because of the lack of police surveillance. Their location on the periphery, the entrances to the city, and in the center—in the areas where the most active commercial, administrative, and transportation activities are concentrated—becomes a strategic factor during intense conflicts. Access to the city can be closed as it was in the Middle Ages, and urban activities can be seriously disrupted. The opposition's territory is fundamentally middle-class neighborhoods, which are less strategic in that they are removed from key activities and not easily accessed without a car.

If we analyze the social background of people who occupy the streets of Caracas on a daily basis, and the physical characteristics of the spaces where they carry out their activities, we would observe a highly polarized city, and a city under siege. We could draw a political map of Caracas indicating Chavista territories and those of the opposition, including poor and affluent neighborhoods and public spaces that are not politically defined. Specific reference would be made to gates, electrical wiring, guard posts, and even barricades in homes, buildings, streets, and neighborhoods to safeguard the private property of the middle and upper class; public spaces that are deteriorated and unsafe; and streets and other spaces that have been appropriated and transformed for economic purposes by merchants of the informal economy. In sum, Caracas is a segregated city in which the spaces of social intermingling have been divided into spaces for the poor and those for the privileged classes.

The occupation of spaces on the part of those who support President Chávez and those who oppose him have created homogeneous areas in socioeconomic and political terms (García-Guadilla, 1998; Rodríguez and Winchester, 1997; García and Villá, 2001). The unfolding of spatial conflicts in the Caracas of 2003 is not so much ethnic and racial (Park and Burguess, 1925) as it is political and social. The Chavistas and the opposition exclude the "other" from their territory and in the process solidify a segregated pattern of occupation with strong class associations. The poor tend to identify with the Chavistas and to live in the west of Caracas, while those with the most to lose tend to identify with the political opposition and are concentrated in the east. All this points to an antidemocratic dimension in which social and political activity takes place in spaces of fear by citizens who are virtually at war (Rotker, 2000).

The sociopolitical conditions for territorial and political polarization already existed. Since the colonial period, plazas and streets have served as arenas for demanding rights at moments of political or economic crises, such as occurred with the fall of dictator Marcos Pérez Jiménez in 1958 and with the *Caracazo* of 1989. Since 1999, however, the intensity and duration of street protests have meant that spaces have remained politically identified and their use completely changed for a relatively long time or even permanently. This has been the case of the so-called Hot Corner located in the center of Caracas as well as the area outside of the headquarters of Petróleos de Venezuela (PDVSA), both of which have been taken over by Chavistas. The same occurred in the Plaza Altamira, which has been occupied by military officers opposed to Chávez and converted into a center for the mobilization of the opposition.

This defense of space by social and political organizations that support or oppose President Chávez leads to antidemocratic exclusion and the possibility of violence. The spaces involved tend to lose their original urban function, at least at moments of political conflict: highways are not for vehicles to circulate freely but for holding massive protests and vigils (while other public spaces accommodate tents and equipment for modern camping for the purpose of housing thousands of persons on their way to political gatherings). Similarly, instead of serving recreational purposes, plazas are for expressing political support for, or rejection of, the president.

Finally, middle-class youth, who in the past followed U.S. habits of recreation, reinforce the new subculture. Political marches feature the wearing of clothing in the colors of the national flag, music based on national folklore, and symbols and posters with a nationalistic flavor. Increased face-to-face social relations and the rise of a spirit of solidarity among social equals are also part of this subculture based on political marches.[7]

DEMOCRATIC PRACTICES OR
THE DEFIANCE OF DEMOCRATIC LOGIC?

Mobilizations and actions sponsored by social organizations to defend "their democracy" are not always democratic in nature. Many of the same citizen organizations that promoted mobilizations in the past in favor of political reforms and the deepening of democracy are now on the side of either the opposition or the party in power, and on both sides there is a break with the democratic practices and strategies of previous decades

The tenuousness of democracy among social organizations was apparent in their support for the so-called "national civic strike" against President Chávez that lasted from December 2002 until February 2003—a strike that was called without rank-and-file consultation. The ten-week conflict witnessed the conversion of the mass media into political actors that monopolized and distorted information and became, in effect, the most important spokesmen for the strike. At the same time, social organizations were used to legitimize the discredited political parties, as occurred with the conversion of high-level executives from the state-owned oil industry into political leaders and their incursion into the space of civil society as a result of their creation of a nongovernmental organization called Gente de Petróleo (People of Oil). The major leadership role played by business leaders and media owners was undemocratic in that the employees were not consulted when businesses were closed. Furthermore, in addition to forfeiting wages during the strike, many professionals, technicians, and blue-collar workers were dismissed from their jobs as a result of the recession caused by the strike. The organization of professional PDVSA employees as Gente de Petróleo displayed an antidemocratic mentality by instigating the strike and closing the national petroleum industry, thus producing considerable economic losses and environmental damage. The leaders of Gente de Petróleo acted as if they owned the oil industry; at no time were others consulted even though PDVSA was a public company belonging to all Venezuelans.

Other undemocratic actions included the closing of streets and the blocking of traffic on highways. Social organizations such as Queremos Elegir announced schedules for placing obstacles to impede the movement of vehicles. These tactics created tension and intense rejection among the residents who were the most affected, and for this reason the actions were suspended. Significantly, the measures were lifted not because they were antidemocratic or infringed on the constitutional right to move freely through the streets, but because surveys indicated that they were extremely unpopular and threatened to generate violence among neighbors.

Perhaps the most blatant example of an undemocratic strategy was the preparation of "contingency plans" prepared during the weeks prior to January 23, 2003, the anniversary of the beginning of the democratic period in 1958. These veritable war plans reflected an exclusionary mind-set and were a response to the rumor that "the Chavista hordes" and the "Bolivarian Circles" were poised to invade the residences of the middle and upper classes. The source of the rumor was the retired military officers of the opposition grouped in the Frente Institucional Militar (Institutional Military Front). Dispatches released by opposition officers, many of whom had ties with security companies, joined together representatives of middle-class neighborhoods to design a "Community Active Defense Plan" for middle-class apartment buildings and neighborhoods. The document's introduction stated, "This material was developed by a group of neighbors with the consensus and participation of friendly communities and specialists in the area of community security for the purpose of establishing guidelines to increase the effectiveness of the response to emergency situations that might occur in our homes, schools or jobs" ("Community Active Defense Plan," 2003: 3).

The defense plan, more appropriate for fortifications under siege during the Middle Ages than for modern urban buildings, included the use of weapons and Molotov cocktails, locking the gates and doors of buildings, spilling barrels of oil and hot water on assailants, and constructing barricades. Both the popular sectors and the middle class began to arm themselves while blaming one another. One member of the opposition whom I interviewed said that the middle class was arming itself "to defend the sacred rights of property, family and freedom" while the Chavistas were doing so "to attack these rights." The version of Chávez supporters was that they were not "armed" and that they too were "defending their rights."

The plan also called for nocturnal surveillance by the residents themselves because in the majority of cases they did not trust the maids and the private guards who normally performed this task. The plan warned: "Do not trust household servants, specifically those who work during the daytime. Remember that many of these people have been manipulated and some are beginning to see us as enemies. This is a delicate matter and there is no reason to generalize . . . but you must be alert in the face of any evidence" ("Community Active Defense Plan," 2003: 17). It recommended "being prepared for any contingency" and included a highly sophisticated communication system of alerts from green to red, in which local police, the mass media, and neighbors were to be contacted ("Community Active Defense Plan," 2003: 1). Many neighborhoods reinforced the number of guards (who paradoxically, belonged to the lower class), while some residents built barricades and stayed awake all night. Although nothing happened, the middle class in general perceived poor people as the "enemy."

The antidemocratic face of social organizations is based on the fear of the "other," which is defined as "undemocratic." In the case of the privileged sectors, the "other" is excluded even from the category of "civil society," while for the nonprivileged the other is the "oligarch," excluded from the "people" and the "sovereigns." In both cases these social images, reinforced by political polarization in the nation as a whole, served to justify acts of violence, the spatial and social exclusion of the "other," and the denial of the existence of the other "civil society."

According to public opinion surveys carried out in 2002–2003, the Venezuelan middle and upper classes view the typical poor person as a criminal and characterize his organizations as violent. In the context of social and political polarization, the organizations identified by the mass media as the backbone of "civil society" tend to exclude the popular organizations of the low-income population, particularly those aligned with Chávez. The opposition perceives these sectors as being organized around the so-called Bolivarian Circles, which are allegedly violent and armed. This perception ignores the pluralism and heterogeneity of the Circles (see chapter by Valencia in this volume). In general, government supporters prefer to call themselves "the people" and "the sovereigns" and perceive the middle and upper classes as corrupt and exploitative. In their eyes, the middle and upper classes are the "squalid ones" and the "oligarchs." This characterization ignores the heterogeneity of the opposition, its main area of consensus being opposition to Chávez and the defense of class interests.

In contrast to these antidemocratic strategies, democratic strategies have also emerged including the call to activate aspects of participatory democracy embodied in the constitution, such as the consultative referendum and recall. The opposition organized a campaign for a referendum on the Chávez government as a way of calling a halt to the 2002–2003 general strike once it had proven completely unsuccessful. The process of gathering signatures for the recall election in late 2003 demonstrated the democratic potential of opposition social organizations, notwithstanding the issue of whether civil society was going beyond its natural functions by taking on the role of political actors.

CONCLUSION

The notions regarding the exceptionalism of Venezuelan democracy and civil society overlooked the socioeconomic and political-ideological polarization that had been underway since the 1960s. The exceptionalism thesis exalted civic culture and civil society, which it considered the pillars of democracy. The assumption of power of President Chávez, who proposed a sociopolitical project directed at the popular sectors that implicitly excluded the middle and upper classes, placed in doubt the exceptional nature of Venezuelan democracy and above all its alleged capacity to avoid the exclusion of sectors of society. In recent years, the ideological, political, and social polarization that is even expressed territorially has given rise to a crisis of citizenship in which private and collective interests, and public and private spaces, have become increasingly confused. Moreover, anti-Chávez strategic alliances between opposition social organizations and political parties have cast doubt on the alleged autonomy of the former, leading to a loss of rank-and-file power and the strengthening of the vertical and personalist decision-making process.

Even though we have focused on social organizations identified with the political opposition to President Chávez, the same pattern of politicization and alliances with the progovernment political party, the Movimiento Quinta República (Fifth Republic Movement—MVR), has been emerging within pro-Chavista social organizations in order to counteract the broad front of opposition groups. An example was the convergence of pro-Chávez social organizations such as the Comités de Tierra around the Unidades de Batalla Electoral (Electoral Battle Units), which were linked to the MVR and canvassed in favor of the "No" vote in the presidential recall election of August 2004. In this case, as in that of the social organizations of the opposition, intolerance and exclusion of "the other" tended to substitute, albeit momentarily, pluralistic, democratic, and collective interests. In contrast, human rights organizations were among the few in Venezuela that did not take a political stand throughout the conflicts beginning in 2002. Their approach to democracy based on "rights" kept them focused on their objectives and facilitated a possible role as mediators.

The vacuum left by this loss of autonomy and the discrediting of traditional political parties and other institutions has led to the distortion of the identities of social actors and their role in the face of the crisis. The social organizations of both the opposition and the popular sectors have locked themselves into alliances with political parties, however discredited and delegitimized. Occasionally, the organizations of civil society have attempted to play the role generally assigned to political parties, thus confusing their identity and leaving their own long-term interests unprotected. In other cases, political actors have disguised themselves as nongovernmental organizations or foundations that have usurped the role of political parties. This usurpation of functions is in large part a consequence of the absence of a common sociopolitical project that would clearly define the roles of individual actors. The power vacuum has also encouraged the social organizations of the opposition to place their hope in the military and has stimulated undemocratic civilian-military alliances. This casts doubts on the alleged maturity of the nation's democratic political culture, as is embodied in the exceptionalism thesis, and the democratizing potential of social organizations, particularly when they feel their interests are threatened.

Since 2002, the opposition as well as Chávez's followers have concentrated their efforts on street mobilizations, rather than promoting a civic-democratic culture. Both sides lack an alternative project capable of uniting the citizenry. The Bolivarian Constitution of 1999 may come to constitute one such all-inclusive project, even though paradoxically it has been used up until now to strengthen the positions of one of the two sides in the current conflict. The constitution opened new possibilities for social organizations in defense of an autonomous status and interaction with the state, political parties, and corporatist actors. These goals need to be furthered within the context of an inclusive and participatory democracy grounded in human rights that minimizes polarization and promotes tolerance.

NOTES

This paper is based on field work financed by the Fondo Nacional de Ciencia, Tecnología e Investigación (FONACIT). The project is titled "Constitutionalization of New Actors and New Citizenships: Resolution of Sociopolitical Conflicts in Venezuela" and is being carried out in the Universidad Simón Bolívar under the coordination of María Pilar García-Guadilla.

1. The term "social organization" here refers to organizations that are actively mobilized in defense of social interests. In Venezuela this category takes in many of the social movements of the past. During the period under study, the social organizations of the ideologically heterogeneous opposition formed part of the Coordinadora Democrática (Democratic Coordinating Committee— CD), which organized more than 150 protest marches against Chávez between its founding in January 2001 and the end of 2003. The CD was composed of twenty-five political parties, the Confederación de Trabajadores de Venezuela (Venezuelan Workers' Confederation—CTV), the Federación Venezolana de Cámaras y Asociaciones de Comercio y Producción (Venezuelan Federation of Chambers and Associations of Commerce and Production—FEDECAMARAS), and about twenty nongovernmental organizations. Some of its members (e.g., Queremos Elegir) predate the drafting of the constitution of 1999 and were very active in that process. New ones include the Ciudadania Activa and the Frente Institucional Militar, consisting of retired military officers.

2. For the purposes of this chapter, "civil society" is defined as the part of organized society that is distinct from the state and the market and excludes political parties. The constitution of 1999 makes few references to "civil society," instead using the terms "society," "organized society," "communities," "social organizations," and particularly "the sovereigns."

3. The fallacy of the exceptionalism thesis was also clear from the limited credibility of traditional political parties, which had previously been considered models for Latin America, and institutional fragility, which has been aggravated by the failure to achieve a consensus with regard to the new institutions created by the 1999 constitution.

4. The appropriation of the term "civil society" by the middle and upper classes to the exclusion of nonprivileged sectors is to a certain extent the consequence of the discursive polarization of President Chávez. The term is used as part of the effort to promote individualistic, proneoliberal values.

5. A minority sector of the middle class supports the government and is grouped in the organization called "Middle Class in Positive."

6. Some human rights and environmental organizations are not identified with pro- or anti-Chávez camps and their positions vary according to the issue.

7. The "patriotic" and "nationalistic" subculture that has recently emerged in the marches of the middle-class opposition differs from that of the lower class with regard to the appropriation of landmarks and traditional and modern spatial symbols. In a society strongly divided along class lines, traditional national symbols such as the Plaza Bolívar in the center of the city, the National Pantheon, the Presidential Palace of Miraflores, the National Assembly, and the Paseo Los Próceres have been appropriated by progovernment forces for their symbolic and patriotic value. At the same time, highways, plazas, and public buildings, including the symbolic spaces of the modern petroleum culture, have been appropriated by the middle and upper classes that oppose Chávez.

REFERENCES

Bresser Pereira , Luiz Carlos and Nuria Cunill (eds.)
1998 *Lo publico no estatal en la reforma del Estado.* Paidós-CLAD.
"Community Active Defense Plan"
2003 MS. Caracas.
Ellner, Steve
1999 "Obstáculos a la consolidación del movimiento vecinal venezolano: la brecha entre lo nacional y lo local." *Revista Venezolana de Economía y Ciencias Sociales* 5 (1): 33–57.
García, Pedro José and Marc Villá
2001 "De la sociabilidad vigilante a la urbanizada privativa." *Perfiles Latinoamericanos* 10 (19): 57–82.
García-Guadilla, María Pilar
1998 "Ajuste económico, desdemocratización y procesos de privatización de los espacios públicos en Venezuela." *Revista Interamericana de Planificación* 30 (119–120): 77–89.
2002 "Actores, organizaciones y movimientos sociales en la Venezuela el 2002," in Marisa Ramos Rollón (ed.), *Venezuela: rupturas y continuidades del sistema político (1999–2001).* Salamanca: Ediciones Universidad de Salamanca.
2003 "Civil Society: Institutionalization, Fragmentation, Autonomy," in Steve Ellner and Daniel Hellinger (eds.), *Venezuelan Politics in the Chávez Era: Globalization, Social Polarization, and Political Change.* Boulder, CO: Lynne Rienner.
García-Guadilla, María Pilar and Ernesto Roa
1996 "Gobernabilidad, cambio político y sociedad civil: el proceso constituyente en Venezuela." *Revista Venezolana de Economía y Ciencias Sociale* 2 (2–3).
1997 "La red de organizaciones sociales liberales y la democracia en Venezuela." *Cuadernos del CENDES* 14 (35): 55–80.
García-Guadilla, María Pilar and Nadeska Silva
1999 "De los movimientos sociales a las redes organizacionales en Venezuela: estrategias, valores e identidades." *Politeia* no. 23: 7–28.
Gómez Calcaño, Luis
1997 "Nuevos actores y viejas prácticas: asociaciones de vecinos y partidos políticos." Paper presented at the Forty-ninth meeting of the Congreso Mundial de Americanistas, Quito.
Habermas, Jurgen
1984 *Teoría de la acción comunicativa: complementos y estudios previos.* Madrid: Editorial Cátedra.
Lander, Edgardo
1995 "Movimientos sociales urbanos, sociedad civil y nuevas formas de ciudadanía," in Edgardo Lander (ed.), *Neoliberalismo, sociedad civil y democracia: ensayos sobre América Latina y Venezuela.* Caracas: Universidad Central de Venezuela.
Melucci, Alberto
1995 *Nomads of the Present.* Philadelphia: Temple University Press.
Park, Robert and Ernest Burguess
1925 *The City.* Chicago: University of Chicago Press.
Rabotnikof, Nora
2001 "La caracterización de la sociedad civil: perspectiva de los bancos multilaterales de desarrollo." *Nueva Sociedad* no. 171.
Ramos Rollon, María Luisa
1995 *De las protestas a las propuestas: identidad, acción y relevancia política del movimiento vecinal en Venezuela.* Caracas: Editorial Nueva Sociedad.

Restrepo, Darío
1998 "Eslabones y precipicios entre la participación y la democracia." Paper presented to the conference Participación, ciudadanía y democracia. Comisión Presidencial para la Reforma del Estado, Caracas.

Roberts, Kenneth
2003 "Polarización social y resurgimiento del populismo en Venezuela," in Steve Ellner and Daniel Hellinger (eds.), *La política venezolana en la época de Chávez: clases, polarización y conflicto.* Caracas: Nueva Sociedad.

Rodríguez, Alfredo and Lucy Winchester
1997 *Ciudades y gobernabilidad en América Latina.* Santiago: Ediciones Sur.

Rotker, Susana
2000 *Ciudadanías del miedo.* Caracas: Rutgers–Nueva Sociedad.

Santana, Elías
1988 "La política de los vecinos: experiencias del movimiento comunitario como fuerza democrática y de cambio frente a la crisis," in *El venezolano ante la crisis.* Caracas: Ediciones Amón C.A. Instituto IDEA.

Silva, Nadeska
1999 *Democracia, descentralización y concepciones de ciudadanía en Venezuela.* Master's thesis, Universidad Simón Bolívar.

Part V

ELECTORAL POLITICS, SOCIAL CHANGE, AND U.S. REACTION

For the left in Latin America, elections have produced contradictory outcomes. The electoral arena is also one in which the United States has attempted to exercise its influence and determine the results. In the case of Chile, the United States supported a coup, and in Nicaragua it financed the opposition to the Sandinistas. Yet in Venezuela the electoral arena has been an important political vehicle for change and has served to affirm the legitimacy of the Chávez political program. Chapter 9 examines the recent recall vote and calls for a reassessment of the role of the left in electoral politics. Chapter 10 examines the policies the United States has pursued in opposing the Chávez government.

CHAPTERS 9 AND 10: ELECTORAL POLITICS, SOCIAL CHANGE, AND U.S. REACTION

Daniel Hellinger's chapter provides an important reassessment of the role of elections in Latin American revolutionary movements. For many, the electoral defeat of the Sandinistas in Nicaragua called into question the role of elections as an instrument in producing or sustaining social change. Hellinger reconsiders this debate in light of the recent string of elections in Venezuela that have sustained and, in fact, reinvigorated the Bolivarian Revolution. His work provides a timely analysis of the recall elections of August 15, 2004, and the regional voting held on October 31 of the same year. He assesses the political climate in Venezuela leading up to the electoral contest and analyzes the role of class and regional factors in the outcome. He describes the strengths and weaknesses of Chávez's electoral strategy and the declining influence of opposition forces grouped in the Coordinadora Democrática (Democratic Coordinator—CD). The massive outpouring during the recall election highlights the strength of the Chavistas, while the abstention evident in the October regional elections points to a potential weakness of the movement.

Christopher Clement's chapter examines how the United States has reacted to the government of Hugo Chávez. He questions the central tenets of U.S.-sponsored "democracy promotion" as it was applied to Latin America in the 1980s, whenever social protests and outright rebellion challenged the established order. Beyond its obvious political content, the U.S. support for democracy promotion was seen as a way of facilitating the emergence of neoliberal economic policy in the region. Clement's chapter provides a succinct critique of the Reagan-era National Endowment for Democracy (NED) and the "undemocratic" policies it has pursued in Venezuela under the Chávez presidency. He traces the network of institutions that receive NED funding in the United States and Venezuela and shows how it attempts to bolster the undemocratic opposition to Chávez. He ends by questioning the likelihood of U.S. tolerance for democratically elected governments in Latin America if figures like Chávez are elected in other countries throughout the continent.

Chapter Nine

When "No" Means "Yes to Revolution": Electoral Politics in Bolivarian Venezuela

Daniel Hellinger

The lessons of history suggest that pluralist constitutional structures present myriad ways for opponents to block radical overhaul of social and economic structures. Antimajoritarian checks and balances make redistribution of wealth and changes in property regimes difficult to implement. When these mechanisms fail, the capitalist class seems willing and able to abandon constitutional politics and fall back on the state's night-watchman, the military. In dependent nations, the weight and resources of the hegemon can be brought to bear to influence the outcome. Often, however, institutional and extraconstitutional tools of reaction are unnecessary in polyarchies.[1] Elections themselves seem to suck the life blood out of revolutionary movements.

The Venezuelan recall election of August 15, 2004, evidently accelerated rather than retarded revolutionary momentum. On that day Venezuelans went to the polls in extraordinary numbers to vote on an opposition petition to revoke (hence, *revocatorio*) President Hugo Chávez's electoral mandate two years before he would complete his term. To achieve this objective and thereby terminate the Bolivarian Revolution, the opposition Coordinador Democrática (CD) needed to win more votes than the president had received in his second electoral victory of July 2000 (following the adoption of the new constitution). Not only did the CD fail to exceed that number, but the No option triumphed with 59 percent of the vote. The majority said yes to the Chavista revolutionary project.

This chapter will examine the ways that electoral politics and defense of a revolutionary regime were made compatible in Venezuela. After a review of some theoretical perspectives on elections and social change, a comparison of the Venezuelan case with earlier episodes of electoral politics in a revolutionary context (Nicaragua and Chile), and a review of the political and constitutional issues that had to be resolved to allow the recall election to take place, we will examine polling data that demonstrate the class polarized nature of the vote. We will also assess the sustainability of the Chavista success story by comparing aggregate results for the recall and the subsequent regional elections of October 31. Despite the sweeping victory of Chavista candidates in these elections, the level of mobilization of progovernment voters fell significantly. Although this can be attributed in part to electoral fatigue, I argue that it also reflects the incomplete institutionalization of the participatory, "protagonist" democracy often posed by Chávez as an alternative to representative democracy. Failure to advance on this front may make Chavismo vulnerable to defeat in future elections and referendums.

In fact, turnout for the December 2005 National Assembly elections was only 25 percent. The opposition, which at the last moment decided to boycott the election, claimed that low turnout showed that the government had lost legitimacy. Pro-Chávez forces, which won 100 percent of Assembly seats as a result of the boycott, argued that the abstention rate was inflated by the demoralization of the opposition, certainty of a Chavista victory, and bad weather. Furthermore, they pointed out, the proportion of the electorate that voted for the Movimiento Quinta República (Fifth Republic Movement—MVR) or an allied party was comparable to that achieved by winning parties in the pre-1998 era. Neither the *oficialista* nor opposition interpretation of abstention should be accepted at face value. The opposition boycott most certainly was motivated by polls showing the Chavista coalition likely to win more than two thirds of seats. Although international observers from the OAS and the European Union reinforced opposition criticism by calling attention to the lack of trust in "wide sectors" of Venezuelan society, they praised the integrity of the National Electoral Council and, in recognition of its concessions to opposition demands, criticized the boycott.

My contention is not that elections and liberal regimes are politically neutral and open to all democratic outcomes, including revolutionary ones. The key to harnessing an electoral process to a revolutionary process in Venezuela was the organic linkage of electoral mobilization with other forms of social class mobilization. Chávez has yet to solve the problem of institutionalizing the relationship between the popular democratic forces that formed in defense of his presidency and the MVR, the Chavista party. The participation of the former is needed to prevent Chavismo from degenerating into familiar forms of clientelism and populism, but a party is needed to organize Chavista forces on the electoral battlefield. The recall, regional, and Assembly elections reveal difficulty in reconciling these two elements of Chavismo.

ELECTIONS AND REVOLUTIONARY CHANGE

Elections are as much mechanisms for state control of citizens as vice versa. Drawing on de Tocqueville and Foucault, Benjamin Ginsberg argues,

> The election and the prison, along with mass education and the factory, were the great institutions of social control introduced in the eighteenth and nineteenth centuries to deal with the entry of the masses onto the political and economic stage. Since the nineteenth century, governments have ruled through electoral mechanisms even when they have sometimes been ruled by them. (1982: 2)

An analogy can be drawn, adds Ginsberg, to an automobile for which a single pedal controls both the brake and the accelerator: "The principal mechanism by which citizens attempt to control the state simultaneously helps both to limit popular intervention in the governmental process and to increase the state's authority and power" (1982: 3).

Elections usually focus the attention of political leaders on the task of winning or holding onto office, not social transformation. Political activists tend to put aside other mobilization strategies in favor of generating votes. Candidates, acting as political entrepreneurs, vie with one another for nominations, encouraging divisiveness as activists side with different forces or debate among themselves the wisdom of engaging in electoral politics. In dependent nations, elections provide openings for imperialist actors in the world system to influence the struggle for power. "It is clear that the electoral front is not the most favorable field for the revolution to advance," wrote two Marxist journalists covering the Venezuelan recall campaign. Although they expected Chávez to win, they warned, "Here the vote of the most active elements, who participate directly in marches, assemblies, meetings, and trade unions, counts as much as the vote of the politically inactive layers more subject to the propaganda of the bourgeois media" (Martin and Sanabria, 2004).

Latin American experience provides ample reason to be cynical about the revolutionary potential of electoral processes and pluralist politics. Nicaragua is a case in point. William Robinson described the 1990 election defeat of the Sandinistas by the U.S.-supported Unión Nacional Opositora (National Opposition Union—UNO) coalition as nothing less than an electoral coup. He did not conclude from this, however, that elections were hopeless or unnecessary in a revolutionary process:

> What makes the Nicaraguan experience important for other countries and peoples is not that the FSLN [Frente Sandinista de Liberación Nacional] lost elections but that massive foreign interference completely distorted an endogenous political process and undermined the ability of the elections to be a free choice

regarding the destiny of the country. U.S. intervention undercut the Nicaraguan people's right to exercise self-determination. (1992: 150)

Because it was a plebiscite, the Venezuelan recall election posed the question of power more starkly than in Nicaragua or, before that, in Chile during the Unidad Popular experience (1970–1973). The key electoral contests (1972 and 1973) in Chile were (respectively) municipal and congressional elections, and the 1990 contest in Nicaragua was a presidential election. However, there were ways in which these earlier elections were also plebiscitary. In both cases, the parties and the electorate had clearly polarized into coalitions in support of and opposition to the government and its revolutionary agenda, just as in contemporary Venezuela. The two elections in Chile were watched closely to determine whether the government of Salvador Allende could win a plebiscite to overhaul the constitution, which was essential to its conception of a "Chilean way to socialism." In Nicaragua, the 1990 election presented voters with a clear option: to continue with or terminate a revolutionary project that, however sapped of momentum, was clearly defined by the United States and internal opposition as a threat to the dominant capitalist model. The Nicaraguan case is especially relevant to Venezuela because, similar to Chávez's conception of "protagonist democracy," the Sandinistas' conception of democracy combined representative and participatory notions.[2] An "electoral coup" is also a good way of describing the intentions of the Venezuelan version of UNO, the Coordinadora Democrática (CD), and its supporters in Washington.

THE RECALL

The Coordinadora Democrática, which dissolved after its defeat in the recall, was a coalition of opposition parties, business groups, and other organizations. It included a number of labor leaders associated with the Punto Fijo regime ended by Chávez's victory in the presidential election of December 1998. Ironically, the legal basis for its effort to recall President Chávez is a provision of the new "Bolivarian Constitution" of 1999. The constitution is based on an uneasy mixture of pluralist and participatory provisions. Representatives chosen through a pluralist electoral process are supposed to engage in a high degree of consultation with organizations in civil society. The possibility of recalling elected officials is one of the most important provisions designed to lend a protagonist role to the mass public—what Chávez calls "el soberano."

Although Chávez is undeniably a charismatic figure, mass allegiance to the Bolivarian Constitution transcends his personal popularity. The constitution itself was subject to considerable input from civil society (Pastor and Martínez, 2001) and afterward was mass-distributed. Chávez never tired of talking about its provisions in his national speeches and *Aló Presidente*, his weekly talk program. The mass uprising that contributed mightily to his restoration to power after the short-lived coup of April 11, 2002, was as much a defense of the constitution as a defense of the president himself. The abrogation of much of the charter by the junta installed by the revolt turned many of its initial supporters (especially in the military) against the new regime.

The recall process was not the opposition's first attempt to remove Chávez from office. Others included the forty-eight-hour April coup, a two-month civic strike and sabotage of the vital oil industry begun in December of that year, and the *guarimba* of February 27 to March 2, 2004, when a campaign of civil disobedience brought about disruptions, sometimes violent, throughout the eastern half of Caracas. In each case, supporters of the president countermobilized to meet opposition threats. Although kept relatively in check, street violence and deaths, especially during the events leading to the April coup, raised the specter of civil war, which probably served to some degree to encourage several elite compromises that paved the way for the recall.

Given the degree of polarization, it is not surprising that a high degree of mistrust characterized the entire process. A bitter fight over the composition of the Consejo Nacional Electoral (National Electoral Council—CNE) was resolved in 2001, when it was agreed that it would be composed of two members identified with each side and a chairman known to be a supporter of Chávez but respected as a jurist.[3] When on May 29, 2003, the government and the CD signed an agreement accepting the idea of a referendum on President Chávez's mandate as permitted by Article 72 of the constitution, the CNE was faced with the formidable task of refereeing the recall petition process. Under Article 72 the opposition needed to submit petitions with signatures amounting to more than 20 percent of registered voters, in this case 2,451,821. The opposition gathered and submitted its petitions with over 3 million signatures in November 2003.

The CNE accepted only 1,900,000 million signatures as valid, half a million short. Over 800,000 of the rejected names appeared on petitions on which a single person appeared to have filled out all but the signatures. According to the CNE's rules, published in September 2003, petitions were to include the "name, last name, identity card number, date of birth, name of organization or voter registry, original signature by hand and digital fingerprint, of each petitioner of the recall referendum, in legible form." Furthermore, "The petition for a referendum is a very personal act, which is why authorizations to sign on behalf of another voter will not be permitted."[4] These provisions do not expressly prohibit organizers from filling out parts of petitions, but the CNE chose to interpret the rules broadly. In highly polarized Venezuela, finding one's name on a petition awaiting only a signature was surely intimidating.

The opposition accused the CNE majority of being a pawn of Chávez, a charge largely echoed in the international media. The CD carried the dispute into the courts, and this elicited legal countermaneuvering from the MVR. The case landed on the docket of two different chambers of the highly politicized Supreme Court. The two chambers issued conflicting rulings, sending the matter to a hearing before the full court. Fortunately for the divided court, the CD and the government, spurred by international pressure and mediation, signed a compromise agreement to allow a "repair" process (*reparos*) to take place. Many Chavistas were angered and claimed that the CNE's rules of September did not provide for such a widespread, systematic follow-up. However, Article 31 of these rules did envision the possibility of a process to allow voters to verify or withdraw signatures.[5]

On the weekend of May 28–30, 2004, voters were permitted to withdraw or reconfirm 1.2 million contested signatures. The hurdle was made higher by a countermobilization by the Chavistas, an operation called Comando Ayacucho headed by leaders drawn from the MVR and the four smaller parties that made up the government coalition. Ayacucho's goal was to find 200,000 citizens willing to claim that their signatures were fraudulent, but in the end only 74,112 people denied that their signatures had been freely given. On June 4 the CNE verified that the opposition had confirmed 614,968 of the contested signatures, 15,738 more than needed. Ayacucho was also charged with gathering enough signatures to recall twenty opposition legislators, but it submitted enough to put only nine CD legislators in jeopardy.[6] Certainly, the CD had reason to be optimistic.

To revoke President Chávez's mandate, the opposition needed to win more Yes votes than the president had received in the July 2000 presidential elections. The trigger number was 3,757,773. To win, then, the opposition would have to mobilize not only the 2.5 million who had voted for other candidates in 2000 but also another 1,200,000 from the ranks of disillusioned Chávez supporters, abstainers, and new voters. The CD's optimism sprang from polls throughout 2003 showing that the president's approval ratings had fallen below 40 percent. The low approval ratings seemed to reflect popular discontent with an economy that continued to stagger and with social insecurity. In addition, the CD could count on support from the United States, especially from the National Endowment for Democracy (NED), which funneled over US$1 million dollars to opposition groups in 2003.

The failures of Ayacucho induced Chávez to reorganize his forces for the recall battle, giving birth to Comando Maisanta, named for Chávez's great-grandfather, a nationalist guerrilla fighter. In a brilliant use of historical discourse, Chávez equated the No campaign with the Battle of Santa Inés of 1859, which took place near the president's home town in Barinas. In this battle, General Ezequiel Zamora, the populist caudillo and martyr, utilized tactical retreats to draw his conservative enemies into a deadly, strategic trap. The Chávez retreat to the electoral battlefield was probably improvised, but it proved to be no less a master stroke.

Chávez took direct control of the effort and drew more heavily on the ranks of his mass base. His supporters were to organize themselves into neighborhood-level electoral platoons with ten members each, in turn grouped into electoral battle units. However, even in Maisanta there remained tensions between base committees and mid-level "commanders." Many Maisanta commanders were artists, intellectuals, and communicators of good will but limited political experience. Some were politicians with the same deficiencies as the Ayacucho leaders. In Caracas, a swearing-in ceremony for mid-level Maisanta commanders was canceled because of discontent in several militant poor barrios (Harnecker, 2004; Martin and Sanabria, 2004).

After some difficult negotiations and interventions by Chávez himself, Maisanta was able to take root and gain momentum, even where the local leadership was not always up to the task. Spontaneously, often organizing where people worked rather than where they lived, going door to door rather than following electoral lists, a grassroots movement formed in response to the president's call to action. As Marta Harnecker (2004: 43) has described it, the electoral battle units "allowed hundreds of thousands of supporters of the process to join together to carry out a concrete political task independently, regardless of the quality or lack of party leadership in their locale."

Here was the key to victory in the recall, the way so many new voters were mobilized for electoral combat. In walking strongholds of Chavismo in Caracas and other cities, one could not help but be impressed by the high levels of enthusiasm and politicization of ordinary Venezuelans. Most poor Venezuelans were animated by the same spirit that had moved them to descend from the barrios to Miraflores on April 11, 2002, and after sixteen months of ambitious, visible, and palpable social programs they had material interests to reinforce their support for a president who seemed to have come from their own ranks.

In contrast to the Sandinistas, who turned away from mass organizing toward more traditional campaign tactics in the 1991 election, Chávez wisely adopted a more participatory strategy. This strategy was available to him because unlike the Sandinistas he was willing and able to accelerate economic and social programs often at odds with neoliberal orthodoxy, eschewing the imposition of sacrifices upon his core, mass constituency. Of course Venezuela had something that Nicaragua lacked: oil rents, enhanced by favorable global market conditions. However, this was not entirely a matter of luck. Chávez shaped market conditions through his leadership in revitalizing the Organization of Petroleum Exporting Countries (OPEC), and he reversed the generous terms offered foreign capital in the last years of the Punto Fijo era (the *apertura petrolera*; see Mommer, 2003).

Maisanta delivered an overwhelming victory because it made an extraordinary effort to mobilize the citizenry. Almost 10 million Venezuelans voted, 3 million more than in the national election of July 2000 and 70 percent of the eligible population. Hundreds of thousands of Venezuelans, mostly drawn from the ranks of the poor, were persuaded to obtain or replace lost identity cards. Colombians who had migrated in the boom years before 1990 finally sought citizenship and were eligible to cast their votes. On both sides, voter education campaigns instructed citizens on how to make sure they were registered, locate the correct polling place, and prevent fraud. According to figures from the CNE (www.cne.gov.ve [accessed December 22, 2004]), the number of registered voters increased from just below 12.2 million in November 2003 to over 14 million nine months later.

Campaign propaganda appeared across the country. In Caracas, "No" signs were most prominent in the west, fluttering from ranchos in the barrios hugging the hillsides and in huge housing blocks such as the militant *23 de enero*. In the more affluent eastern suburbs, especially where the capital imperceptibly sprawls across the border dividing the Federal District from the neighboring state of Miranda, "Sí" signs were more visible, reflecting the class polarized nature of the contest. Venezuelans living overseas, mostly Yes voters, traveled by air to consulates to vote. On election day, voters on both sides, awakened by bugle calls and knocks on the door by organizers, turned out in massive numbers to line up at the polls before dawn. Many waited seven or eight hours in the tropical sun, giving the world images resembling the lengthy, winding queues that were indelibly stamped on our memories when South Africans voted for the first time after the collapse of apartheid.

Political polarization formed around race, not just class. Venezuelan social structures have long been fluid. *Pardos* (people of partially African descent) and *mestizos* have found their way into the ranks of the elite, but the visible face of the opposition is strikingly white. Chávez, in contrast, has the face of Venezuela *popular*, Afro-Indian as much as European. Race is of course as much a social construction as a biological given. Chavistas conceive themselves as the inheritors of a deeply imbedded tradition of populist caudillism emblematic of the bloody nineteenth-century Federal War. There is little doubt that Chávez's slogan "¡No volverán!" evoked in many Venezuelans resistance to a return to power of a discredited ruling class that not only lived differently but in their minds' eye *looked* different.

ELECTORAL OBSERVATION, LEGITIMACY, AND INSTITUTIONAL AUTONOMY

The agreement between the CD and the government in May 2003 to utilize the recall provisions of the constitution and the decision to allow the "repair" of signatures ruled invalid by the CNE were both fostered by pressure and mediation from (among others) the Organization of American States (OAS) and the Carter Center. These two organizations also took on an important responsibility as the key international observers. Their role in negotiating compromises and undertaking verification of the fairness of the vote was bitterly criticized by some Chavistas (though not by Chávez himself). Some well-known international leftist intellectuals contended that the OAS and the Carter Center were preparing the ground for supporting a charge of fraud in the event of a Chávez victory.

Alexander Cockburn, in *The Nation* (July 12, 2004), accused the OAS and former U.S. President Jimmy Carter of acting on behalf of the opposition to exert "enormous pressure on the country's independent National Electoral Council during the signature-gathering and verification process," describing their actions as part of a plan to "save the rich." James Petras, writing in *CounterPunch* (July 8, 2004), argued,

> Behind the simple and humane façade, Carter has a strategy to reverse progressive regimes and undermine insurgent democrats. Carter and his "team" from his Center probe and locate weaknesses among insecure democrats, particularly those under threat by US-backed opponents and thus vulnerable to Carter's appeals to be "pragmatic" and "realistic"—meaning his barely disguised arguments to accept fraudulent electoral results and gross US electoral intervention.

Despite these fears and warnings, the OAS and Carter confirmed the validity of the results, as a consequence attracting bitter criticism now from the CD. The lesson to be drawn is not that election monitoring or support for "civil society" by such organizations is always benign or is unrelated to the exercise of imperial hegemony. I would suggest that their role exemplifies a typical characteristic of a liberal, capitalist political order, its reliance on the "relative autonomy" (Poulantzas, 1980) of political authority. This relative autonomy of liberal politics sometimes opens space for counterimperialist projects. It was the ability of Chávez to take advantage of contradictions in the capitalist world order that allowed Bolivarianism to triumph over the obstacles posed by outside intervention and the limits of the electoral process. It would be mistaken to believe that such space always exists, but in this case Chávez recognized the opportunity and articulated it to his supporters by using the analogy to the Battle of Santa Inés.

Many critics charge that Chávez won the election the old-fashioned populist way—by buying votes with massive social spending made possible by a
new oil boom. Part of the new oil policy was the creation of a lucrative social
fund by which Petroleos de Venezuela (PDVSA) directly provided money to
subsidize popular markets and to support "missions" aimed at improving
health care and education services in the barrios. Patients were given leaflets
and pro-Chávez T-shirts promoting a No vote at the health clinics set up in
poor areas by the *Barrio Adentro* program, which deploys mostly Cuban medical personnel to provide health services. However, access to services was not
made dependent on allegiance to Chávez as is typical under personalist clientelism. The opposition, lacking any program of its own, found itself promising not to dismantle these programs in the future, a proposition hardly credi-
ble given the shrill attacks on "Cubanization."

The ability of the Chávez government to deliver services in the barrios was
crucial to gaining support from the poorest sectors of the population, especially the informal sectors. Paul Oquist argues that the inability of the Sandinistas to incorporate this sector, which expanded considerably in the context of war and economic privation imposed on Nicaragua by the United
States, significantly contributed to their defeat in 1990. In Managua this fast-
growing sector came to be known as the "apron bourgeoisie" because it enjoyed a relative boom due to profitable trading in the black and gray markets,
which in turn often expanded due to official price controls (1992: 10–20). In
Caracas, tensions between Freddy Bernal, the Chavista mayor of the municipality of Libertador, and ambulant street vendors *(buhoneros)* sometimes escalated into street violence. This tendency has been counteracted to some degree by other factors, including Chávez's insistence that the street vendors are
part of *el soberano*, the extension of citizenship to the many Colombian immigrants working in this sector, and the expansion of neighborhood services.
This combination of factors may explain why Bernal, despite several tense incidents of conflict with Bolivarian grassroots groups, managed to get re-
elected with 70 percent of the vote in October.

If the government campaign abused the privileges of incumbency, its advantage was offset by the opposition's overwhelming support from the private media. Venezuela's four private television networks and most prestigious
newspapers went beyond mere support of the opposition; with the complete
collapse of the old parties, the media themselves became the most institutionalized force of opposition. Not merely biased, they actively organized efforts to oust Chávez via coup, work stoppages, and recall. Certainly, such a
prejudiced information system is incompatible with the basic principle of democracy even in its weak pluralist form.

The international media devoted much attention to the opposition claim of
bias on the part of the CNE and neglected the Chavistas' claims of widespread

fraudulent practices by the CD, including manufacturing of identity cards and pressure from employers. Chávez made many concessions that were questioned by his more militant supporters. For example, in order to ensure that a victory for Yes would result in a new election, the original date was moved from August 19 to August 15. Otherwise, Vice President José Vicente Rangel would have finished the term.

All of the compromises, observation teams, and civic involvement did not prevent the opposition from claiming fraud after August 15. Perhaps no other outcome could have been expected. One of the CD's most influential members, Súmate ("Join Up"), a middle-class organization funded by the NED, had organized an exit poll that purportedly showed a Yes victory. Few independent observers put much credence in the Súmate results, which were very likely skewed by overrepresentation of voters in areas where volunteers were willing to conduct their interviews. Even polls conducted by U.S. public relations companies and by firms linked to the opposition, many of which had shown low levels of approval for the president throughout 2003 and early 2004, were in the final weeks of the recall campaign predicting defeat for the CD.[7]

Having thoroughly routed the opposition, President Chávez faced difficult choices on how to proceed. He proclaimed himself open to dialogue with the opposition but made it clear that negotiations were contingent on recognition of the legitimacy of the recall results. Against all empirical evidence, some sectors of the opposition, including Henry Ramos Allup, the leader of Acción Democrática (Democratic Action—AD), persisted in charging fraud. Some influential Venezuelan intellectuals, including Moisés Naím, editor of *Foreign Policy*, echoed these charges (e.g., Naím, 2004). The largest business confederation, the Federacíon de Cámaras y Asociación de Comercio y Producción (Federation of Chambers and Associations of Commerce and Production—FEDECAMARAS), recognizing the fruitlessness of this approach, seemed ready to deal with the new situation more pragmatically. Ramos found himself forced to participate in the October elections when AD's labor leadership made it clear that it was not inclined to desert the electoral battlefield.

Some zealous Chavistas compromised the integrity of the recall process by recording the names and personal data of signers of the recall petition on a computer CD. An MVR Assembly member, Luis Tascón, posted the list on a website. The "Tascón list" was used to blacklist signers, a practice that President Chávez himself condemned in asking that the list be "buried." Of course, similar practices pervaded the pre-1998 regime, and it is tempting to see the tactic as a justifiable defense against counterrevolutionaries. However, the abuse of the petition process in this way undermines one of the key participatory mechanisms designed to empower ordinary citizens in the Bolivarian Constitution. Besides sowing mistrust about the electoral rules of the game for future elections, such a list may next time be used to intimidate democratic sectors within the revolutionary movement from exercising their right to hold representatives accountable. Given the absence of opposition in the National Assembly elected in December 2005, such a mechanism became even more important in ensuring the protagonistic character of democracy in Venezuela.

CLASS POLARIZATON IN THE RECALL AND REGIONAL ELECTIONS

In Venezuela, the abstention rate in elections is vested with considerable significance for legitimacy. In the first four elections after the inauguration of the Punto Fijo era in 1958, abstention remained below 8 percent, a major factor in the defeat of the leftist guerrilla insurgency of the 1960s. When abstention rose to 18.1 percent in the 1988 election, many observers felt that it signaled a serious deterioration in regime legitimacy, and indeed the Caracazo riots of 1989 seemed to confirm that judgment. The abstention rate in the recall exceeded the low rates of the early decades of the Punto Fijo era, but the circumstances were somewhat different. Many Venezuelans had dropped out of the system in the interim. The country had experienced massive migration from rural to urban areas. New migrants were separated from their previous political moorings in the countryside; they and their descendants in the barrios were never as fully integrated into the Punto Fijo party system as were the working and the middle class (Myers, 2004; Canache, 2004). Many barrio residents lacked the necessary identity cards or had not voted in a decade. Survey evidence also suggests that abstention in the 1990s rose in part because of Chávez's call for voters to stay away from the polls and because of "imbedded systemic dissatisfaction, not lack of motivation to participate due to confidence in the system" (Gil Yepes, 2004: 244). Comando Maisanta brought many poor voters back into the system, but nearly 30 percent of the electorate abstained from a remarkably polarized, high-stakes contest.

At the same time, the turnout demonstrated a mobilization capacity that had been thrown into doubt by low rates of participation in earlier referendums. In December 2000 less than 25 percent of voters had gone to the polls in a referendum on reorganizing the union movement. Although a large majority voted for the reorganization, the low turnout suggested that mass support for sweeping away all aspects of Punto Fijo, in this case the power of the Confederación de Trabajadores de Venezuela (Confederation of Venezuelan Workers—CTV), was not unlimited. Throughout 2002 and 2003, the president's falling approval ratings seemed evidence of popular disillusionment and frustration with continued economic hardship and high social insecurity. To some degree, this perception was contradicted by the response from the barrios to the short-lived coup of April 2002, but would *el soberano* rally to Chávez's defense when the attempt to oust him was undertaken constitutionally? The failures of Comando Ayacucho gave the CD reason to believe that Chávez was vulnerable.

Although the abstention rate did not match the lows achieved in the early years of Punto Fijo, the turnout in the 1998, 2000, and 2004 elections reversed a secular rise in abstention over the preceding 25 years, and the 9.8 million voters who went to the polls in August 2004 represented an increase of more than 3.2 million voters over the 2000 contest. The rise in electoral participation is even more remarkable when one considers that prior to the recall many Venezuelans had never bothered to register or replace lost identity cards. The lowest rates of electoral participation were typically found in the barrios, the areas where President Chávez tended to achieve his highest levels of support, but the obstacles, sociological and legal, were also highest in these areas.

The president's analogy to the Battle of Santa Inés proved apt. As we have already seen, the turnout rate in the recall was nearly 50 percent higher than in the "mega-elections" of July 2000; it was 3.5 times higher than in the labor referendum of December 2000. However, it should be noted that the opposition also contributed to the higher turnout. Despite the increased turnout, the *percentage* of the national vote won by Chávez in 2004 was only a little higher than what he had achieved in 1998 and very similar to that achieved in 2000.

The mobilization of the electorate was clearly spurred by a process of class struggle, which manifested itself in surveys of voter intentions. The most comprehensive analysis of voters was conducted on behalf of the CNE by the opinion research company IMEDIOPSA in late June 2004. The IMEDIOPSA study found the No option significantly ahead, in this case 52.5 percent to 39.2 percent, if anything somewhat underestimating the size of the eventual Chávez victory. In six large states of the coastal highlands plus Caracas (Libertador) and the industrial state of Bolívar, voters in the two poorest categories (D and E) indicated their intention to vote No by large majorities (see table 9.1), quite in contrast to voters in the A, B, and C categories. Unfortunately, June data were unavailable for Zulia, the most populous state, which includes the country's second city, Maracaibo, and is home to some the oldest and most significant installations of the oil industry. However, in a poll done in early August by the same company, respondents in the D and E categories showed a similarly strong preference for retaining the president, while voters in the higher income categories strongly favored Sí.

While a good deal of attention has been focused on the support of the urban poor (e.g., Canache, 2004), it is worth noting that Chávez's advantage among the poorest voters was even more pronounced in eight predominantly rural states. Although a majority of Venezuelans live in the more urbanized

Table 9.1. Voter Preferences for Recall Election by State Type, Gender, Class, Summer 2004

Type of State and Preference	Class					Gender	
	A-B No. (%)[d]	C No. (%)	D No. (%)	E No. (%)	Total No. (%)	Men No. (%)	Women No. (%)
Urban[a]							
No (%)[e]	19 (19)	148 (34)	581 (64)	584 (64)	1,329 (54)	641 (52)	642 (52)
Yes (June)	62 (75)	256 (58)	365 (24)	223 (24)	906 (37)	442 (36)	493 (40)
Rural[b]							
No	19 (20)	220 (44)	691 (64)	752 (71)	1,681 (62)	864 (63)	818 (61)
Yes (June)	56 (69)	229 (46)	294 (27)	237 (22)	816 (30)	415 (30)	401 (30)
Andean[c]							
No	15 (50)	74 (46)	183 (50)	185 (54)	457 (51)	258 (56)	199 (45)
Yes (June)	11 (37)	71 (44)	149 (41)	122 (35)	354 (39)	163 (35)	191 (43)
Zulia[d]							
No	3 (25)	17 (25)	89 (54)	120 (70)	229 (55)	118 (56)	111 (55)
Yes (Aug.)	8 (67)	49 (73)	73 (44)	47 (28)	177 (43)	89 (42)	88 (43)

Source: IMEDIOPSA Survey for the CNE, June 2004, Aug. 2004 for Zulia.
[a] Anzoátegui, Aragua, Bolívar, Carabobo, Lara, Miranda, Vargas, Municipality of Libertador (central Caracas, in no state). Data for Zulia was unavailable for June.
[b] Apure, Barinas, Cojedes, Falcón, Guárico, Monagas, Portuguesa, Sucre, Yaracuy
[c] Mérida, Táchira, Trujillo.
[d] Zulia results are for August.
[e] Percentages do not add up to 100 because "Undecided" and "Not Voting" are included in the base total for June poll, "Undecided"("No report or "not voting") for August poll (Zulia).

states, the depth of support for Chávez in rural areas may provide a reserve of strength in future, more contested elections, especially if the government continues its land reform policies. The exception here would be the three Andean states, where class is correlated more weakly with preferences on the recall. This may be a reflection of the more traditional regional culture, which is more mestizo (European and Indian) and less African-influenced.

A first test of the capacity of the Bolivarians to sustain their electoral mobilization capacity after the recall came in the October 2004 regional elections to elect governors and mayors. On the surface, the results seemed unambiguously positive for Chávez. Chavista candidates won twenty-one of twenty-three governorships and the metropolitan Caracas government. Pro-government candidates won control of over 70 percent of city governments. The Chavistas won in the states of Carabobo[8] and Miranda, opposition strongholds. Miranda was an especially bitter loss for the CD, as Governor Enrique Mendoza, a possible future presidential candidate, was defeated. The opposition did retain control of the mayoralties in some middle-class municipalities (Chacao, El Hatillo, Baruta, Los Salias, El Páez) in Miranda, but it lost four mayoralties that it had held in municipalities that had voted heavily No (see tables 9.2 and 9.3).

Certainly internal divisions and demoralization hurt the opposition; some sectors advocated abstention, while others, including Acción Demócratica and Primero Justicia, a middle-class neoliberal party strongest in metropolitan Caracas, participated in the hope of establishing their credentials as the leading anti-Chávez force.[9] However, divisions and frustration on the opposition side do not account for the precipitous decline in turnout. Rates of turnout in areas that voted heavily No were unimpressive. A certain degree of electoral fatigue was to be expected, but there were other factors at work that ought to give pause to anyone who would interpret the results as an unambiguous victory for Chavismo.

The discredited Commando Ayacucho had designated nominees for the regional elections, in many instances imposing candidates on a resistant local base. Despite appeals from grassroots leaders, Chávez opted to go forward with these same nominations, pleading insufficient time to organize an internal process. The Chavista electorate mostly complied with its leader's endorsements. However, as tables 9.2, 9.3, and 9.4 indicate, Chavista gubernatorial and mayoral candidates generally attracted many fewer voters than had cast No ballots six weeks earlier. In some cases, the opposition mobilized a higher percentage of the Yes vote total for its mayoral candidates than Chavistas did with regard to the No total.

High abstention was notable in Bólivar, the Capital District, and Vargas, all areas where there existed significant conflict between grassroots activists and Chavista politicians. In Vargas, the imposition of an MVR candidate generated

Table 9.2.   No Vote in the Recall and Vote for Governor in October Elections by State

State	Vote for No		Abstention (%)	Gubernatorial Vote (GV)		Abstention (%)	GV/ No Vote[a]
	No.	(%)		No.	(%)		
National	5,800,629	59.1	30.1	NA	NA	est. 55	
Amazonas[b]	28,522	70.3	32.3	NA	NA	NA	.71
Anzoategui	261,877	54.1	32.3	187,209	57.3	51.2	.86
Apure	103,642	67.6	28.8	88,587	66.9	37.7	.53
Aragua	413,174	68.0	28.5	217,796	67.7	58.7	.73
Barinas	186,901	69.2	30.3	135,674	76.2	49.7	.50
Bolívar	293,027	66.4	34.1	146,329	58.8	61.0	.72
Carabobo	435,244	56.8	31.2	311,189	51.3	43.8	.69
Cojedes	78,143	67.0	27.8	54,142	56.1	36.8	.83
D. Amacuro	35,446	70.4	38.5	29,441	61.3	38.3	NA
Metro Caracas[c]	NA	NA	NA	388,356	60.3	NA	.61
Falcón	193,639	57.2	29.6	118,718	59.5	56.0	.63
Guarico	183,007	71.0	30.3	115,010	78.5	54.5	

Lara	424,394	64.8	27.5	289,945	73.6	54.3	.68
Mérida	176,438	53.8	26.2	135,895	60.7	48.5	.77
Miranda	542,095	50.9	28.4	345,752	51.9	54.2	.64
Monagas	186,763	61.0	27.9	144,326	58.3	40.8	.77
N. Esparta[d]	81,887	<50.0	29.6	56,350	43.5	42.4	.69
Portuguesa	226,569	72.9	26.8	128,370	59.0	46.6	.57
Sucre	208,865	66.9	35.3	140,407	62.2	50.9	.67
Táchira	209,818	50.6	29.2	169,587	57.5	48.5	.81
Trujillo	179,329	66.3	28.0	101,141	54.3	48.3	.56
Vargas	91,184	64.2	37.0	38,920	55.2	64.2	.43
Yaracuy	136,099	60.2	26.4	101,481	50.7	32.9	.75
Zulia[d]	605,383	53.1	32.9	391,927	44.4	47.7	.65

Source: Dirección de Estadísticas Electorales, CNE. October election data are preliminary results.

[a] GV/No Vote yields a decimal equivalent to the proportion (percentage) of the August No vote obtained by the government-supported candidate in the October 31 regions.

[b] Amazonas held its gubernatorial election four months later.

[c] Metropolitan Caracas includes Libertador, also known as the Capital District, and three other municipalities in the State of Miranda.

[d] Opposition candidates won in these states.

Table 9.3. Sustaining Electoral Mobilization from August Recall to the October 31 Mayoral Elections in the State of Miranda and the Municipality of Libertador (Caracas)

Municipality	Vote in August		Abstention Rate (%)	Vote for Leading Opposition Candidate in October		Abstention Rate (%)	Mayoral Vote/ Yes or No[a]
	No.	(%)		No.	(%)		Yes or No[a]
Majority for Yes							
Baruta	113,679	79.4	25.3	71,160	78.8	52.9	62.6
Chacao	39,901	80.0	31.0	26,876	79.6	53.4	67.6
Carrizal[b]	10,741	52.9	26.0	3,582[b]	36.3	50.5	33.3 (69)[b]
El Hatillo	24,014	82.1	22.5	7,183	38.6	50.7	29.6
Los Salias	24,014	71.0	21.3	14,455	65.1	47.2	60.2
Sucre[c]	131,781	52.9	31.6	67,191[c]	50.9	60.5	51.0
Majority for No							
Acevedo[d]	20,971	69.6	28.3	10,294	47.3	45.9	49.1
Andrés Bello[d]	6,442	66.9	26.0	3,904	50.1	38.1	60.1
Brion[d]	13,126	64.4	26.3	8,292	56.3	45.0	63.2
Buroz	6,233	69.7	25.6	4,710	67.7	41.1	75.6

Cristobal Rojas	25,254	69.9	25.4	11,476	49.4	48.8	45.4
Guaicaipuro	60,239	56.7	28.8	33,746	51.6	53.5	56.0
Independencia	35,487	77.6	30.5	15,351	50.4	51.4	43.3
Lander[d]	35,035	76.5	26.7	15,544	52.9	44.5	43.8
Páez[e]	8,424	62.9	27.8	2,725[e]	23.6	35.7	32.3 (67)[e]
Paz Castillo	22,510	77.5	34.0	11,866	57.2	51.4	52.7
Pedro Gual[d]	4,923	59.0	23.9	3,444	46.8	31.9	70.0
Plaza	50,248	66.5	26.1	17,095	40.7	56.9	34.0
Simón Bolívar	10,844	74.5	23.6	3,516	32.4	41.2	32.4
Urdaneta	26,236	71.9	32.7	10,764	42.3	50.8	40.6
Zamora[e]	34,531	59.0	28.9	10,109	29.3	55.3	29.3 (50)[e]
Libertador	516,840	56.0	30.7	284,085	73.9	68.1	55.0

Source: Dirección de Estadísticas Electorales, CNE; preliminary results for October.

[a] Percentage of the August Yes [No] vote obtained by the leading opposition candidate in the October mayoral election.

[b] No vote for mayor was reported in Carrizal; the vote for deputy to the state assembly is used instead. AD and Primer Justicia (MPI) divided the opposition vote, with MPI winning; combined opposition vote was 69 percent of the Yes vote.

[c] José Vicente Rangel, MVR incumbent and son of the vice president, defeated an MPI candidate. His vote was equivalent to 62 percent of the No vote.

[d] An incumbent opposition mayor was replaced by a Chavista.

[e] Divided Chavista candidacies; the combined vote as percent of the No vote is shown in parentheses. Opposition (AD) won mayorality in Páez with 92 percent of the Yes vote.

highly visible resistance from electoral battle units. The government alliance won the gubernatorial election, but it barely mustered 43 percent of the No vote total in this heavily urban, poor coastal state. In Sucre, a very poor agricultural state, the incumbent Chavista governor was a former *puntofijista* politician from the Movimiento al Socialismo (Movement toward Socialism—MAS) with a reputation for corruption. He survived the vote largely because of the president's backing and because divisions within the opposition were greater than those within Chavismo. Not atypically, he won comfortably even though he obtained only two-thirds of the No vote. In the hotly contested governors' races in Miranda, Monagas, and Carabobo, opposition candidates retained a higher proportion of the recall vote totals than did the government candidates. In Miranda, where divisions in the opposition were exceptionally bitter, the Chavista candidate defeated his opponent (Mendoza) by the narrowest of margins.

Mayoral races in the Caracas area also showed a mixed pattern. Chavistas wrested back control of the metropolitan Caracas regional government and retained control over Libertador (Caracas proper), but overall abstention soared past 68 percent in the latter case. Chavista victories were sometimes due to idiosyncratic factors, such as divided opposition candidacies. In one case, Municipio Páez, a divided opposition defeated equally divided government forces. Only in a few cases did the MVR far surpass the opposition in holding onto the recall voter base. Abstention rates were very high across the board. Relatively low rates of abstention (29 to 33 percent) could be found in both opposition (e.g., Carrizal and El Hatillo) and government (e.g., Simón Bolívar and Plaza) strongholds. Conversely, high rates (over 50 percent) could be also found in strongholds on both sides.

The opposition's most important victory by far was in Zulia, the most populous state and largest oil producer, with a strong regional tradition. Dominated by the oil industry and the site of intense conflict over land reform, Zulia was an uncertain battleground in the recall, but it ultimately went narrowly for No. In the regional elections, Chavistas held onto the mayor's office in Maracaibo by a scant 199 votes, and electoral abstention was over 49 percent, up from 32.4 percent in August. The Chavistas had few other happy results. The incumbent opposition governor, a former member of AD, Manuel Rosales, defeated a retired general, Alberto Gutiérrez, for whom Chávez had campaigned heavily. Votes for Rosales totaled over 91 percent of the Yes total, while Gutiérrez tallied only 65 percent of the No vote.

If we examine selected mayoral races, we see that Chavista hegemony is clearly weaker in Zulia than in any other area of the country, even Miranda (see tables 9.3 and 9.4).[10] Although the No option won in several Zulia municipalities (e.g., Colón, Simón Bolívar, Cabimas), majorities were generally below national levels. In other oil towns (e.g., Santa Rita, Lagunillas, Val-

Table 9.4. Sustaining Electoral Mobilization of the Chavista Vote from August Recall to the October 31 Mayoral Elections in Selected Municipalities.

Municipality	No Vote		Abstention Rate (%)	Voting Trends from the Recall to the October 31 Mayoral Elections		Abstention Rate (%)	M/No[a]
	No.	(%)		No.	(%)		
Zulia							
Cabimas[b]	58,250	56.0	27.2	33,095	42.3	43.1	56.8
Colón[b]	16,977	57.3	35.7	6,810	46.9	27.0	40.1
Lagunillas[b]	28,325	44.3	30.9	11,542	25.9	50.8	40.7
Mara[c]	33,084	65.3	33.1	7,900	18.5	44.2	23.9
Maracaibo[‡]	228,924	48.6	32.4	171,648	49.6	49.7	75.0
San Francisco	69,528	59.9	36.3	24,529	26.8	49.7	35.3
Santa Rita[b]	10,389	49.0	27.5	6,904	35.4	35.5	66.5
Simón Bolívar[b]	9,227	52.1	28.2	5,371	36.7	39.0	58.2
Valmore-Rodríguez[b]	10,373	48.5	30.4	5,170	43.8	45.1	49.8
Bolívar							
Caroní[c]	150,751	68.2	31.2	55,081	49.4	62.8	36.5
Heres[d]	65,946	40.1	34.0	21,414	35.5	61.4	32.5
Anzoátegui							
Anaco[b]	19,661	54.3	36.1	12,882	44.7	47.7	65.5
Freites[b]	14,246	53.3	29.8	7,611	36.0	43.1	53.4
Monagas							
Maturín[b,d]	96,356	60.7	28.3	75,208	59.8	42.3	78.1
Piar[b]	11,624	64.8	25.4	10,492	68.8	35.9	90.3
Santa Barbara[b]	3,175	64.2	22.9	2,697	59.6	28.9	84.9

Source: Dirección de Estadísticas Electorales, CNE.
[a] Percentage of the August No vote obtained by the leading opposition candidate in the October mayoral election.
[b] Municipalities located near or in significant oil fields.
[c] Industrial areas: petrochemical in Mara, metallurgical in Caroní.
[d] Capital with industrial areas.

more Rodríguez), the Yes option actually won. Where the No option triumphed handily was in more industrialized municipalities such as Mara (65.3 percent), home of a major petrochemical complex just north of Maracaibo, and in San Francisco (59.9 percent), a large, poor suburb south of the city.

Undoubtedly, elections in these regions were affected by fallout from the defeat of the oil company work stoppage of 2002–2003 and the subsequent discharge of eighteen thousand PDVSA employees. Many of these employees, disproportionately from the skilled and professional sectors, were evicted from homes that PDVSA provided as a benefit of employment and were bitterly aligned against the president. Workers who stayed on the job performed heroic feats to restore production and were deeply committed to Chávez, but precisely because they fought in such fashion to defend the Bolivarian Revolution they could not be taken for granted. In the October mayoral elections, in several cases rifts appeared between government-endorsed candidates and those linked to the labor movement. In Colón, San Francisco, Mara, Cabimas, Santa Rita, Valmore Rodríguez, Simón Rodríguez, and Lagunillas, government-endorsed candidates for a variety of reasons (division, higher levels of abstention, poor candidates) registered far less than 50 percent of the No vote total. Besides losing the gubernatorial race, the forces of Chavismo failed (outside of Maracaibo) to carry most municipalities near oil and gas fields (See table 9.4).

In the period prior to 1998 the labor sector was the site of significant movements to democratize Venezuelan society and develop an alternative to *puntofijismo* (Hellinger, 2003). This fact has been obscured outside of Venezuela by the alignment of top leaders, notably Carlos Ortega of the old CTV, with the CD and its involvement in the coup of April 2002. Divisions within Causa R, the political party that spearheaded that movement, submerged this project, but parts of the Nuevo Sindicalismo (New Unionism) movement survived. In addition, significant portions of the CTV have been able to adapt to new circumstances (Ellner, 2003), and leaders of unions aligned with the Bolivarian Unión Nacional de Trabajadores (UNT) have proven themselves far from passive in relations with the government.

One must be cautious about drawing conclusions about the behavior of unionized workers. The Chavistas triumphed handily in the recall election in the eastern oil-producing states of Anzoátegui and Monagas and in central states associated with manufacturing. The No option also carried Zulia, but it is worth noting that in the IMEDIOPSA survey, respondents in the C category overwhelmingly indicated that they would vote to recall Chávez. Many of these respondents would have been skilled workers and professionals employed (or formerly employed) by the state oil company. Victory for No in Zulia more than anywhere else depended on overwhelming support for the president among the poorest voters. In Bolívar, where the New Unionism is strongest, Chavista candidates won the governorship and most mayoral races, but they carried only one-third of the No vote over to the local contests in the most industrialized and urban parts of the state (see table 9.4). Everywhere in the country, voters in the working-poor (D) classification were slightly less likely to vote No than were the poorest (E) Venezuelans.

The available data do not permit definitive conclusions about the overall tendency of employees in the formal sector, especially unionized workers. It would seem that these workers gave President Chávez a conditional vote of confidence in the recall, perhaps recognizing it as a way of defending the Bolivarian Constitution, blocking the return of the reactionary forces of the past, and continuing the material benefits delivered to their communities. However, like the activists who were mobilized into Bolivarian Circles and some middle-class groups, organized workers remained deeply suspicious of political parties, including the MVR. Such an interpretation would be consistent with Steve Ellner's observations (2003: 176–178) that the surest supporters of Chávez are the urban poor and that "the labor movement posed more of a challenge to the government than did the political parties of the opposition" (2003: 177). I would add that poor Venezuelans in the hinterland, though less numerous, are even more secure bastions of Chavismo.

ELECTORAL POLITICS AND REVOLUTIONARY CHANGE IN VENEZUELA

In her comparative study of the Nicaraguan experience, Rose Spalding enumerated five characteristics that make it easier for a revolutionary regime "to negotiate with economic elites, even as it pursues redistributive reform" (1994: 191): weak oligarchical control, an organizational void in the private sector, relatively low threat perceptions among local propertied classes, firm political consolidation of the regime, and sustained economic growth. Four of these conditions seem to exist in Venezuela, which perhaps explains why the compromises needed to hold the recall could take place. Seven decades of oil-based rentier politics certainly left Venezuela with a weak traditional oligarchy. The collapse of the Punto Fijo party system left the private sector in an organizational void, without an effective vehicle for contesting Chávez. Besides serving to some degree as a prophylactic against U.S. intervention, Venezuela's oil export economy provided, if not sustained economic growth, resources to undertake redistributive reform. Early on, outside of politicians from the Punto Fijo system, it is doubtful that most Venezuelan elites fully perceived the threat to their interests. By the time that became evident, with the radical decree laws of November 2001, Chávez had already swept aside many of the political structures through which these elites had defended their interests before 1998.

With his victory in the recall, Chávez may have achieved the fifth of Spalding's criteria, political consolidation, but that does not mean that Bolivarianism has achieved hegemony. Four of ten Venezuelans who voted opted for recall. Three in ten eligible voters abstained. Given the rates of poverty in Venezuela, these sectors must include large numbers of those poor Venezuelans called "el soberano" by the president. And within the Bolivarian movement there are signs of internal opposition. Many of these activists are the ones who ensured that the recall, as an election, would serve as an accelerator of, not a brake on revolution.

Some sectors of international and national capital have sought to negotiate with the Chávez government. The oil, banking, and construction sectors all had material reasons to repair relations with a government that advocates incubating domestic petroleum-related businesses, funding massive housing construction, and absorbing excess liquidity by borrowing domestically. International investment firms such as Morgan Guarantee actually raised the nation's bond ratings after the recall. Oil consulting firms indicated that given the prevailing high prices and the prospect of improved political stability, the industry was prepared to accept the new rules of the game (including royalty payments) and do business.

After the recall, Chávez faced some important strategic decisions from a position of strength. A confrontational stance with capital risked economic and international isolation; too accommodating a stance risked sapping the revolution of its creativity and mass appeal. President Chávez gave indications that he interpreted his victory as a mandate to "deepen" the Bolivarian Revolution. For example, he ordered the armed forces to carry out a survey of unused land as part of an ambitious effort to replace unproductive *latifundios* with peasant cooperatives and resettled urban poor. This bold move risked violent confrontation with landowners and posed, as is the case with any agrarian reform, extraordinary challenges. It is one thing to redistribute land, another to provide credit, infrastructure, and secure markets in rural areas. High oil prices may provide a cushion in what will be a difficult transitional period, moderating the impact of economic disruptions that might otherwise try the patience of the electorate.

The opposition, we have seen, also increased its capacity to mobilize votes in the recall. It too failed to sustain this capacity, but should it be able to regain some of its mobilizational power it might be able to take advantage of the constitutional provisions allowing referendums, recalls, and initiatives. For example, one right-wing populist proposal is to distribute shares of PDVSA to individual citizens, a proposal that might be made attractive to a population that continues to experience serious privation. Such tactics are more promising for opponents to the extent that Bolivarian electoral mobilization declines toward the levels of 2000.

Politically, Chávez still faced the difficult task of consolidating an institutional vehicle for his revolutionary project. One legacy of Punto Fijo democracy is deeply rooted antiparty sentiment. Chávez won in 1998 and 2000 as the candidate of the MVR in an alliance, the Polo Patriótico (PP). For the first three years, he leaned heavily on the political sagacity of Luis Miquilena, a leftist skilled in the bargaining and trade-offs of the clientelist Punto Fijo era. The MVR seemed then to have eclipsed the Movimiento Bolivariano Revolucionario (Revolutionary Bolivarian Movement—MBR–200). But the MVR under Miquilena became more a legislative faction than a vehicle for social mobilization, so Chávez in 2001 sought to reinvigorate the MBR–200 (prompting Miquilena's departure) and promoted the formation of Bolivarian Circles, popular assemblies, a process aided by the mass response to the coup of April 11, 2002 (see Hansen, Hawkins, and Seawright, 2003). The formation of Maisanta was a further step in that direction, but the tensions between mobilization politics and electoral politics reasserted themselves in the regional elections of October. They were visible again in the process of choosing progovernment candidates for the Assembly elections of 2005.

Roberto Hernández Montoya (2004), a writer and president of the Rómulo Gallegos Center of Latin American Studies, argues that Venezuela's process has avoided the problem of "revolution degenerating into government." "We have overcome in Venezuela the dangers of Stalinism or the tragedy of the so-called Democratic Kampuchea, led by Pol Pot. And also, on the other side of hubris, we have overcome the poltroonery of social democracy, as in Venezuela's Acción Democrática and [Spain's Social Democratic] Felipe González." In other words, thus far Chavismo has not settled for the kind of reformism that eschews deeper social and economic reforms promised by revolutionary movements.

Electoral politics have played a role in avoiding either unwanted result, but there is no guarantee that they will continue to forestall either tragedy or torpor. Venezuela remains extraordinarily polarized, and authoritarian tendencies can be seen in both camps. Furthermore, there remains a danger that elections could pull the revolution toward "poltroonery," that is, that they will become once again occasions for opportunist politicians to exercise clientelism and to co-opt mass democracy. One test for democracy in Venezuela will be whether the politicians and bureaucrats of the MVR convert the missions into patronage vehicles to cement their own control. The Bolivarian conception of protagonist democracy envisions an active civil society that is able to shape legislation and participate in choosing judges, human rights defenders, and ombudsmen. The institutional apparatus and legal structure for identifying authentic representatives of civil society will be difficult to create in a way that avoids corporatism and demobilization of activists who resisted the April 2002 coup and defeated the recall. It remains to be seen whether the

MVR or any other party can transform itself into a vehicle for popular recruitment and control over candidates and officials.

CONCLUSION

Should the vote of the engaged count more than the vote of the more passive elements, including those in whose name the revolution is made? If the hegemony of a revolutionary project is to be achieved, somehow, those who are to be liberated in a revolutionary process must become engaged in its defense at the ballot box, not just in the streets. In this study we have seen that the recall election of August 15, 2004, in Venezuela was extraordinarily class-polarized, especially around the dimension of living conditions and distribution of wealth. The working class more traditionally defined, which remains one center of power in Venezuela, seems less uniformly Chavista than the urban and rural poor. The triumph of Chávez shows that elections need not dampen revolutionary momentum. However, the results of the local elections that followed the recall indicate that maintaining this momentum depends on a continuing commitment to social justice and to creation of political institutions that make protagonist democracy a reality.

NOTES

1. The term "polyarchy" was coined by Robert Dahl (1971) to describe the structural characteristics of pluralist polities. William Robinson (1996) demonstrates the U.S. predilection for this type of weak democracy as was made especially clear in the cases of Chile, Nicaragua, the Philippines, and Haiti.

2. The historic program of the Frente Sandinista de Liberación Nacional (FSLN) envisioned a democracy predicated on combining representative democracy, participatory democracy, and individual rights. Its program incorporated an explicit commitment to "pluralism" as it broadened its alliance in the final struggle for power. In the first five years of the revolution, these principles took concrete form in the creation of mass organizations that were represented in a Council of State. In 1984, hoping to reinforce international legitimacy, the government held national elections, which it won overwhelmingly. Vanden and Prevost (1993: 92–97) argue that from that point on the regime moved steadily away from participatory principles toward the weaker pluralist form of democracy. The mass organizations were promised direct participation in the governing process, but by 1990 the FSLN had become a much more conventional political party. Aided greatly by the National Endowment for Democracy (NED) and other overt and covert operations by Washington, in the context of war fatigue, UNO successfully exploited the Sandinista failures.

3. The opposition's confidence in the chairman, Francisco Carrasquero, did not survive the process intact.

4. Regulations were reproduced by Venezuelanalysis on its website, www.venezuelanalysis .com/docs.php?dno=1003 (accessed December 20, 2004).

5. See "De los reparos," Article 31, *Normas para regular los procesos de revocatorios de mandates de cargos de elección popular*, September 25, 2003.

6. These recalls were still being disputed and had not been held by the end of 2004.

7. For example, the Datos poll conducted by Antonio Gil Yepes in late June showed Chávez winning 51 percent of the vote (See Sánchez, 2004).

8. Although no convincing direct evidence has surfaced, the opposition has the strongest circumstantial case for electoral fraud in Carabobo, where candidates associated with Salas Feo swept first position in each district for the state assembly, but Salas Feo himself lost.

9. In this respect, Primero Justicia clearly trumped AD among the middle class of the Caracas area, but it has yet to show that it can mobilize voters at the same national scale as even a greatly weakened AD.

10. One exception may be the small state of Nueva Esparta, dependent on a devastated tourist industry on Margarita Island and traditionally an AD stronghold.

REFERENCES

Canache, Damarys
2004 "Urban Poor and Political Order," pp. 33–49 in J. McCoy and D. J. Myers (eds.), *The Unravelling of Representative Democracy in Venezuela.* Baltimore, MD: Johns Hopkins University Press.

Dahl, Robert A.
1971 *Polyarchy: Participation and Opposition.* New Haven, CT: Yale University Press.

Ellner, Steve
2003 "Organized Labor and the Challenge of Chavismo," pp. 161–178 in S. Ellner and D. Hellinger (eds.), *Venezuelan Politics in the Chávez Era.* Boulder, CO: Lynne Rienner.

Gil Yepes, José Antonio
2004 "Public Opinion, Political Socialization, and Regime Stabilization," pp. 231–262 in J. McCoy and D. J. Myers (eds.), *The Unravelling of Representative Democracy in Venezuela.* Baltimore, MD: Johns Hopkins University Press.

Ginsberg, Benjamin
1982 *The Consequences of Consent: Elections, Citizen Control and Popular Acquiescence.* Reading, MA: Addison-Wesley.

Hansen, David R., Kirk A. Hawkins, and Jason Seawright
2003 "Dependent Civil Society: The *Circulos Bolivarianos* in Venezuela." Paper prepared for the 25th International Congress of the Latin American Studies Association, Las Vegas, NV, October 7–9.

Harnecker, Marta
2004 "After the Referendum Venezuela Faces New Challenges." *Monthly Review* 56 (November): 34–48. www.monthlyreview.org/1104harnecker.htm (accessed December 20, 2004).

Hellinger, Daniel
2003 "Political Overview: The Breakdown of *Puntofijismo*," pp. 27–54 in S. Ellner and D. Hellinger (eds.), *Venezuelan Politics in the Chávez Era.* Boulder, CO: Lynne Rienner.

Hernández Montoya, Roberto
2004 "How to Prevent Revolution from Degenerating into Government." *Venezuelanalysis.* www.venezuelanalysis.com (accessed December 20, 2004).

Martin, Jorge and William Sanabria
2004 "Venezuela's Presidential Recall Referendum." *In Defense of Marxism*, July 4. www.marxist.com/Latinam/venez_santaines_en.html (accessed December 20, 2004).

Mommer, Bernard
2003 "Subversive Oil," pp. 131–146 in S. Ellner and D. Hellinger (eds.), *Venezuelan Politics in the Chávez Era.* Boulder, CO: Lynne Rienner.
Myers, David J.
2004 "The Normalization of Punto Fijo Democracy," pp. 11–32 in J. McCoy and D. J. Myers (eds.), *The Unravelling of Representative Democracy in Venezuela.* Baltimore, MD: Johns Hopkins University Press.
Naím, Moisés
2004 "World View: Sad Hints of a Bloody Future." *Newsweek International*, August 30. www.msnbc.msn.com/id/5783808/site/newsweek (accessed January 9, 2005).
Oquist, Paul
1992 "Sociopolitical Dynamics of the 1990 Nicaraguan Elections," pp. 1–40 in V. Castro and G. Prevost (eds.), *The 1990 Elections in Nicaragua and Their Aftermath.* Lanham, MD: Rowman & Littlefield.
Pastor, Roberto Viciano and Rubén Martínez Dalmau
2001 *Cambio Político y Proceso Constituyente en Venezuela (1998–2000).* Caracas: Vadell Hermanos.
Poulantzas, Nicos
1980 *State, Power, Socialism.* London: New Left Books, Verso Edition.
Robinson, William I.
1992 *A Faustian Bargain: U.S. Intervention in the Nicaraguan Elections and American Foreign Policy in the Post–Cold War Era.* Boulder, CO: Westview.
1996 *Promoting Polyarchy: Globalization, US Intervention and Hegemony.* Cambridge, UK: Cambridge University Press.
Sánchez, Martin
2004 "New Polls Show Venezuela's Chavez Winning Recall Referendum." *Venezuelanalysis.* www.venezuelanalysis.com (accessed December 20, 2004).
Spalding, Rose
1994 *Capitalists and Revolution in Nicaragua: Opposition and Accommodation, 1979–1993.* Chapel Hill: University of North Carolina Press.
Vanden, Harry E. and Gary Prevost
1993 *Democracy and Socialism in Sandinista Nicaragua.* Boulder, CO: Lynne Rienner.

Chapter Ten

Confronting Hugo Chávez: U.S. "Democracy Promotion" in Latin America

Christopher I. Clement

After the overthrow of the dictatorship of General Marcos Pérez Jiménez in 1958, the two dominant parties in Venezuela, Acción Democrática (Democratic Action—AD) and Comité de Organización Política Electoral Independiente (Independent Electoral Political Organizing Committee—COPEI), agreed to mediate and alternate power through electoral mechanisms. The protracted political stability enjoyed by Venezuela's government came to an end in 1989 with massive protests against government-implemented austerity measures, which had contributed to declining standards of living. By 1992, the country faced two attempted military coups. Hugo Chávez, a key figure in the attempted coups, went on to win the 1998 presidential elections. Chávez promised to implement sweeping political reforms and expand political participation. His leadership not only contributed to the end of the domination of the AD and COPEI but also became a turning point in U.S.-Venezuelan relations.

Venezuela's third coup took place in April 2002. After the coup, news reports and political commentary highlighted the United States's long-standing displeasure with Hugo Chávez's leadership. Although the Bush administration denied involvement in the coup, it continued to provide advice and financial support to many of Chávez's opponents under what it considered "democracy promotion." Despite significant domestic popularity of the Chávez government and substantial political reform under his leadership, U.S. officials have interpreted Chávez's leadership and the ongoing events as a sign of deteriorating democracy in Venezuela. Few accounts have explained why the Bush administration believes that its criticism of Chávez, its initial support for the coup, and its continuing funding of his opponents advance rather than undermine democracy. This targeting of a democratically elected government raises serious questions about the objectives and content of U.S. democracy promotion in Latin America.

Some writers on U.S. foreign policy have suggested that recurrent images of Latin American peoples as temperamental, immature, and incapable of self-government have frequently served as pretext and justification for U.S. intervention in the region (Johnson, 1980; Hunt, 1987). Similarly, Martha Cottam has suggested that the U.S. public and its officials often ascribe negative moral traits to Latin American leaders when they come into conflict with U.S.-defined regional policies (Cottam, 1994). A wide assortment of cultural sources (e.g., literature, newspapers, and films) can serve as the materials for constructing U.S. foreign policy as having a noble and higher moral purpose. Recently, Roxanne Lynne Doty and Michael Shapiro have both emphasized the importance of the written and spoken narratives of U.S. leaders, bureaucrats, statesmen, and academicians in making U.S. foreign policy (Doty, 1996; Shapiro, 1988). These narratives provide a glimpse into the way U.S. officials and intellectuals construct the "realities" of politics and society in the Third World and advance the United States as ultimately progressive and democratic in its foreign-policy objectives.

Here I shed light on the argument of a prevalent intellectual discourse on democratic transitions that suggests a lack of confidence in party politics is responsible for turbulence and instability in "third-wave democracies" (i.e., countries undergoing democratic transitions). This discourse resonates well with the views of U.S. foreign-policy leaders and bureaucrats, who frequently employ rhetoric that justifies U.S. interventions as "prodemocratic." I also suggest that this parallel between intellectual discourse and foreign-policy rhetoric becomes especially visible when rifts occur between foreign leaders and U.S.-defined global security interests. The implications of these practices are critical for understanding how the Chávez government came to be branded "semiauthoritarian" and for examining the content of U.S. democracy promotion in Venezuela. In the conclusion, I address some of the assumptions behind U.S. democracy promotion and suggest that the ongoing intervention in Venezuela should make us cautious about U.S. toleration of democratic governments in the region.

WRITING DEMOCRACY PROMOTION IN LATIN AMERICA

Much of what Washington calls democracy promotion developed throughout the 1980s as a response to rapidly changing events in Latin America. A rising tide of protests and armed rebellions against other U.S.-backed dictatorships led prominent figures in the Reagan administration to believe that political change in Latin America was unavoidable. The National Endowment for Democracy (NED) was one instrument created to manage these changes so that the outcomes would be compatible with U.S. interests. With the backing of the Reagan administration, Congress established the NED in 1983 as an agency run by private individuals but funded by the government. In Chile, Assistant Secretary of State Elliot Abrams and other U.S. government officials worked through the NED to devise an electoral transfer of power from the Pinochet dictatorship to centrists in the opposition movement. The strategy was conceived by its proponents as a means for permitting the return to democracy and heading off a possible leftist overthrow of Pinochet. NED and other U.S. governmental funding of the United Nicaraguan Opposition (UNO) in Nicaragua's 1990 election also led to a victory that dislodged the U.S.-maligned Frente Sandinista de Liberación Nacional (Sandinista National Liberation Front—FSLN) (see Robinson, 1996). Elsewhere in Latin America, the relaxation of tensions with the Soviet Union and electoral victories by moderates led the Reagan and Bush Sr. administrations to view the return to democracy as compatible with U.S. interests (Carothers, 1993).

U.S. democracy promotion was and continues to be grounded in a new ideological zeal for democratic governance. Many U.S. officials presumed elections would yield moderate, civilian governments which would invariably back and enhance two key pillars of globalization: free market integration and U.S.-anchored security arrangements.[1] But as political liberalization expanded and included previously marginalized social actors throughout the 1990s, market liberalization faced greater contestation (Teichman, 2001). The rapid and deleterious effects of global economic integration contributed to the growth of militant labor and peasant groups and radicalized indigenous movements, which challenged traditional parties for political space (Veltmeyer, Petras, and Vieux, 1997: especially chapter 11). By the end of the decade, protests against political corruption and economic decline had fueled several attempted coups and pockmarked the region's transition to market democracy.

At the same time, leading intellectuals of democratic studies told tales of fragile and helpless democracies throughout the Third World and postcommunist societies in which weak or ineffective parties had failed to manage popular resentment. Unlike U.S. public officials, these intellectuals did not assume democracies automatically yielded regimes supportive of free market policies or the U.S.-backed world order. The literature of democratic studies emphasized the need for political institutions that could deliver the desired outcomes (see, e.g., Schmitter and Karl, 1996). The resuscitation and development of political parties were considered central to deepening the link between democratization, the free market, and international stability. At a conference sponsored by the NED, political parties, were declared "key institutions in all democracies," were reported to be "widely regarded as being in decline" (International Forum for Democratic Studies, 1996). The political scientist Juan

Linz asserted, "Today, in all countries of the world, there is no alternative to political parties in the establishment of democracy. No form of nonparty representation that has been advocated has ever produced democratic government" (International Forum for Democratic Studies, 1996). Peter Mair added, "However fragmented, weak, or undisciplined, however poorly rooted in society, however unstable and vociferous, parties are a very real and necessary part of the politics of new democracies" (International Forum for Democratic Studies, 1996).

In several academic publications underwritten by the NED, strong parties and deeper commitments to market reforms are sanctioned as the solution to turbulence and instability while resistance to either is censured as antidemocratic. In their study of political parties and democracy, Larry Diamond and Richard Gunther (2001: x) proceed by first objectifying societies they regard as lacking in deeply rooted democratic values. While noting that disaffection with political parties is widespread, they still insist that:

> [the] implications of disaffection are much more serious in countries where democracy is not consolidated—most of the third-wave democracies of Asia, Latin America, Africa, and the post-communist world. Where the legitimacy of democracy is not deeply rooted at all levels of society, dissatisfaction and disaffection with democracy are much more likely over the long term to give rise to preferences for, or diminished resistance to, the return of some form of authoritarian rule.

In another publication underwritten by the NED, Laurence Whitehead cautions: "The resilience of communist rule in mainland China, as well as the weakening of democracy in Colombia and Venezuela, indicated that such convergence [of political and economic liberalization] was likely to encounter opposition and resistance" (Whitehead, 2002: 182). Dismissing Hugo Chávez's electoral victory in 1998 as seemingly an "untypical throwback," Whitehead concludes, "three years later the political and economic benefits of an unquestioning endorsement of a liberalized world system seem more doubtful" (2002: 183). But resistance to globalization will reportedly lead to abandoning and reversing political and economic opening and reducing the scope for dissent (2002: 188). Whitehead therefore stresses the importance of regimes' pushing ahead with market reforms despite political pressures and urges the United States to maintain its commitment to economic and political liberalization.

The Inter-American Dialog (IAD), a think tank that has received numerous NED grants for its research on Latin America, issues similar directives in its policy recommendations. The foreword of an IAD 2003 policy report entitled *The Troubled Americas* states (2003: iii),

> We see little evidence so far of a regional backlash against market economics and democratic politics, but we are concerned that Latin America's citizens and government are losing confidence in the economic and political reforms that, in the past dozen years, have taken hold in most of the region. The challenge, we argue, is to recast and amplify, not jettison, the reform agenda.

The IAD thus describes the design and efficacy of economic and political reforms as unproblematic and points to Latin America's "citizens and government" as lacking faith in the market and democracy. The report concludes, "Washington has considerable power to shape events and determine outcomes in Latin America. Stronger leadership from Washington could help address other regional economic challenges" (2003: 26).

PRACTICING DEMOCRACY PROMOTION IN LATIN AMERICA

Some commentaries have charged the United States with focusing too heavily on trade and illicit narcotics trafficking in Latin America while neglecting regional political problems (IAD, 2003; Robinson, 1991). Over the past two decades, however, the United States has provided substantial political aid for democracy promotion through the NED. Between the Reagan and Clinton administrations, NED funding and programs in Latin America remained at similar levels despite widespread transitions to democracy. From 1985 to 2000 the NED spent over US$93 million in Latin America. Although funding declined slightly during the Clinton administration, Latin America remained a major region for NED funding and programs. Only Central Europe and the former Soviet Republics intermittently surpassed Latin America in such funding. Under George W. Bush, NED annual funding levels in Latin America have also been similar to those of previous presidential administrations.[2]

When some members of Congress argued that the NED no longer served any purpose after the Cold War and moved toward ending public funding, NED Chair John Brandemas stated (NED, 1996: 2),

> Because the Endowment is a small, nongovernmental organization, it does not operate under the constraints of federal institutions that must (and should) serve U.S. diplomatic interests. The Endowment is thus able to act in certain countries where the involvement of an official U.S. government agency may complicate our diplomacy and conflict with our desire to help democratic activists.

The NED's *1997 Strategy Document* (NED, 1997) further noted that the organization needed to remain at the "cutting edge" of democratic change to sustain its funding from Congress. In the organization's 2002 *Strategy Document*, the NED (2002a) explained that most of its resources not only were directed at authoritarian systems, but also "semi-authoritarian" ones that fell "somewhere between dictatorship and genuine political openness and competition of electoral democracy" (NED, 2002a: 3).

The NED believed that it had a special role to play in "crafting a comprehensive response" in "semi-authoritarian" systems. The key objectives in these cases were strengthening the independent media, civil society, and political parties and building "effective governing coalitions, and business associations, trade unions, and policy institutes that can mediate between the state and the market and effect real economic reform" (NED, 2002a: 4). Venezuela's government was explicitly identified as a semiauthoritarian system targeted by NED programs. As relations between the United States and Chávez worsened, this characterization would be repeated to justify NED funding of his opponents.

TEPID RELATIONS WITH
THE CLINTON ADMINISTRATION

During the Clinton administration, Chávez's visits to Iraq and his praise for Fidel Castro met with some criticism. Just prior to one of these trips, the State Department spokesperson Richard Boucher said, "We do think it's a rather dubious distinction to be the first democratically elected head of state to go meet with the dictator of Iraq" (*Agence France Presse*, 2000a). Chávez also diverged from Washington over regional counternarcotics operations and economic integration. In 1999 he refused to permit U.S. military aircraft involved in antinarcotics operations to fly over Venezuelan airspace. But in public the administration still maintained a cordial relationship with the Chávez government. U.S. Ambassador to Venezuela Donna Hrinak stated, "Venezuela is an active partner in building an integrated hemisphere through the economy, through a consolidated democracy and through sustainable development" (*Agence France Presse*, 2000b).

The official statements at least acknowledged the Chávez government as a democracy. In contrast, the International Republican Institute (IRI), the Republican Party's international organization and a core NED grant agent, scrutinized Chávez's presidential bid and expressed anxiety over Venezuela's democratic future. An IRI report acknowledged that while opinion polls showed Chávez in the lead, the IRI believed that Chávez's armed revolt against the Pérez government made his credentials "questionable." Without citing any irregularities in voter registration, political violence, or restrictions on civil liberties during the election campaign, the IRI still concluded with a warning (1998):

Accustomed to a stable and democratic Venezuela, many U.S. policymakers have yet to confront the possibility that the country may veer away from the democratic path being followed by most Latin American countries. The consequences of such a development would be profound: the United States imports more oil from Venezuela than from any other country and bilateral trade has been expanding rapidly in the 1990s. For these reasons, the travails of Venezuelan democracy bear watching.

To the IRI and other NED grantees, the potential of a Chávez presidency signaled a serious erosion of party politics in Venezuela. Indeed, Chávez's political project appears to be clearly out of step with the NED's mission of promoting democracy through "party-building." He has built his political profile by relying on an "antiparty" discourse in which the traditional party domination of Acción Democrática (Democratic Action—AD) and Comité de Organización Política Electoral Independiente (Independent Electoral Political Organizing Committee—COPEI) are considered a source of political corruption and an impediment to democracy. Following his victory at the polls, he decreed a referendum for a constituent assembly that would draft a new constitution. As Steve Ellner explains, Chávismo and the political reforms under way in Venezuela resemble the populism employed by parties throughout Latin America during the 1930s and 1940s, but the constitutional changes also create the potential for direct popular participation in Venezuela's politics (Ellner, 2001).

NED spending in Venezuela during the period illustrates that the organization responded to Chávismo almost from the start. In 1999 Venezuela ranked the highest of eleven countries in the region for NED-funded programs. The IRI received the most funding out of all NED grantees in Venezuela during the period and it responded to Chávez's push for a new constitution by using a US$194,521 grant for developing a network to offer input into the drafting process (NED, 1999: 56). Its country-project overview (IRI, 2004) explains that, "the perception that the country's traditional political parties are out of touch with the concerns of the citizenry and are largely responsible for its misery is the chief reason for this disdain. An opportunity exists to work with Venezuelan political parties to help them play their essential role more effectively." A US$292,297 grant from the NED helped the IRI "train national and local branches of existing and/or newly formed political parties on party structure, management, organization, communications, and other topics" (NED, 1999: 56).

The American Center for International Labor Solidarity (ACILS), another core grantee of the NED representing organized labor in the United States, was also active in Venezuela. In 1998, ACILS provided the Confederación de Trabajadores Venezolanos (Confederation of Venezuelan Workers—CTV), which is dominated by the AD, with US$54,289 so that it could play a greater role in Venezuela's economic and political debates (NED, 1998: 57). In 1999 pro-Chávez labor leaders introduced a resolution into the constituent assembly that would require all federated and confederated labor leaders to step down until elections were held. The CTV leadership responded by carrying out substantial internal reforms, which relieved some of the tension (Ellner, 2001: 22–23). During this period, a US$246,926 grant to the CTV was described as helping to conduct internal elections by providing training and promoting widespread support and participation (NED, 1999: 56). Although total funding of NED programs in Venezuela declined sharply the following year, ACILS, the IRI, and a number of other grantees were still active. ACILS provided another US$60,084 to the CTV "to effect reforms intended to increase rank and file control over decision making" (NED, 2000: 54).

HEIGHTENED TENSIONS UNDER THE BUSH ADMINISTRATION

Some predicted that the incoming Bush administration would toughen U.S. policy toward Chávez (Marquis, 2000). Indeed, relations between Washington and Caracas continued to sour through 2001. When traveling to Iran, Chávez urged members of the Organization of Petroleum Exporting Countries (OPEC) to refrain from increasing oil production. He insisted that OPEC members would not give in to pressure even if it came from the United States (*Deutsche Presse-Agentur*, 2001). On the eve of a visit by Fidel Castro, the Venezuelan government ordered the U.S. military mission in Caracas to vacate its office space. The final straw may have come in late October, when Chávez described the U.S. military actions in Afghanistan as "fighting terrorism with terrorism." Days later, U.S. Ambassador Donna Hrinak was called back to Washington to brief the administration on its current relationship with Venezuela.

Chávez was facing political turmoil at home as well. Throughout the year, his opponents carried out a number of protests, alleging that his political reforms were really a means of consolidating dictatorial power. Shortly after Hrinak's return to Venezuela, the AD called another demonstration. AD member Henry Ramos stated, "Our principal weapon is our right to demonstrate against this pitiful situation which is dragging Venezuela through dirt, humiliated and discredited not only at home but abroad as well" (*New York Times*, 2001). Several members of Chávez's Fifth Republic Movement were wounded by rubber bullets when the Caracas police (controlled by Mayor Alfredo Peña, a Chávez opponent) opened fire because they were attempting to block the protest march.

In early January the *Washington Post* reported that the Bush administration expressed its solidarity with Venezuelan newspapers after Chávez had allegedly infringed on freedom of speech. Peter Hakim, the director of the Inter-American Dialog, used the resignation of Venezuela's ambassador to the United States to chide Chávez: "Deteriorating ties with the U.S. are being blamed on [Ambassador] Arcaya. It demonstrates the irrationality of Chávez, when the problem is in Caracas, not in Washington" (*Washington Post*, 2002). About this same time, allegations of Chávez's support for Colombia's rebels began surfacing in the U.S. press. From January until the coup in April, the White House explicitly questioned Chávez's commitment to democracy, human rights, and hemispheric security.

On February 5 Chávez was mentioned when Secretary of State Colin Powell spoke before the U.S. Senate Foreign Relations Committee. When Senator Jesse Helms asked Powell to comment on Chávez's support for "narco-terrorists" in Colombia, Powell responded (United States Senate Foreign Relations Committee, 2002),

> Briefly, we have been concerned with some of the actions of Venezuelan President Chávez and his understanding of what a democratic system is all about. And we have not been happy with some of the comments he has made with respect to the campaign against terrorism. He hasn't been as supportive as he might have been. And he drops in on some of the strangest countries to visit. We've expressed our disagreement on some of his policies directly to him. And he understands that it is a serious irritant in our relationship.

Powell also disclosed that the U.S. embassy in Venezuela had attempted to express its displeasure directly to Chávez, but found him "quite defensive." In fact, after Ambassador Hrinak returned from Washington she reportedly had a "very difficult meeting" in which Chávez was told to "keep his mouth shut on these important issues" (Slevin, 2002).

The verbal attack on Chávez became harsher the next day when CIA Director George Tenet spoke before the Senate Intelligence Committee. Republican Senator Pat Roberts asked Tenet to underscore how "a fellow named Hugo Chávez, who I think would be another Castro" might be "a threat to the U.S. within our own hemisphere." Tenet described Chávez as "a tough actor for us" who "probably doesn't have the interest of the United States at heart." He then deferred to Assistant Secretary of State for Intelligence and Research Carl Ford, who engaged Roberts in deriding Chávez (United States Senate Select Committee on Intelligence, 2002):

> Ford: Well, it seems to me—and I'm not an expert on Chávez or South America—but when you can't solve your basic, fundamental economic problems that Venezuela with the natural resources that it has available, you got to blame somebody. And I think that he's found that it's easier and more politically correct for him in Venezuela to blame us.

Roberts: Well, that's what Castro does.

Ford: That's right. That's why he joins with Castro in several occasions in voic-
ing concerns about the US. That doesn't bother me so much, as long as it's just
words. But there are also indications that he is sympathetic and helpful to the
FARC in Colombia and various other groups. So that I'm sure that all of us are
going to be watching very closely to see what goes on in Venezuela and with
President Chávez in particular.

In March 2002 NED President Carl Gershman spoke before the Senate
Subcommittee on Foreign Operations and repeated the NED's classification
of Venezuela's government as semiauthoritarian. The efforts of the IRI and
the National Democratic Institute (NDI, the Democratic Party's international
organization and NED core grantee) in Venezuela before and after the coup
show that two of Gershman's recommendations are especially relevant:
"work to expand the constitutional, legal, and political space for civil society,
NGOs, and opposition political party development" and "focus on building
up subcultures of democratic activism that try to achieve incremental gains,
but that can also provide leadership if and when opportunities arise for more
substantial breakthroughs" (United States Senate Subcommittee on Foreign
Operations, 2002).

INTENSIFICATION OF DEMOCRACY PROMOTION

In 2000 Venezuela had fallen to sixth place out of ten Latin American and
Caribbean countries in number of NED-funded programs. Just one year later,
NED funding in Venezuela went from a total of US$257,831 to US$877,435.
Venezuela was the highest-ranked out of all the countries in the region (NED,
2000; 2001). The NDI received a US$210,500 grant and opened an office in
Venezuela. The rationale and objective of NDI's program described the state
of Venezuela's democracy in alarming tones (National Democratic Institute
for International Affairs, 2004):

> Once considered South America's most stable democracy, Venezuela is experi-
> encing a period of dramatic political change. The rise of former coup leader
> Hugo Chávez and the demise of the traditional political parties reflect the fact
> that many Venezuelans are losing faith in the democratic process.

The NDI's January to March 2002 quarterly report on Venezuela asserted
that, "to help salvage democracy in Venezuela, an effective political party
system must be rebuilt" (National Democratic Institute for International Affairs, 2002: 1). Shortly after opening its office, it worked closely with several
groups opposed to Chávez, including Proyecto Venezuela (a group associated

with 1998 presidential contender Henrique Salas Romer) and Primero Justicia (Justice First—PJ).

The ACILS also provided another grant totaling US$154,377 to the CTV. According to the NED's *2001 Annual Report*, ACILS funding "played a critical role in mediating the controversial results [of the CTV's elections] after pro-government unions attempted to disrupt the process" (NED, 2001: 49). The NED also provided the Education Assembly Civic Association with a US$55,000 grant for reforming educational policy. Leonardo Carvajal, the group's head, said that the funds were used for the stated purpose but claimed it was one of the first organizations to carry out antigovernment marches. Carvajal was also considered for the position of minister of education in the two-day coup government (Caesar, 2002: 2).

With a Republican in the White House, IRI programs (which had shrunk to a mere US$50,000 in 2000) dramatically increased to almost US$340,000 in 2001. During this year, the IRI office in Venezuela established a firm working relationship with opposition figures, among them Francisco Arias Cárdenas, an erstwhile Chávez cohort who had competed against him in the 2000 election, and Caracas Mayor Alfredo Peña. The IRI's quarterly report on its activities in Venezuela discloses that Cárdenas visited its headquarters in Washington on October 18 and "spoke of the shortcomings of President Chávez's administration and the desperate need for change in Venezuela" (IRI, 2001: 8). The report also reveals that in December 2001 the former Republican Party press secretary Mike Collins conducted an IRI training session on communication strategies for Cárdenas's Unión para el Progreso and encouraged the group to move its weekly press conferences out of its headquarters and into the streets. The IRI also had discussions with Peña about possibly forming his own party. During a December 5 meeting with Peña, Collins suggested that he "soften his aggressive image in order to appeal to a wider range of voters" and discussed "ways in which Peña could differentiate himself from the president and put forth a positive message" (IRI, 2001: 7). Similar contacts were also made with the AD and COPEI. The IRI conducted workshops for these two parties and for PJ.

From February 17 to 23 Elizabeth Winger Echeverri, the IRI's senior program officer for Latin America, visited Venezuela and met with leaders of PJ, AD, COPEI, and other IRI affiliates. Meetings also included U.S. embassy officials and the Federación Venezolana de Cámaras y Asociaciones de Comercio y Producción (Venezuelan Federation of Chambers and Associations of Commerce and Production—FEDECAMERAS), led by Pedro Carmona. After the meetings, IRI reported that it had "received firm commitment of party leaders to place a new, more urgent emphasis on the importance of party strengthening in the context of the present political turbulence" (IRI, 2002a: 4). Another meeting sponsored by the IRI brought these parties to Washington, DC, in March 2001, just a month before the coup.

THE COUP AND THE AFTERMATH

After the coup on April 11, Carmona assumed power and selected individuals from COPEI, PJ, and the CTV for the new government (Corn, 2002). The White House and the IRI praised the coup and justified it on the grounds that Chávez had allegedly instigated his supporters to attack demonstrators and later resigned. IRI President George Folsom applauded "the bravery of civil society leaders—members of the media, the Church, the nation's educators and school administrators, political party leaders, labor unions, and the business sector—who have put their lives on the line in their struggle to restore genuine democracy to their country" (IRI, 2002b). State Department spokesperson Philip Reeker stated the United States looked "forward to working with all democratic forces in Venezuela to ensure full exercise of democratic rights. The essential elements of democracy, which have been weakened in recent months, must be restored fully" (Ross, 2002). During a State Department meeting on April 12, Assistant Secretary of Western Hemisphere Affairs Otto Reich told attendees that the United States did not approve of coups or encourage the one in Venezuela but that Chávez had had it coming. The next day, U.S. Ambassador to the Organization of American States (OAS) Roger Noriega chastised member states for being more concerned with events in Venezuela over the past twenty-four hours than Chávez's "antidemocratic" behavior (DeYoung, 2002a).

Carmona's attempt at shutting down the National Assembly and Supreme Court and Chávez's return to office on April 14 prompted a dramatic modification of these sentiments. Christopher Sabatini, the NED's senior program director for Latin America, maintained that NED recipients who came out in support of the Carmona government had been under the impression that Chávez had resigned (Corn, 2002). Folsom's praise had also drawn sharp criticism from NED president Carl Gershman. Without actually retracting his earlier statement, Folsom followed up by stating that "IRI's statement was not an endorsement of extra-constitutional measures to forcibly remove an elected President, and IRI never contemplated the notion that the will of the Venezuelan people would be circumvented by extra-constitutional measures, such as the closure of the National Assembly and the Supreme Court" (IRI, 2002c). On April 16 White House spokesperson Ari Fleischer stated that the Bush administration did not encourage a coup and still believed that Chávez had resigned, regardless of his denial (DeYoung, 2002b). During the weekend of the coup, Reich had cautioned Carmona against dissolving the National Assembly and stressed the need to maintain the appearance of democratic continuity (Marquis, 2002a). Washington condemned the coup only after Carmona went against its advice.

Nevertheless, the White House continued to place the blame for Venezuela's political crisis squarely on Chávez. On the day of his return, National Security Adviser Condoleezza Rice issued a stern warning that "the whole world is watching" and that Chávez should "right his own ship that has been moving in the wrong direction for quite a long time" (Witworth, 2002). The depiction of the United States as rescuing an imperiled Venezuelan democracy also continued. Lino Gutiérrez, deputy assistant secretary for hemispheric affairs, declared (2002),

> In the past, Venezuela has been a leader in the hemisphere—a champion of democracy, a supporter of regional integration efforts, and a close friend of the United States. It is time for Venezuelans to return to that leadership role in the hemisphere. And the way to do that is to create the conditions at home to preserve and encourage democratic activity.

But the White House had also become more public in its insistence that all parties and individuals involved in Venezuela's political disputes abide by democratic principles and seek a change in government through constitutional means. When Chávez's opponents called for his ouster again in late 2002, the U.S. embassy in Caracas stated that the United States would oppose any illegal or violent actions aimed at the "constitutional and democratically-elected government of Venezuela" (Forero, 2002). Some speculated that this cautious handling of events in Venezuela stemmed from the United States's need to rely on Venezuelan oil in the likely event of war with Iraq (Kaste, 2002).

It appears that the White House prefers to handle Chávez by electoral means rather than by supporting another coup. In December 2002 White House spokesperson Ari Fleischer stated that the "the only peaceful and politically viable path to moving out of the crisis is through the holding of early elections." He added that Venezuelans could seek resolution of the conflict through the ballot boxes, including the use of referendum to recall the president (Dao, 2002). Both the IRI and NDI continue to sustain their contacts with Chávez's opponents. After the coup, the State Department's Bureau of Democracy, Human Rights, and Labor (DRL) designated a US$1 million grant to the NED for its programs in Venezuela. In 2002 Venezuela remained the most heavily funded of all NED programs in the region, with a total of US$1,099,352. The IRI received almost US$300,000 for its party-building efforts (NED, 2002b). Three large grants were also provided to the Center for International Private Enterprise (CIPE), a core affiliate of the NED.

When the NED's funding of Chávez's opponents surfaced in the U.S. press, Sabatini admitted that the goal was to create political space for the opposition but also insisted that the NED "had no opinion of Chávez" (Marquis, 2002b). But several of the grant proposals to the DRL and the NED reveal clear contempt for Chávez. CIPE's proposal was perhaps the most acerbic (NED, 2002–2003):

The current political crisis in Venezuela has been brought about by the deplorable performance of the Hugo Chávez government, which has demonstrated both militaristic and Marxist tendencies while consistently undermining democratic institutions in the country. It is therefore imperative to seek consensus among civil society groups that will help build an alternative vision for Venezuela that will be characterized by greater democratic participation and input.

Grant proposals submitted by five separate groups all contained the same opening paragraph:

Once known for its consensus-based politics and respect for democratic liberties, Venezuela now teeters on the verge of widespread social and political conflict. Elected in 1998 and again in 2000 under a new constitution, President Hugo Chávez tapped into a growing popular sense of frustration and anger against Venezuela's political class, promising a revolution that would sweep out the "squalid" oligarchy. Once in office, Chávez's revolutionary rhetoric, public disregard for democratic processes and institutions and vitriolic attacks on his opponents escalated political and social tensions and hardened the opposition.

The NED also provided a US$53,400 grant to Sumate, the principal organizing vehicle for the presidential recall referendum. Sumate's grant proposal began with the same opening paragraph and further explained, "With Endowment support, the Venezuelan group Sumate will conduct a nation-wide elections education campaign related to the referendum. With the assistance of other election-related groups in the region, Sumate will train voters throughout Venezuela on the voting process and encourage participation in the referendum voting process" (NED, 2003–2004).

Just two months before the recall referendum, Roger Noreiga (now serving as Assistant Secretary of State for Western Hemisphere Affairs) told members of the U.S. Senate that "the Venezuelan people have demonstrated a commendable civic spirit worthy of their rich democratic traditions" (United States Senate Foreign Relations Committee, 2004). Despite Noriega's assertions, Venezuelans rejected the recall referendum in August 2004. The opposition immediately accused Chávez of fraud and demanded an investigation. The United States was quick to support calls for an investigation, but recognized Chávez's victory after confirmation by international election observers.

The failed coup and the results of the recall referendum have not changed the minds of U.S. officials. By January 2005, the Bush administration was working on toughening its stance against Chávez by urging "friendly countries" to "speak up against his authoritarian and anti-democratic rule" (*Washington Times*, 2005). Condoleezza Rice also referred to Chávez as "a democratically elected leader who governs in an illiberal way" (*The Washington Post*, 2005). During the December 2005 legislative elections, the United States stepped up its attempts to discredit the Chávez government. Venezuela's National Electoral Council (Consejo Nacional Electoral—CNE) worked with monitors from the OAS to address the opposition's concerns over the transparency of the election system and voter secrecy. While the CNE was still taking steps to address the issues, several parties associated with the NED abruptly pulled out of the elections and called for a boycott. Twenty-five percent of the eligible voters turned out for an election in which Chávez's party won the majority of the seats. Although observers from the OAS and European Union did not question the results, U.S. officials interpreted low voter turnout as a sign of disaffection. State Department spokesperson Adam Ereli insisted that the Chávez government recognize low voter turnout "reflects a broad lack of confidence in the impartiality and transparency of the electoral process" (*States News Service*, 2005a). An unidentified State Department official also declared that "One-party legislatures are hardly consistent with our understanding of a well-functioning democracy" (*States News Service*, 2005b).

Two months later, Secretary of Defense Donald Rumsfeld claimed Chávez's election to office was similar to Adolf Hitler's (*Agence France Presse*, 2006). By early March, U.S. officials openly declared an "inoculation strategy" to handle Venezuela's purportedly growing military and diplomatic ties with North Korea and Iran. Rice chided Venezuela for being a "sidekick" of Iran and disclosed that the United States would work with "other countries to make certain that there is a united front against some of the things that Venezuela gets involved in" (Richter, 2006).

CONCLUSION

Some have argued that U.S. democracy promotion has the potential of blindly placing idealistic values such as human rights and elected governments ahead of concrete security interests. From this perspective a foreign policy overly concerned with the domestic political virtue of other nation-states might restrict the ability of the United States to make alliances that are strategically necessary (see Schweller, 2000). It has also been suggested that the United States has not sufficiently heeded the potential of despotic leaders remaining or coming to power through elections (Zakaria, 2003); "illiberal democracies" are partly the consequence of a foreign policy that focuses excessively on supporting elections abroad without fully acknowledging the possibility of undemocratic outcomes.

I offer a markedly different critique of U.S. democracy promotion. Indeed, the policy is premised on the ideological assumption that democratic governance optimizes global capitalism and international stability, but the above argument pays little attention to the narrow and orthodox intellectual forces that underpin the practice of democracy promotion. The preoccupation with party building and the "semiauthoritarian" tag used in Venezuela and elsewhere demonstrates a growing awareness that political liberalization does not necessarily result in populations or regimes that readily fall in line with free-market principles or U.S.-defined global security priorities. Experimentation and departures from the authorized model of political liberalization are frequently identified as threats to democratic consolidation. Hugo Chávez's trenchant critique of party politics in Venezuela and his sweeping political reforms run counter to the conventional written narratives of democratization.

Moreover, idealism has not been the sole (or even the principal) impulse behind the practice of democracy promotion. Contrary to the assertions of Zakaria and other critics, U.S. foreign policy has not promoted democracy simply because it is moral. The practice is deployed primarily when U.S. interests can be secured by using a targeted country's electoral system (or other constitutional mechanisms) to accomplish regime change. Furthermore, while these interventions may not be driven by morality they are associated with moral rhetoric that casts the intransigent leaders (even elected ones) as dubious political actors with undemocratic intentions. The statements of several members of the Bush administration make clear that Washington considers tensions with Venezuela the result of a government in Caracas which lacks an "understanding of what a democratic system is all about." Other official statements and the NED's grant descriptions also suggest that a victory by Chávez's U.S.-backed opponents will not only "return" the country to democracy but also repair Venezuela's "close friendship" with the United States.

It has been argued that democracies rarely wage war against one another and seek pacific settlement of disputes (Russett and Oneal, 2001). But David Forsythe has highlighted how U.S. covert operations during the Cold War targeted elected governments (e.g., Guatemala in 1954, Brazil in 1964, and Chile in 1973) because they were suspected of aiding Soviet communism (Forsythe, 1992). Given Forsythe's thesis, I suggest that the United States employs a subjective and contingent conception of democracy that occasionally leads it to deny the credentials of other democratic governments and behave aggressively toward them. Neither U.S. officials nor many academicians are unable to fully grasp how someone like Chávez could win several elections in Venezuela. More importantly, they simply cannot comprehend why an elected leader would dare criticize neoliberalism, condemn U.S. actions in Afghanistan, and obstruct U.S. global security directives. U.S. officials and these academicians thus turn to simplistic descriptions of Chávez (e.g., "semi-authoritarian," "a democratic leader who governs in an illiberal way") and comparisons to Castro and Hitler to discredit the elected government of Venezuela. In the short term, the United States uses such terminology to isolate Venezuela by depicting its government (along with Cuba's) as a vestige of authoritarianism in a hemisphere governed mostly by democracies. In a broader sense, these verbal strategies justify the United States' penchant for sponsoring regime change in Latin America. For now, the primary method of accomplishing this task is "democracy promotion."

Indeed, democracy promotion is markedly different from military and covert operations. Perhaps one could also argue that the shift from violent interventions to democracy promotion marks progress, since U.S.-backed regime change in Latin America now culminates with elected governments rather than repressive military juntas. But the historical record demonstrates that direct U.S. military action and the propping up of repressive dictatorships have been the most common methods of intervention in Latin America and elsewhere in the Third World (Schmitz, 1999; Chomsky and Herman, 1979). As more figures like Chávez win elections in Latin America (e.g., Evo Morales's victory in Bolivia), it is likely that the United States will become more hostile to the region's leadership. U.S. public officials will probably rely on electoral mechanisms within Latin American states to forestall or contain such victories. But we cannot rule out the possibility that the United States may resort to other methods if this strategy is ineffective.

NOTES

1. As Robinson (1996) explains, globalization is about harmonizing fiscal, monetary, and social policies across borders to ease the transnational circulation of capital. Many intellectuals and public officials in the United States believe democracy (or, as Robinson calls it, "polyarchy") is the most capable and reliable form of government for carrying out these policies.

2. These observations are gleaned from the funding numbers disclosed in the National Endowment for Democracy's annual reports from 1985 to 2001. The Agency for International Development (AID) has also been another important source of aid to Latin America. Most of this aid, however, is provided ad hoc and possesses multiple objectives (e.g., conflict resolution, economic development, and cultural).

REFERENCES

Agence France Presse
2000a "U.S. Blasts Venezuela's Chávez for Planned Visit to Iraq." August 7, 2000. Online. Lexis-Nexis Academic. March 11, 2004.
2000b "U.S. Still Considers Venezuela a Partner." November 5, 2000. Online. Lexis-Nexis Academic. March 11, 2004.
2006 "Rumsfeld Says Chávez Rise 'Worrisome.'" February 2, 2006. Online. Lexis-Nexis Academic. February 16, 2006.
Alexander, Robert Jackson
1964 *The Venezuelan Democratic Revolution: A Profile of the Regime of Rómulo Betancourt.* New Brunswick, NJ: Rutgers University Press.

Caesar, Mike
   2002 "As Turmoil Deepens in Venezuela, Questions regarding NED Activities Remain
   Unanswered." *Americas Program*, December 9.
Carothers, Thomas
   1993 *In the Name of Democracy: U.S. Policy toward Latin America in the Reagan Years.*
   Berkeley: University of California Press.
Chomsky, Noam and Edward Herman
   1979 *Washington Connection and Third World Fascism.* Boston, MA: South End.
Corn, David
   2002 "Our Gang in Venezuela?" *The Nation*, August 5.
Cottam, Martha
   1994 *Images and Intervention: U.S. Policies in Latin America.* Pittsburgh, PA: University of
   Pittsburgh Press.
Dao, James
   2002 "U.S. Clarifies Stand on Venezuelan Vote." *New York Times*, December 17. Online.
   Lexis-Nexis Academic. January 21, 2004.
Deutsche Presse-Agentur
   2001 "Venezuela's President: No OPEC Production Increase at June Meeting." May 21,
   2001. Online. Lexis-Nexis Academic. January 21, 2004.
DeYoung, Karen
   2002a "U.S. Seen as Weak Patron of Latin Democracy." *The Washington Post*, April 16. Online. Lexis-Nexis Academic. January 21, 2004.
   2002b "U.S. Details Talks with Opposition: Administration Insists It Did Not Encourage a
   Coup." *The Washington Post*, April 17. Online. Lexis-Nexis Academic. January 21, 2004.
Diamond, Larry and Richard Gunther
   2001 "Introduction," in *Political Parties and Democracy*. Larry Diamond and Richard Gunther (eds.). Baltimore, MD: Johns Hopkins University Press and the National Endowment for
   Democracy.
Doty, Roxanne Lynn
   1996 *Imperial Encounters: The Politics of Representation in North-South Relations.* Min-
   neapolis: University of Minnesota Press.
Ellner, Steve
   2001 "The Radical Potential of Chavismo in Venezuela: The First Year-and-a Half in
   Power." *Latin American Perspective* 28 (5): 5–29.
Forero, Juan
   2002 "Losing Control: Venezuela Approaches the Brink." *The New York Times*, September
   22. Online. Lexis-Nexis Academic. January 21, 2004.
Forsythe, David
   1992 "Democracy, War, and Covert Action." *Journal of Peace Research* 29 (4): 385–395.
Gutiérrez, Lino, U.S. Deputy Assistant Secretary
   2002 *State Department Briefing: US-Venezuela Relations.* April 2. Online. Lexis-Nexis Academic. January 21, 2004.
Hunt, Michael
   1987 *Ideology and U.S. Foreign Policy.* New Haven, CT: Yale University Press.
IAD (Inter-American Dialog)
   2003 *The Troubled Americas.* Online. www.iadialog.org/publications/.
International Forum for Democratic Studies
   1996 *Political Parties and Democracy.* Washington, DC: National Endowment for Democracy. www.ned.org/forum/reports/parties

IRI (International Republican Institute)

1998 *Venezuela Political Situation Update—June 1998*. www.iri.org/countries.

2001 *Quarterly Report: Venezuela, October—December 2001*. Obtained by venezuelafoia .info through the Freedom of Information Act (FOIA). www.venezuelaFOIA.info.

2002a *Quarterly Report: Venezuela, January—March 2002*. Obtained by venezuelafoia.info through the Freedom of Information Act (FOIA). www.venezuelaFOIA.info.

2002b *IRI President Folsom Praises Venezuelan Civil Society's Defense of Democracy*. www .iri.org/pub. Obtained on August 14, 2002. The document is no longer available on the website.

2002c *Statement on Venezuela, May 6, 2002*. www.iri.org/pdfs/venezuela.

2004 *IRI in Venezuela*. www.iri.org/countries.

Johnson, John

1980 *Latin America in Caricature*. Austin, TX: University of Austin Press.

Kaste, Martin

2002 "Relations between the US and Venezuela Improving as That Country Seeks to Provide an Abundance of Oil to the U.S." *National Public Radio*. October 24. Online. Lexis-Nexis Academic. January 21, 2004.

Levine, Daniel

1977 "Venezuelan Politics: Past and Future," pp.7–44 in Robert Bond (ed.), *Contemporary Venezuela and Its Role in International Affairs*. New York: New York University Press.

Marquis, Christopher

2000 "Bush Could Get Tougher on Venezuela's Leader." *New York Times*, December 28. Online. Lexis-Nexis Academic. March 11, 2004.

2002a "U.S. Cautioned Leader of Plot against Chávez." *New York Times*, April 17. Online. Lexis-Nexis Academic. March 11, 2004.

2002b "U.S. Bankrolling Is under Scrutiny for Ties to Chávez Ouster." *New York Times*, April 25. Online. Lexis-Nexis Academic. January 21, 2004.

Martz, John

1984 "Venezuela, Colombia, and Ecuador," pp. 381–401 in Jan Knippers Black (ed.), *Latin America: Its Problems and Its Promises*. Boulder, CO: Westview.

National Democratic Institute for International Affairs

2002 *Quarterly Report: Venezuela, January to March 2002*. Obtained by venezuelafoia.info through the Freedom of Information Act (FOIA). www.venezuelaFOIA.info.

2004 *Latin America and the Caribbean: Venezuela*. www.ndi.org/worldwide/lac/ venezuela.

NED (National Endowment for Democracy)

1996 *Annual Report*. Washington, DC: National Endowment for Democracy.

1997 *Strategy Document*. Washington, DC: National Endowment for Democracy. Online at www.ned.org/publications.

1998 *Annual Report*. Washington, DC: National Endowment for Democracy.

1999 *Annual Report*. Washington, DC: National Endowment for Democracy.

2000 *Annual Report*. Washington, DC: National Endowment for Democracy.

2001 *Annual Report*. Washington, DC: National Endowment for Democracy.

2002a *Strategy Document* Washington, DC: National Endowment for Democracy. www.ned.org/publications.

2002b *Annual Report*. Washington, DC: National Endowment for Democracy.

2002–2003 *NED Report to the US Department of State on Special Venezuela Funds, June 2002–September 2003*. Obtained by venezuelafoia.info through the Freedom of Information Act (FOIA). www.venezuelaFOIA.info.

2003–2004 *Grant Agreement No.2003-548.0, September 12, 2003–September 30, 2004.* Obtained by venezuelafoia.info through the Freedom of Information Act (FOIA). venezuelaFOIA .info.

New York Times
2001 "Venezuelan Demonstrators Attacked by Government Loyalists." November 23, 2001. Online. Lexis-Nexis Academic. January 21, 2004.

Richter, Paul
2006 "U.S. More Intent on Blocking Chávez." *Los Angeles Times*, March 10, 2006. Online. Lexis-Nexis Academic. April 4, 2006.

Robinson, Linda
1991 *Intervention or Neglect: The United States and Central America beyond the 1980s.* New York: Council on Foreign Relations Press.

Robinson, William
1996 *Promoting Polyarchy: Globalization, US Intervention, and Hegemony.* New York: Cambridge University Press.

Ross, Sonya
2002 "U.S. Closely Watching Political Developments in Venezuela following Ouster of President." *Associated Press.* April 12. Online. Lexis-Nexis Academic. January 21, 2004.

Russett, Bruce and John Oneal
2001 *Triangulating Peace: Democracy, Interdependence, and International Organizations.* New York: Norton.

Schmitter, Philippe and Terry Lynn Karl
1996 "What Democracy Is . . . and Is Not," pp.49–61 in Larry Diamond and Marc Plattner (eds.), *The Global Resurgence of Democracy.* Baltimore, MD: Johns Hopkins University Press.

Schmitz, David
1999 *Thank God They're on Our Side: The United States and Right-Wing Dictatorships, 1929–1965.* Chapel Hill: University of North Carolina Press.

Schweller, Randall
2000 "US Democracy Promotion: Realist Reflections," pp. 41–61 in Michael Cox, John Ikenberry, and Takashi Inoguchi (eds.), *American Democracy Promotion: Impulses, Strategies, and Impacts.* New York: Oxford University Press.

Shapiro, Michael
1988 *The Politics of Representation: Writing Practices in Biography, Photography, and Policy Analysis.* Madison: University of Wisconsin Press.

Slevin, Peter
2002 "Political Crisis in Venezuela Worries White House; Declining Popularity of Country's President Threatens Stability of Key Oil Supplier." *Washington Post*, February 23. Online. Lexis-Nexis Academic. January 21, 2004.

States News Service
2005a "U.S. Expresses Concern about Legislative Elections in Venezuela." December 6. Online. Lexis-Nexis Academic. February 14, 2006.
2005b "Venezuelan Electoral Environment Prompts International Concern." December 7. Online. Lexis-Nexis Academic. February 14, 2006.

Teichman, Judith
2001 *The Politics of Freeing Markets in Latin America: Chile, Argentina, and Mexico.* Chapel Hill: University of North Carolina Press.

United States Senate Foreign Relations Committee
2002 *Hearing on FY '03 Foreign Affairs Budget Request.* February 5. Online. Lexis-Nexis Congressional. March 19, 2004.

2004 *Hearings on the State of Democracy in Venezuela.* www.senate.gov/~foreign/hearings/2004/hrg040624p.html.

United States Senate Select Committee on Intelligence

2002 *Hearing on External Threats to US National Security.* February 6. Online. Lexis-Nexis Congressional. March 19, 2004.

United States Senate Subcommittee on Foreign Operations

2002 *Promoting Democracy in the Aftermath of September 11: A Statement by Carl Gershman, President, National Endowment for Democracy to the Senate Subcommittee on Foreign Operations.* March 6. Online. Lexis-Nexis Congressional. March 19, 2004.

Veltmeyer, Henry, James Petras, and Steve Vieux

1997 *Neoliberalism and Class Conflict in Latin America.* New York: St. Martin's.

Washington Post

2002 "Venezuelan Ambassador's Abrupt Departure, a Sign of Turbulent Ties and Times." January 16. Online. Lexis-Nexis Academic. January 21, 2004.

2005 "Rice Stays Close to Bush Policies in Hearings." January 19. Online. Lexis-Nexis Academic. February 16, 2006.

Washington Times

2005 "U.S. to Speak Out on Chávez Policies." January 14. Online. Lexis-Nexis Academic. February 14, 2006.

Whitehead, Laurence

2002 "The Hazards of Convergence," pp. 183–209 in Laurence Whitehead (ed.), *Emerging Market Democracies: East Asia and Latin America.* Baltimore, MD: Johns Hopkins University Press and the National Endowment for Democracy.

Witworth, Damian

2002 "US Urges Venezuelan Leader to Ditch Left-Wing Agenda." *The Times (London),* April 15. Online. Lexis-Nexis Academic. January 21, 2004.

Zakaria, Fareed

2003 *The Future of Freedom: Illiberal Democracy at Home and Abroad.* New York: Norton.

Bibliography

Acosta Saignes, Miguel
  1967 *Vida de los esclavos negros en Venezuela*. Caracas: Ediciones Hesperides.
Alexander, Robert Jackson
  1964 *The Venezuelan Democratic Revolution: A Profile of the Regime of Rómulo Betancourt*. New Brunswick, NJ: Rutgers University Press.
Bautista Fuenmayor, Juan
  1981 *Historia de la Venezuela política contemporánea.* 8 vols. Caracas.
Bergquist, Charles
  1986 *Labor in Latin America: Comparative Essays on Chile, Argentina, Venezuela, and Colombia*. Stanford, CA: Stanford University Press.
Betancourt, Rómulo
  1979 *Venezuela: Oil and Politics*. Boston, MA: Houghton Mifflin. First published in Spanish 1956.
Briggs, Charles and Mantini-Briggs, Clara
  2003 *Stories in the Time of Cholera: Racial Profiling during a Medical Nightmare*. Berkeley: University of California Press.
Brito Figueroa, Federico
  1979 *Historia Económica y Social de Venezuela*. 3 vols. Caracas: Universidad Central de Venezuela.
  1985 *El problema tierra y esclavos en la historia de Venezuela*. Caracas: Universidad Central de Venezuela.
Burggraaff, Winfield
  1972 *The Venezuelan Armed Forces in Politics, 1935–1959*. Columbia: University of Missouri Press.
Buxton, Julia
  2001 *The Failure of Political Reform in Venezuela*. Aldershot, UK: Ashgate.
Carrera Damas, Germán
  1983 *Una nación llamada Venezuela*. Caracas: Monte Avila.
Chávez Frías, Hugo
  2005 *Understanding the Venezuelan Revolution: Hugo Chávez Talks to Marta Harnecker.* New York: Montly Review Press. First appeared in Spanish 2002.

Coronil, Fernando
   1997 *The Magical State: Nature, Money and Modernity in Venezuela.* Chicago: University of Chicago Press.
Diaz, Arlene
   2004 *Female Citizens, Patriarchs, and the Law in Venezuela, 1786–1904.* Lincoln: University of Nebraska Press.
Diccionario de la Historia de Venezuela
   1997 4 vols. Caracas: Fundación Polar.
Ellner, Steve
   1993 *Organized Labor in Venezuela, 1958–1991: Behavior and Concerns in a Democratic Setting.* Wilmington, DE: Scholarly Resources.
   1995 "Venezuelan Revisionist History, 1908–1958: New Motives and Criteria for Analyzing the Past." *Latin American Research Review* 30 (1): 91–122.
   1999 "The Heyday of Radical Populism in Venezuela and Its Aftermath," pp. 117–137 in Michael Conniff (ed.), *Populism in Latin America.* Tuscaloosa: University of Alabama Press.
   2005 *Neoliberalismo y antineoliberalismo en América Latina: el debate sobre estrategias.* Caracas: Editorial Tropykos.
Ellner, Steve and Daniel Hellinger (eds.)
   2003 *Venezuelan Politics in the Chávez Era: Class, Polarization, and Conflict.* Boulder, CO: Lynne Rienner.
Ewell, Judith
   1984 *Venezuela: A Century of Change.* Stanford, CA: Stanford University Press.
   1996 *Venezuela and the United States: From Monroe's Hemisphere to Petroleum Empire.* Athens: University of Georgia Press.
Friedman, Elisabeth J.
   2000 *Unfinished Transitions: Women and the Gendered Development of Democracy in Venezuela 1936–1996.* University Park: Pennsylvania State University.
Gallegos, Rómulo
   1948 *Doña Barbara.* New York: Peter Smith. First published in Spanish 1931.
García, Jesús Chucho
   2001 "Comunidades afroamericanas y transformaciones sociales," in Daniel Mato (ed.), *Estudios Latinoamericanos sobre cultura y transformaciones sociales en tiempos de globalización.* Buenos Aires: CLACSO.
Gott, Richard
   2005 *Hugo Chavez and the Bolivarian Revolution.* New York: Verso.
Guss, David
   2000 *The Festive State: Race, Ethnicity, and Nationalism as Cultural Performance.* Berkeley: University of California Press.
Hansen, David R. and Kirk A. Hawkins
   2006 "Dependent Civil Society: The Círculos Bolivarianos in Venezuela." *Latin American Research Review* 41 (1): 102–132.
Hellinger, Daniel
   1991 *Venezuela: Tarnished Democracy.* Boulder, CO: Westview.
Herrera Salas, Jesús María
   2003 *El Negro Miguel y la primera revolución venezolana.* Caracas, Vadell Hermanos Editores.
Hillman, Richard
   1994 *Democracy for the Privileged: Crisis and Transition in Venezuela.* Boulder, CO: Lynne Rienner.

Ishibashi, Jun
2003 "Hacia una apertura del debate sobre el racismo en Venezuela: exclusión e inclusión estereotipada de personas 'negras en los medios de comunicación," in Daniel Mato (coord.), *Políticas de identidades y diferencias sociales en tiempos de globalización.* Caracas: FACES-Universidad Central de Venezuela.

Karl, Terry Lynn
1987 "Petroleum and Political Pacts: The Transition to Democracy in Venezuela." *Latin American Research Review* 22 (1): 35–62.
1997 *The Paradox of Plenty: Oil Booms and Petro-States.* Berkeley: University of California Press.

Lander, Edgardo
1996 "Urban Social Movements, Civil Society and New Forms of Citizenship in Venezuela." *International Review of Sociology* 6 (1): 51–65.
1996 "The Impact of Neoliberal Adjustment in Venezuela 1989–1993." *Latin American Perspectives* 23, no. 3 (Summer): 50–73.

Levine, Daniel H.
1973 *Conflict and Political Change in Venezuela.* Princeton, NJ: Princeton University Press.
1994 "Goodbye to Venezuelan Exceptionalism." *Journal of Interamerican Studies and World Affairs* 36 (Winter): 145–182.

Lieuwen, Edwin
1963 *Venezuela.* London: Oxford University Press.

Lombardi, John
1971 *The Decline and Abolition of Negro Slavery in Venezuela, 1820–1854.* Westport, CT: Greenwood.
1982 *Venezuela: The Search for Order, the Dream of Progress.* New York: Oxford University Press

López Maya, Margarita
1996 *E.E.U.U. en Venezuela: 1945–1948.* Caracas: Universidad Central de Venezuela.

López Maya, Margarita and Luis Lander
2005 "Popular Protest in Venezuela: Novelties and Continuities." *Latin American Perspectives* (March): 92–108.

Martz, John
1966 *Acción Democrática: Evolution of a Modern Political Party in Venezuela.* Princeton, NJ: Princeton University Press.

Morón, Guillermo
1964 *A History of Venezuela.* London: G. Allen.

Mommer, Bernard
2003 "Subversive Oil," in Steve Ellner and Daniel Hellinger (eds.), *Venezuelan Politics in the Chávez Era: Class, Polarization, and Conflict.* Boulder, CO: Lynne Rienner.

Pérez Alfonzo, Juan Pablo
1974 *Petróleo y dependencia.* Caracas: Síntesis Dos Mil.

Picón Salas, Mariano
1962 *A Cultural History of Spanish America, from Conquest to Independence.* Berkeley: University of California Press. First published in Spanish in 1944.

Rabe, Stephen G.
1982 *The Road to OPEC: United States Relations with Venezuela, 1919–1976.* Austin: University of Texas Press.

Roseberry, William
1983 *Coffee and Capitalism in the Venezuelan Andes.* Austin: University of Texas Press.

Salas, Yolanda
1987 *Bolívar y la historia en la conciencia popular*. Caracas: Universidad Simón Bolívar.
Tinker Salas, Miguel
2003 "Races and Cultures in the Venezuelan Oil Fields," in Vincent Peloso (ed.), *Work, Protest and Identity in Twentieth Century Latin America*. Wilmington, DE: Scholarly Resources.
2004 "Culture, Power and Oil: The Experience of Venezuelan Oil Camps and the Construction of Citizenship," in González Gilbert, Raul Fernández, Vivian Price, David Smith, and Linda Trinjh Vo (eds.), *Labor versus Empire: Race, Gender and Migration*. New York: Routledge.
2005 "Fueling Concern: The Role of Oil in Venezuela." *Harvard International Review* 26, no. 4 (Winter): 54–60.
Trinkunas, Harold A.
2005 *Crafting Civilian Control of the Military in Venezuela: A Comparative Perspective*. Chapel Hill: University of North Carolina Press.
Ungar, Mark
2003 "Contested Battlefields: Policing in Caracas and La Paz." *NACLA Report on the Americas*, September/October, 30–36.
Uslar Pietri, Arturo
1963 *The Red Lances*. New York: Knopf. First published in Spanish 1940.
Valencia Ramírez, Cristóbal
2006 "Venezuela in the Eye of the Hurricane: Landing an Analysis of the Bolivarian Revolution." *Journal of Latin American Anthropology* 11 (1): 173–186.
Wilpert, Gregory
2003 "Collision in Venezuela." *New Left Review* 21: 101–116.
Wright, Winthrop R.
1990 *Café con Leche: Race, Class and National Image in Venezuela*. Austin: University of Texas Press.
Yarrington, Doug
1997 *A Coffee Frontier: Land, Society and Politics in Duaca Venezuela, 1830–1936*. Pittsburgh, PA: University of Pittsburgh Press.

Index

About the Contributors

Christopher I. Clement is a visiting professor in the politics department at Pomona College. His doctoral dissertation dealt with U.S. influence on the 1989 elections in Chile and the 1990 elections in Nicaragua. His current research examines stereotypes of Latin Americans perpetuated by U.S. public officials and their effect on democratic governance in the Western Hemisphere.

Steve Ellner has taught at the Universidad de Oriente since 1977. He is coeditor with Daniel Hellinger of *Venezuelan Politics in the Chávez Era: Class, Polarization, and Conflict* (2003) and the author of *Organized Labor in Venezuela, 1958–1991: Behavior and Concerns in a Democratic Setting* (1993) and *Venezuela's Movimiento al Socialismo: From Guerrilla Defeat to Electoral Politics* (1988).

María Pilar García-Guadilla has a PhD from the University of Chicago and is professor in the postgraduate program in political sciences at the Universidad Simón Bolívar. She is the head of the Interdisciplinary Research Laboratory on Civil Society, Conflict Resolution and Decision Making Policies and has published extensively on democratization, citizenship, and social movements. Currently, she coordinates a major research project on postconstitutional social movements, participatory democracy, and conflict resolution in Venezuela.

Daniel Hellinger is a professor of political science at Webster University (St. Louis), a coeditor (with Steve Ellner) of *Venezuelan Politics in the Chávez Era: Class, Polarization, and Conflict* (2003), president of the Venezuelan

Studies section of the Latin American Studies Association, and a participating editor of *Latin American Perspectives*.

Jesús María Herrera Salas is a professor of social and political science at the Universidad Simón Bolívar in Caracas. He has published *El Negro Miguel y la primera revolución venezolana* and several articles on the interrelations between culture and power.

Edgardo Lander is professor of social sciences at the Universidad Central de Venezuela. In recent years he has been working on democracy in Latin America and the global implications of free trade. He is the editor of *La colonialidad del saber: Eurocentrismo y ciencias sociales* (2000).

Dick Parker is a Welsh historian educated in England. He has taught at the University of Warwick and the University of Chile and is currently professor of Latin American studies in the Sociology School at the Universidad Central de Venezuela.

Cristóbal Valencia Ramírez is a Ph.D. student in anthropology at the University of Illinois at Urbana-Champaign.

Miguel Tinker Salas is professor of history and Latin American and Chicano/a studies at Pomona College. He has previously published on the Mexico-U.S. border, including *In the Shadow of Eagles: Sonora and the Transformation of the Border during the Porfiriato* (1997). He has published several articles on Venezuela, oil, and culture, and his book entitled *The Enduring Legacy: Oil, Culture and Citizenship in Venezuela* will soon be published.